THE POETICS OF UTOPIA

THE POETICS OF UTOPIA

Shadows of Futurity in Yeats and Auden

Stewart Cole

BLOOMSBURY ACADEMIC
LONDON • NEW YORK • OXFORD • NEW DELHI • SYDNEY

BLOOMSBURY ACADEMIC
Bloomsbury Publishing Plc
50 Bedford Square, London, WC1B 3DP, UK
1385 Broadway, New York, NY 10018, USA
29 Earlsfort Terrace, Dublin 2, Ireland

BLOOMSBURY, BLOOMSBURY ACADEMIC and the Diana logo are trademarks of
Bloomsbury Publishing Plc

First published in Great Britain 2023
This paperback edition published in 2024.

Copyright © Stewart Cole, 2023, 2025

Copyright © 1928, 1933, 1939, 1939, 1945, 1939, 1952 by W.H. Auden, renewed
Reprinted by permission of Curtis Brown, Ltd. All rights reserved.

Stewart Cole has asserted his right under the Copyright, Designs and Patents Act,
1988, to be identified as Author of this work.

For legal purposes the Acknowledgments on p. viii constitute an extension
of this copyright page.

Series design by Eleanor Rose
Cover design by Rebecca Heselton
Cover image: The Cloud Shadow by Algernon Cecil Newton, reproduced by permission of
the Master and Fellows of Clare College, University of Cambridge

All rights reserved. No part of this publication may be reproduced
or transmitted in any form or by any means, electronic or mechanical, including
photocopying, recording, or any information storage or retrieval system, without prior
permission in writing from the publishers.

Bloomsbury Publishing Plc does not have any control over, or responsibility for, any
third-party websites referred to or in this book. All internet addresses given in this
book were correct at the time of going to press. The author and publisher regret any
inconvenience caused if addresses have changed or sites have ceased to exist, but can
accept no responsibility for any such changes.

A catalogue record for this book is available from the British Library.

A catalog record for this book is available from the Library of Congress.

ISBN: HB: 978-1-3502-9385-4
PB: 978-1-3502-9389-2
ePDF: 978-1-3502-9386-1
eBook: 978-1-3502-9387-8

Typeset by Newgen KnowledgeWorks Pvt. Ltd., Chennai, India

To find out more about our authors and books visit www.bloomsbury.com
and sign up for our newsletters.

CONTENTS

List of Figures	vii
Acknowledgments	viii
INTRODUCTION: SHADOWS OF FUTURITY	1
Chapter 1 "EVER NEW AND EVER ANCIENT": THE PASTORAL UTOPIAS OF EARLY YEATS	35
Chapter 2 "HISTORY IS VERY SIMPLE": DESIRE AND THE MEANINGS OF UTOPIA IN LATER YEATS	65
Chapter 3 "THE GOOD PLACE HAS NOT BEEN": THE PURSUIT OF UNITY IN EARLY AUDEN	95
Chapter 4 "THE UNGARNISHED OFFENDED GAP": UTOPIA AND NEGATIVE POETICS IN LATER AUDEN	125
Chapter 5 DRAPED IN BLACK: EKPHRASIS AND THE END(S) OF UTOPIA	155
CONCLUSION: SHADOWS OF FUTURITY	187
Works Cited	207
Index	213

FIGURES

1. Cover of the November 1937 issue (the "Auden Double Number") of *New Verse* — 20
2. Etching by Yeats's father John Butler Yeats of King Goll — 43
3. Illustration from the 1925 version of *A Vision* depicting the phases of the moon — 85
4. Auden and Christopher Isherwood at Victoria Station, London, en route to China in January 1938 — 120
5. Auden's Romanticism chart — 144
6. Yeats at the BBC, London, March 1937 — 167

ACKNOWLEDGMENTS

Early phases of this research were supported by a Canada Graduate Scholarship from the Social Sciences and Humanities Research Council (SSHRC), and later phases were supported by the Faculty Development Program at the University of Wisconsin Oshkosh. My thanks to both these entities. Sincere thanks are also due to Malcolm Woodland, Andrew DuBois, Michael Cobb, and Jeffery Donaldson, all of whom provided invaluable insights on an earlier draft of the manuscript, and to Brian Lander and James Langer for their helpful comments on more recent sections. I am also grateful for feedback received at the Modernist Studies Association and Society for Utopian Studies conferences at which I presented aspects of this work. W. H. Auden's literary executor, Professor Edward Mendelson, has been personally generous with his time in addition to serving, through his own brilliant work, as an apt and inspiring scholarly model for all who venture to write on Auden. I owe him a debt of gratitude.

This book could not have been written without the lifelong support that my family—and particularly my mother, Judi Reside-Service—has shown for my academic endeavors.

My deepest thanks are reserved for Pascale McCullough Manning, who is always my first and best reader, listener, and interlocutor, and whose love and partnership lie at the root of my thinking about poetry, utopia, and all things aspirational.

The author and publisher gratefully acknowledge the permission granted to reproduce the copyright material in this book.

"Musée des Beaux Arts," and "In Memory of W. B. Yeats," copyright 1940 and © renewed 1968 by W. H. Auden; "The Shield of Achilles," copyright 1952 by W. H. Auden and © renewed 1980 by The Estate of W. H. Auden; "Atlantis," copyright 1945 and © renewed 1973 by W. H. Auden; "The Watershed," copyright 1934 and © renewed 1962 by W. H. Auden; "Paysage Moralisé," copyright 1937 and © renewed 1965 by W. H. Auden; and "In Time of War" from *Collected Poems* by W. H. Auden, edited by Edward Mendelson, copyright © 1976 by Edward Mendelson, William Meredith and Monroe K. Spears, Executors of the Estate of W. H. Auden. Used by permission of Random House, an imprint and division of Penguin Random House LLC. All rights reserved.

Poems from the *Collected Poems* and *Selected Poems* of W. H. Auden copyright © 1928, 1933, 1939, 1939, 1945, 1939, 1952 by W.H. Auden, renewed. Reprinted by permission of Curtis Brown, Ltd. All rights reserved.

Material from *The English Auden* copyright © 1977 by the Estate of W.H. Auden. Reprinted by permission of Curtis Brown, Ltd. All rights reserved.

"Sailing to Byzantium" and "Lapis Lazuli" by W. B. Yeats are reproduced by permission of United Agents LLP on behalf of W. B. Yeats.

INTRODUCTION: SHADOWS OF FUTURITY

The twentieth century's most oft-repeated statement about poetry comes from W. H. Auden: "poetry makes nothing happen." Appearing in 1939, on the eve of the Second World War, it finds the poet seeming to affirm that his art can have no impact on the disastrous course of global affairs, that in times of geopolitical crisis poetry can amount to little more than (as he put it in another context) "fiddling while Rome burns" (*English* 329). Auden's apparent dismissal of poetry's real-world efficacy has taken on an aphoristic authority in the culture at large, frequently cited in journalistic contexts, by those who agree and disagree with it alike, as a claim that requires reckoning with.[1] It is too often neglected, however, that Auden makes his assertion of poetry's causal impotence within the framework of an elegy for William Butler Yeats, and so, rather than being plucked out to pithily encapsulate debates around the value of poetry in a world driven by quantitative logics, it should be understood in its fuller poetic context, as one line amid a sixty-five-line tribute to Yeats not only as an ambivalently influential predecessor but also as the great poet of Auden's age most likely to disagree with it. For Yeats himself often made extraordinary claims for poetry (and art in general) as exerting a patterning influence upon the course of history, repeating in many forms the assertion that "the laws of art ... are the hidden laws of the world" (*Early* 120). In the context of Yeats's work, such an assertion implies not just that the extra-perceptive artist builds his work from what he gleans from a deep communion with the world, but also that his work somehow exerts a determining influence upon world events. As he wrote in his 1900 essay "The Symbolism of Poetry": "I am certainly never certain, when I hear of some war, or of some religious excitement or of some new manufacture, or of anything else that fills the ear of the world, that it has not all happened because of something that a boy piped in Thessaly" (*Early* 116). This is art—and throughout Yeats's early writings, all art is metonymic of poetry—unequivocally making something happen, and it is precisely against such assertions of art's causal force that Auden formulates his famous aphorism.

But the picture set out in the preceding paragraph—of Yeats the late Romantic indulging in fantasies of poetry's worldly power, with Auden the clear-eyed Modern arriving to straighten the record—is far from complete. When Auden claims, in his comic essay "The Public v. the Late Mr. William Butler Yeats" (written just after the first draft of the elegy), that "if not a poem had been written, not a picture painted, not a bar of music composed, the history of man would be materially unchanged" (*Prose II* 7), any close reader of his 1930s work must be skeptical of his sincerity. For not only did he place this statement in the mouth of the Defence attorney in an essay whose dialogic form allows the Prosecution equal space to embody the opposite viewpoint, but he also published the essay at the end of a decade during which he himself repeatedly expresses the hope that art might alter the moral landscape of the world, helping us to distinguish between good and evil and thus leading us closer to social unity. His repudiation of such hopes comes only after his move to the United States—a move that precipitated his return to the Anglican communion and his subsequent shift in aspirational emphasis from social unity to union with the divine. Yeats actually follows a similar trajectory, as his work before the turn of the twentieth century embodies the hope that poetry might help to forge Ireland into unity, while his later work reflects the abandonment of these cultural nationalist aspirations in favor of a view of poetry as expressing the poet's unique attunement to the cyclical forces of history—his status as harbinger "Of what is past, or passing, or to come."

Even in their later periods, however—having largely repudiated their youthful hopes for poetry as a force for concrete sociopolitical change—both Yeats and Auden persist in depicting in their work worlds and states of being more ideal than the societies in which they lived, visions of melioration that evidence both poets' enduring conviction that poetry has a crucial role to play in the imagining and imaging of better futures. This book is built upon the premise that despite their considerable formal and ideological differences, what crucially unites Yeats and Auden is their propensity, throughout their bodies of work, to adopt poses of what I call affirmative futurity: desiring, wishing, hoping, aspiring, even prophesying—modes of looking forward that emphasize the future as above all a space of potentiality and promise. Given the sheer prevalence of this affirmative future-orientation in the two poets' work, I see them as embodying (albeit in various ways at different stages in their careers) a *poetics of utopia*, whereby both poetry itself and the vocation of writing it stand as crucial manifestations of the impulse to strive after better ways of life in more ideal futures. While this book is specifically about Yeats and Auden, however—reading their poems, essays, and other writings in relation to prevailing currents of thought in their times to trace their various iterations of a utopian poetics in its shifting manifestations over the course of their careers—it also takes these two signal poets as exemplars in the hope of urging us to consider how poetry, particularly in the twentieth century and beyond, may be an almost inherently utopian artform. This is not to say that Yeats and Auden can be taken as representative of modern poetry as a whole; no two poets could be, and they in particular are both too exceptional in the breadth of their engagement with poetry's relation to the collective and too at odds with avant-garde currents in modern poetry to serve as stand-ins for such a diverse field of artistic production. Nor am I claiming that two English-language poets from a relatively narrow cultural-linguistic milieu encompassing England and Ireland can possibly attest to the full range of ways in which questions of poetry's status as a social artform have been broached cross-linguistically.[2] What I am claiming, however, is that the myriad ways in which Yeats and Auden conceive of poetry's relationship to its dwindling audience, its place within increasingly atomized societies, and its potential role as a unifying force that could both oppose that atomization and newly galvanize an audience can serve as the basis for a framework within which to view modern poetry more generally, particularly in its aspirational dimensions.

But just as Yeats and Auden cannot be taken as overly representative, they should not be unduly conflated. While they are contemporaries at crucial stages of their careers, Yeats (1865–1939) and Auden (1907–1973) do occupy separate poetic generations, and though one of their key moments of overlap ("In Memory of W. B. Yeats" generally and "poetry makes nothing happen" in particular) serves as one of the provocatory nexus points of this study, they do also inhabit what Pascale Casanova terms separate "literary spaces"—that is, while the English-American Auden spends his career within the orbit of the literary metropoles of London and New York, Yeats operates within and in relation to such metropolitan spaces (London in particular) while also, as an Irishman, spending a significant portion of his career helping to transform Ireland not only from a colonial to a postcolonial nation but also from a marginal literary space to a more dominant one.[3] As this book will make clear in treating Yeats's work in a specifically Irish context, his poetics of utopia as it variously manifests over the course of his career is inseparable from his involvement in the struggle for Irish nationhood—a nationalist impetus that of course does not apply to Auden. At the same time, however, over the course of the story that this book tells about poetry, utopia, and their convergences in Yeats's and Auden's work, we will see unmistakable, instructive similarities in both the forces they respond to and the forms their aspirations take as they strive to envision for their art a significant role in shaping improved futures.

Why Utopia?

From among the many possible ways of characterizing the affirmative future-orientation that is my focus, I have chosen the term "utopia" for several reasons. First, its use in designating a literary genre allows it to encompass those texts—remarkably frequent in the two poets' oeuvres, like Yeats's "The Lake Isle of Innisfree" and "Byzantium," and Auden's "On This Island" and "Atlantis"—which envision, describe, and/or inhabit the sorts of ideal "no-places" (*outopias*) and "good places" (*eutopias*) to which the word punningly refers. Despite quite commonly depicting such places, poetry—and especially modern poetry—is not often acknowledged among the annals of utopian literature, and this book aims to redress that omission. Second, the structural and organizational connotations that inhere in the word "utopia"—the idea of a society minutely planned down to the last detail—make it a useful way of figuring the similar rigor with which poems themselves are organized; and indeed Auden himself highlights this connection in his claim (which I examine in considerable detail in Chapter 4) that "every good poem is very nearly a utopia" (*Dyer's* 71). In other words, a poem is like a little verbal society, which though it may present through its subject matter any number of impressions from paradisal to hellish, nonetheless strives for internal coherence—for harmoniousness, however defined by the given aesthetic occasion. Thus the concept of utopia can shed light not only on poetry's *content*, but on its foregrounding of *form* as well, offering a means by which we might conceive of an inherent connection between at least some acts of poetic composition and the drive for more ideal social formations. Third, the concept of utopia is multivalent enough to encompass, or at least to meaningfully inform, an investigation of all the instances of affirmative futurity that we find in Yeats's and Auden's work.[4] This multivalency is particularly evident in the tendency among scholars in contemporary utopian studies to distinguish between utopia as a *genre*—in a line descending from Thomas More's 1516 *Utopia*—and utopia as a future-oriented *impulse* that manifests well beyond the genre's fairly narrow and programmatic parameters. This distinction is elaborated by Fredric Jameson, who in his *Archaeologies of the Future* posits "two distinct lines of descendancy from More's inaugural text: the one intent on the realization of the Utopian program, the other an obscure yet omnipresent Utopian impulse finding its way to the surface in a variety of covert expressions and practices" (3). In Jameson's schema, the programmatic line includes "revolutionary political practice, when it aims at founding a whole new society" as well as "exercises in the literary genre," while the line of impulse includes more moderate "social democratic and 'liberal' forms" of political theory—particularly "when they are merely allegorical of a wholesale transformation of the social totality"—along with many "more obscure and more various" glimmerings of "Utopian investment" (3–4). Rather than see these lines as fully discrete, however, I take this basic distinction as setting out a continuum, with concrete utopian activism at one end and the faintest of utopian desires at the other, along which Yeats's and Auden's expressions of a utopian poetics might be variously situated.

Nor do I take Jameson's useful account as authoritative, as throughout this study I engage with many prominent theorists of utopia from the early twentieth century to the present whose work has served to both broaden and nuance the category of utopia, helping to open the conceptual space within which this book's claim for poetry as a utopian artform can be situated. The idea of utopia as an impulse is widely held (including by Jameson) to have originated with Ernst Bloch, whose related concept of the "Not Yet" highlights the latency of the future within the present and the past and thus the fundamental inextricability of these temporal registers. As Jack Zipes puts it, in Bloch's thinking, "Literature and art contain the anticipatory illumination of that which has not yet become, and the role of the writer and artist is similar to that of a midwife who enables latent and potential materials to assume their own unique forms" (Bloch *Utopian* xix). This is similar to the position of Bloch's contemporary Lewis Mumford, whose *The Story of Utopias* (1922) posits a human "will-to-utopia"—i.e., a propensity to affirmative futurity that means we "live in two worlds" (21)—and asserts an indispensable role for the arts in bringing the conjectural futures of our utopian imaginings into actuality: "if the inspiration for the good life is to come from anywhere, it must come from no other people than the great artists" (201). Mumford is also first to place Yeats in a utopian context, exalting him as embodying the artist's "proper relation to the community" and lauding the work of Yeats, Æ, and others in the Celtic Revival as "one of the most promising attempts to establish a concrete utopia which shall rise out of the real facts of the everyday environment and, at the same time, turn upon them and mold them creatively a little nearer the heart's desire" (204). Joining Bloch's utopian "impulse" and Mumford's "will-to-utopia" among conceptions of utopia that see it as a near-intrinsic emanation of human consciousness is Karl Mannheim's formulation, set out in his *Ideology and Utopia* (1929), of the "utopian mentality." Defining as utopian "that type of orientation which transcends reality and which at the same time breaks the bonds of the existing order," Mannheim thus contrasts such states of mind with those he characterizes as "ideological," setting out a dichotomy the two sides of which serve to either reinforce or subvert the status quo (192). This emphasis on the critical, subversive function of utopia, inherent in the work of all the thinkers mentioned thus far, is particularly acute in that of Bloch's close friend and Frankfurt School colleague Theodor Adorno, whose theorization of utopia eschews ascribing to it any positive manifestation along the lines of an impulse, a will, or a mentality. Instead, building on the lacunar connotations of Bloch's conception of the Not Yet, Adorno conceives of utopia in almost entirely negative terms, as essentially that which highlights, through its ineffable otherness from the world as currently constituted, the fundamental impoverishment of that world. Throughout his posthumously published *Aesthetic Theory* (1970), Adorno ascribes this enigmatic conception of utopia to art in particular:

> Because for art, utopia—the yet-to-exist—is draped in black, it remains in all its mediations recollection; recollection of the possible in opposition to the actual that suppresses it; it is the imaginary reparation of the catastrophe of world history; it is freedom, which under the spell of necessity did not—and may not ever—come to pass. (134)

Art's utopian function thus inheres in the way it serves to underscore, by its very existence, the absence from life of the spectral fulfillment and conciliation to be found in the aesthetic artifact. As we will see, this idea is of particular relevance to poetry, an artform that is often thought (by Yeats and Auden and more generally) to model, through its internal unities, aspects of the greater social unity sought by utopian reformers.

With Adorno's negative account of utopia, the opening-out of the concept that can be traced through Bloch, Mumford, and Mannheim reaches perhaps its limit point. This is the culmination of a genealogy of utopian thinking that stands in stark opposition to what Russell Jacoby calls the "blueprint tradition" of utopianism—the utopian tendency, from More to B. F. Skinner, to meticulously plot out the ideal society, down to details such as the dimensions of its buildings and the clothing of its inhabitants (32). As Jacoby argues, not only do such blueprint utopias lose in applicability what they gain in specificity ("History soon eclipses them"), but they are also responsible—both because they "betray, and sometimes celebrate, a certain authoritarianism" and because actually existing authoritarianisms have often evoked blueprintist utopian schemes—for the negative connotations that adhered to "utopia" throughout the latter decades of the twentieth century (and still often do) (32). This is no doubt why the Blochian counter-tradition—or what Jacoby terms the "iconoclastic tradition" of utopianism—is dominant among scholars of utopia today: because it allows us to preserve the critical, subversive, and transformative power of utopian thinking while extricating it from those still-clinging authoritarian connotations. From the perspective of analytical usefulness, however, the reluctance of the iconoclastic or impulse utopian tradition to define or even typify utopia does stand as a notable downside, as it can come to seem that any impetus to change the world might be regarded as utopian if viewed in a sufficiently sanguine light. The closest thing to a workable definition of utopia to have emerged out of this vein of thought is Ruth Levitas's statement—reiterated in various forms over the course of her landmark book *The Concept of Utopia* (1990)—that "Utopia is the expression of desire for a better way of being" (8). Though in a vacuum the breadth of this definition might attenuate its usefulness, when taken up in light of the present book's specific focus on poetry—with its myriad generic, formal, and conceptual anchors to utopia—it will prove indispensable in the way it both centralizes the motive force of desire (which, as we will see, both Yeats and Auden conceived as lying at the root of their work) and allows for the sheer diversity of ways in which that utopian desire can manifest in an artform as expressively flexible as poetry.

Poetry, Modernism, and Utopia

While Levitas and many of the other thinkers discussed in the preceding paragraphs passingly acknowledge poetry's status as a repository of utopian thinking, none specifically addresses how and why poetry in particular—with its specific means of marshalling formal and figurative resources—can serve as an apposite medium in which to embody (to borrow a phrasing from Jameson) the desire called utopia. This neglect of poetry is also marked in the recent wave of scholarship that explores the extraordinary prominence and diversity of engagements with utopia in modernist literature and culture. Across three recent edited essay collections—Rosalyn Gregory and Benjamin Kohlmann's *Utopian Spaces of Modernism: British Literature and Culture, 1885–1945*; Alice Reeve-Tucker and Nathan Waddell's *Utopianism, Modernism, and Literature in the Twentieth Century*; and David Ayers et al.'s *Utopia: the Avant Garde, Modernism, and (Im)possible Life*—only two of a combined fifty-three-chapter contributions take poetry as their primary point of focus. Of those two, one treats not modernist work at all but rather the legacy of modernist-era utopianism as expressed in contemporary "Language" poetry.[5] But the one that does engage directly with modernism—a fascinating essay on T. S. Eliot and Wallace Stevens by Douglas Mao—touches meaningfully upon key aspects of this book's argument that not just poetry but modern poetry in particular, by virtue of its historical situatedness in a time of both great sociopolitical and spiritual upheaval and growing uncertainty about the status of poetry as a cultural force, proves a fertile ground in which to uncover novel and complex expressions of the utopian impulse—modes of what Bloch calls "anticipatory illumination" or "pre-appearance": stances of affirmative futurity that repudiate the status of the given as all that is, reaching forward to more ideal hypotheticals that, through the very act of grasping, might just be drawn nearer to the possible.

Focusing on Eliot's and Stevens's 1930s and 1940s work by way of examining the two poets' mutual commitment to what he terms "the unseen"—specifically *in*visible objects of knowledge and belief (i.e., God in Eliot's case and a "supreme fiction" in Stevens's)—Mao explores how both sought to exalt the unseen as a more ideal alternative to "new kinds of political regimes [that] were in effect seeking to refute the hypothesis of a need for the unseen by providing a viable ultimate object in the seen world: the party, the revolution, the leader, the new social order itself" (195). In casting Eliot as "not a utopian" (196) and characterizing Stevens's vision of a more ideal society as "utopian but (apart from its implicitly liberal tonality) politically uncharacterized" (210–11), Mao's analysis implicitly ascribes to a blueprintist definition of utopia according to which authentic utopia is concretely political, materialist, and therefore hostile to the immateriality and uncertainty of the unseen realm. Claiming that "Both poets' treatments of belief in a sense follow from the question, 'If we were actually to arrive at the kind of society promised by the progressive nineteenth century, what *then*?'" (210)—i.e., that both poets proceed from the conviction that even if they were materially actualized, the sorts of ideal societies set out by blueprint utopians like Edward Bellamy, William Morris, and H. G. Wells would leave their citizens *im*materially impoverished—Mao traces the ways in which they affirm in their poetry the primacy of the unseen amid a sociopolitical climate marked by the ascendancy of -isms appealing to people's fearful desires for the certainty and finality of seen truths. For Stevens, this means elaborating with ever-greater nuance, in poems like *Notes toward a Supreme Fiction*, his conviction that (as Mao puts it) "there is no seeing of reality undeformed by the play of imagination," and as a consequence, "in a rigorous sense the world remains unseen, something we believe in rather than know" (199). For Eliot, on the other hand—whose Christianity precludes him from so exalting the world-making capacities of the human imagination (much as it does the later Auden, as I explore in Chapter 4)—poetry can serve as a means of revealing the luminous eternal order of the unseen realm that shimmers behind the screen of our quotidian, fallen existence. As Mao points out, it is in his poetic dramas that Eliot particularly aspires to this feat of unveiling; in plays such as *The Rock* and *The Family Reunion*, the tangibility of staging allows for climactic moments at which curtains are drawn to reveal the presence of a realm behind and beyond that in which the main human drama takes place—moments that constitute an allegorical representation of Incarnation, "which can be understood as the point at which the timeless order of the unseen breaks into the visible world" (206).[6]

Though the intricacies of Mao's argument both resist quick summary and bear only marginal relevance to my argument here, his emphasis on both Eliot's and

Stevens's determination to frame in poetry a window onto an unseen world of orderly ideality in contrast to the disorderly actuality of the seen one touches upon a number of the key motivating insights of this book. First, poetry is an aspirational medium: poems are brought into the world out of a sense of its incompletion. From the anonymous "Cuckoo Song" to the love sonnets of the Early Modern period to twenty-first-century spoken word, poetry in the English language and beyond attests to a restless impulsive faith in the power of musically shaped utterance to effect some positive alteration in the existing order of things, to conjure into being—whether from mind, spirit, or some other ephemeral beyond-space of potentiality—arrangements of words that might ripple or resonate in an ameliorating way, edging the world nearer, if not to completion, then to fuller conciliation. Second, modern poetry—here flexibly defined as spanning the fraught period from the 1890s of the proto-modernist early Yeats to the decade or so following the Second World War—often expresses this aspirational impetus in at least nebulously sociopolitical terms. Both modern poetry's most ambitious productions (e.g., *The Waste Land*, the *Cantos*, *Trilogy*, the aforementioned *Notes*) and its lyric-scale output frequently announce themselves as engaged commentaries on and interventions into the state of society, whether (as Mao claims of Eliot's and Stevens's interwar work) by contrasting the world as it is with an alternate, more ideal state of things or through more directly critical means. Third, poetry in particular stands apart from the socially engaged literature of the period in other genres by virtue of its *form*, which serves as a kind of spatio-temporal layer of aspiration and critique operating in dialogic parallel to the more strictly semantic layer. Though the two layers (roughly corresponding to the traditional categories of "form" and "content") cannot be disentangled, there is no denying that the form of modern poetry in particular has often been read as figuratively meaningful in itself. *The Waste Land* is of course the exemplar text of this tendency—frequently occasioning claims like "Its exploded poetic form ... seems a delayed effect of the trenches; all that remains of literature and culture is a handful of fragmentary quotations" (Selby 7–8)—but even in more traditionally formed poems, in which the connection between the form of the poem and the state of the society it evokes is less transparently rendered—indeed, even in poems in which such a connection may not be discernable—the surface overtness of poetic form, the fact of poetry's arriving to us garbed in its form, like a *uni*form, means that it is always present to us, embodying ideas about coherence and incoherence, harmony and disharmony, that any mind attuned to the political resonances of poetry cannot but be tempted to find ways of analogizing to the societal sphere.

Form and Utopia

This last point about form requires elaboration. One might argue that not just poetic form but all artistic form—whether literary, visual, performing, architectural, and so on—can be seen to embody this socially resonant dimension. Indeed, an influential vein in aesthetics with Schiller as its most prominent exponent conceives of form as lending rational, unified shape to the irregular multiplicities of nature and thus as manifesting the aspirational impulse to harmony that societies strive (or ought to strive) to embody. In the letters of his *On the Aesthetic Education of Man* (1795), Schiller links form to unity, timelessness, and ultimately, the social whole as embodied in the State, while linking the content or subject matter of art to both the time-bound reality of Nature and the individual as a material being. In his Fourth Letter, he claims that "Every individual man ... carries in disposition and determination a pure ideal man within himself, with whose unalterable unity it is the great task of his existence, throughout all his vicissitudes, to harmonize," going on to assert that this "pure ideal man" finds his form in "the State, the objective and, so to say, canonical form in which Man in time can be made to coincide with Man in idea" (49). The "great task of existence," then, is a kind of existential conciliation of form and content, the process of bringing the ideal, timeless, formal self into harmonious concord with the real, temporal, material self, and this task is mirrored at the social level in the relationship between the individual and the State—the two of which, ideally, will coexist in an analogous condition of harmony. In Schiller's view—and this forms a crucial part of the "aesthetic education" of the book's title—these processes of self- and societal fashioning play out on a microcosmic scale within the work of art, allowing us glimpses into (or, if we happen to be artists, hands-on training in) the dynamic harmonization of form and content, timelessness and the temporal, the State and the individual, Reason and Nature, and so on. In his Ninth Letter, Schiller directly connects art's harmonizing capacity to the creation of more ideal societies, averring that "All improvement in the political sphere is to proceed from the ennobling of the character—but how, under the influence of a barbarous constitution, can the character become ennobled?" and quickly concluding that "This instrument [i.e., the instrument of such improvement] is the Fine Arts" (77). And once again, *form* is the key to art's political instrumentality: Schiller writes of the artist that "He will indeed take his subject matter from the present age, but his form he will borrow from a nobler time—nay, from beyond all time," thus envisioning form as that which allows art not only to transcend the disordered material conditions of its historical moment but, through this act of formal transcendence, to project forward an image of the unity of timelessness and the temporal that can serve to inspire societal improvement (78–9). While Schiller's letters are notoriously elliptical in their shifting terminology (one English translator notes of him that "he is wholly unwilling to use a consistent terminology, and the reader must not expect it of him" (26)), it becomes clear over the course of the book that what he calls the "form impulse"—i.e., what drives us to impose unified form upon the multiplicities of nature—and what he calls the "moral impulse"—i.e., what drives us to overcome our natural barbarism—are essentially synonymous. Of the latter, he makes the compelling claim that "the future is its present"—a claim that, when applied to the former, produces the idea that the form impulse is a fundamentally aspirational one. In Schiller's terms, then, the matter of art is not just time-bound but present-bound ("the artist is the child of his time"), while its form is timeless in its unbounded futurity ("but woe to him if he is also its disciple")—that is, its gestural allegiance to the Not Yet (78).

While this book does not ascribe to either Schiller's idealist conception of form or his positivist conception of the relationship between art and political improvement, it does seek to mine the analytical value of both his theorization of form as essentially aspirational and his implication that the twin impulses he identifies—on the one hand, to lend artistic form to matter, and on the other, to strive toward more ideal social formations—may arise from a common wellspring. Though he does not use the term, it seems clear that Schiller's conception of form can readily be characterized as *utopian*, especially within the context of contemporary utopian studies, where the pervasive emphasis on a utopia as an "impulse" could plausibly be termed Schillerian. Despite embodying an untenable degree of false consciousness in its idealist neglect of the actualization gap between the conceptual productions of impulse and the material conditions enjoyed by citizens of states—i.e., the gap between artistic visions of society and the material realities of actually existing societies, one important manifestation of the base/superstructure problem at the core of Marxist theory—Schiller's aesthetic program is the first to urge our attentiveness to form's utopian dimensions, thus opening up crucial categories for thought in conceiving of utopia in terms that transcend traditional blueprintist, content-centered approaches.[7] This tradition inaugurated by Schiller is particularly important for a study like this one focused on poetry—which, as a medium that foregrounds form to an unusually overt degree, has been neglected not only in such traditional accounts of utopian literature but in the more recent impulse-oriented scholarship. Despite its shortcomings, then, Schiller's approach to form helps to illuminate poetry's distinctness as a utopian medium, one in which form and content, the aspirational and the actual, can interact to project visions of social melioration unique in their vividness and figurative complexity.

It is important to emphasize that this book does not set forth a poetics of utopia according to which, in an oversimplified idealist fashion, form is equated with the aspirational and content with the actual. Nor is poetic form in itself one of this book's central concerns. The foregoing discussion of form is instead intended to highlight that the relative absence of poetry in the copious scholarship on utopian literature represents a significant gap not only because poetry often advances images of more ideal worlds in many ways akin to those advanced in the novels upon which such scholarship overwhelmingly focuses, but also because the over 200-year tradition of theorizing the utopian dimensions of form ought by now to have attuned critics to poetry's singularity as a form-forward utopian medium. As the first book-length study to treat poetry wholly in relation to utopia, *The Poetics of Utopia* frequently attends to the ways in which the tension between the ostensible separateness of form and content and their essential inextricability produces a layered ambivalence that compellingly charts the push and pull of desire and acceptance, wishing and knowing, aspiring and abiding that characterizes expressions of affirmative futurity as they confront the apparent limits of the present. Poems often do not fully mean what they say: their utterances tend to register as less sincere the more overtly shaped they seem by the artifices of form, and the space of performative distance between author and speaker is highly manipulable, allowing for everything from autobiographizing to the adoption of personae entirely remote from the author's experience. This makes poetry an ideal medium in which to try on viewpoints, to test values, and, crucially for its status as utopian literature, to embody in myriad hypothetical forms what Levitas posits as the definitional essence of utopia: "the expression of the desire for a better way of living and being" (191).

"Musée des Beaux Arts" and Utopian Form

As a brief case study in the ways in which the tensile, dialectical relationship between form and content that prevails in poetry makes it a uniquely nuanced and flexible means of expressing the utopian impulse, consider one of Auden's most renowned lyric productions, his 1938 poem "Musée des Beaux Arts":

> About suffering they were never wrong,
> The Old Masters: how well they understood
> Its human position; how it takes place
> While someone else is eating or opening a window or just walking dully along;
> How, when the aged are reverently, passionately waiting
> For the miraculous birth, there always must be
> Children who did not specially want it to happen, skating
> On a pond at the edge of the wood:
> They never forgot
> That even the dreadful martyrdom must run its course
> Anyhow in a corner, some untidy spot
> Where the dogs go on with their doggy life and the torturer's horse
> Scratches its innocent behind on a tree.
>
> In Breughel's *Icarus*, for instance: how everything turns away
> Quite leisurely from the disaster; the ploughman may
> Have heard the splash, the forsaken cry,
> But for him it was not an important failure; the sun shone
> As it had to on the white legs disappearing into the green
> Water; and the expensive delicate ship that must have seen
> Something amazing, a boy falling out of the sky,
> Had somewhere to get to and sailed calmly on. (*Collected* 179, lines 1–21)

On the surface, no one would consider this a utopian poem. If anything, it could be construed as anti-utopian in its clear-eyed affirmation not only of the transhistorical universality of human suffering but of the equally universal human propensity to obliviousness and indifference in the face of such suffering. Nor does the poem seem to advance a vision of art as playing a meliorative or even palliative role in relation to this condition. In framing the "human position" of suffering, it markedly does not take up the idealist posture of lauding the "Old Masters" for producing works that have the power to change minds and thereby, perhaps, reduce the quotient of suffering in the universe. Rather than express the desire for a better way of living and being, then, the poem seems to express resignation in the belief that, at least in the matter of suffering, improvement is impossible. On the one hand, the prominence of animals in the poem—with the speaker highlighting that "the dreadful martyrdom must run its course" while "the dogs go on with their doggy life and the torturer's horse / Scratches its innocent behind on a tree"—attests to a commonsense awareness of the indifference of the nonhuman world to our travails. On the other hand, however, by framing its meditation on human suffering within this more-than-human context, the poem flirts with the implication that not only are suffering and oblivious indifference endemic to our animal nature, but the acts that *cause* suffering—the "martyrdom" and "disaster" depicted in both the poem and the Bruegel paintings that serve as its ekphrastic objects—may be equally, biologically incontrovertible. The poem can readily be seen, then, to embody a dismal fatalism, a kind of atheistic prefiguration of the conviction that Auden would be espousing in more hopeful, Christian terms just a year later, of humanity as essentially fallen. Whereas the post-conversion Auden continually asserts this fallenness as a means of combating the "auto-idolatry" that leaves us insensible to God's grace—a dynamic whose utopian dimensions I explore in detail in Chapter 4—here in "Musée des Beaux Arts" our fallenness is rendered piteously literal in the pagan figure of Icarus, whose graceless plunge serves to figure the farcical emptiness of a lapsarian condition in the absence of God.

This anti-utopian reading of the poem can only be sustained, however, if one neglects to analyze its form, as any such analysis alerts one to the ways in which its structural elements operate in a productive tension with its subject matter to complicate the dominant surface impression of the poem as fatalistic or even quietist in its account of human fallenness. The complex rhyme scheme in particular—rendered inconspicuous by the widely varying line lengths—suggests a harmonious order (or at least the wish for such an order) underlying the poem's catalogue of lives in anguish and disarray. The first stanza's dizzying scheme of ABCADEDBFGFGE leaves only the 'C' ending unrhymed; that the line in question is "Its human position: how it takes place" suggests that, contrary to the indifference to suffering that permeates the poem's imagery, part of suffering's "human position" lies in its uniqueness: each of us suffers distinctly. In other words, the fact of that one line left singularly unrhymed pulls against the poem's apparent emphasis (i.e., the emphasis of its *content*) on suffering as a universal, de-individualized, and therefore widely ignored and ignorable phenomenon. This, in combination with the fact that the poem becomes more tightly woven as it wears on—with the lines becoming notably more even in length and the second stanza's rhyme scheme (HHIJKKIJ) tightening to almost evoke ottava rima—can lead us to see the poem's form as attesting, in Schillerian fashion, to art's propensity to aspire beyond the givens of reality and conjure more harmonious formations.

In her landmark book *On Form*, Angela Leighton evokes Helen Vendler's distinction (which Vendler develops in engaging with the work of Czeslaw Milosz) between "the serenity of form" and "the anguish of content" (22). Quoting Vendler's comment that Milosz's poem "The Poor Poet" presents "the problem of content and form in its most violent aspect, as the serenity of form ... tortures the anguish of content," Leighton shifts to a brief commentary on "Musée des Beaux Arts" that reframes this idea of content *torturing* form in an unexpectedly positive light:

> Form matters in this case, not because it withdraws altogether from "content," but because it "tortures" it. We are back in the "*Musée des Beaux Arts*," but that may be precisely why, in the serene quiet, we might hear the "anguish" all the more clearly. In Auden's poem, that brilliant exposé and defence of aestheticisms of all kinds, the poet forces us to consider the place, art-room or poem-room, where torture is serenely depicted. At the same time, the poem is a searing reminder that this is the room not only of art but also of life, where the daily routines continue, oblivious to horrors. (22)

In Vendler's account, if the content (as in the case of Milosz's and Auden's poems) consists of massacres, anguish, and other forms of extreme suffering, then the "serenity of form" warrants distrust. In other words, to the extent that the poem's formal elements combine to convey a sense of harmoniousness at odds with the violence of its subject matter, they "torture" it, raising ethical questions about the aestheticization of suffering. Auden himself expresses a version of this reservation in his essay "The Virgin and the Dynamo," warning against the insidious capacity of the well-formed artwork to deceive us into believing that "since all is well in the work of art, all is well in history" (to which he quickly adds, "But all is not well there") (*Dyer's* 71). I will return to these remarks and their wider context in Chapter 4, but for now, it is important to highlight Leighton's claim that, in Auden's poem and others, the torturous effect of the serenity of form "may be precisely why, in the serene quiet, we might hear the 'anguish' all the more clearly" (22). With this, Leighton invites us to consider how, rather than serving to indict the formal impulse as ethically dubious, the apparent disjuncture between form and content can be viewed as a kind of complementarity, with form serving to clarify and thus to more profoundly assert the ethical urgency of content. Extending Leighton's suggestion, one might also wonder if the inverse is true—i.e., if the content thus clarified by form serves to affirm, by virtue of that very clarity, the power of aesthetic form (and therefore of art itself) to give lucid, ethically compelling shape to human experience. Viewed in this way—with form clarifying content, which in turn points back at form's power to clarify—the poem is a dialectical artifact, the tension between the serenity of form and the anguish of content a synthetic rather than an agonistic one.

Such a model is not quite sufficient, however, to this book's treatment of poetry as a specifically utopian medium. Although poems—and especially modern ones, written in an era of poetry's dwindling public power—frequently gesture to their own capacities in this dialectical manner, crucial to this book is the claim that they also (and perhaps just as frequently) gesture *beyond* such capacities, embodying an awareness of the limits not only of their representational powers but also of the world in which those powers are exercised, and aspiring beyond that world to a more ideal one in which both sorts of limits will be less keenly felt. Returning to "Musée des Beaux Arts" and Leighton's brief analysis of it, we can see how her claim that "the poet forces us to consider the place, art-room or poem-room, where torture is serenely depicted" highlights the poem's reflexivity about its own limitations, its misgivings as to whether poetry—and by extension art in general, as metonymized by the poem's museum setting—may be guilty of trivializing suffering in lending aesthetic form to it (22). On the other hand, her balancing claim that "the poem is a searing reminder that this is the room not only of art but also of life, where the daily routines continue, oblivious to horrors" emphasizes that the poem's element of self-critique is inextricable from a wider critique of the world that harbors it. In keeping with this book's ambition to do fuller justice to the world-forming aspirations of Auden's work, of Yeats's, and of so much of modern poetry, however, I would extend the terms of Leighton's analysis to account for how the poem embodies not just a critical dimension but a utopian one, expressing in the dialectical interplay of form and content a stance of affirmative futurity that hints—indeed insists—that the world could be a better one. I have already discussed how the poem's apparent emphasis on the universality of both suffering itself and callousness in the face of it is counterpoised by the complex harmoniousness of its rhyme scheme and, most intricately, by the individuating implications of its one line left unrhymed, through which the poem embodies an awareness of the singularity of suffering in contrast to the predominant anonymity of the victims depicted in both it and Bruegel's panoramic paintings. The poem's form thus conjures from the Not Yet both a more harmonious world—one less marked by the factional strife, common to both the biblical world and Bruegel's, that gave rise to paintings like *The Massacre of the Innocents* and *The Numbering at Bethlehem*—and one in which the suffering that does occur is accorded its due compassion. But the poem's aspirational energies do not reside in its form alone. Readers who take the time to attend to how its apparent fatalism about suffering is tempered by the utopian implications of its form might then be moved to notice the instances at which such implications manifest, glancingly, in its content. The first stanza's reference to "the miraculous birth," for instance ("How, when the aged are reverently, passionately waiting / For the miraculous birth, there always must be / Children who did not specially want it to happen"), is rooted in Bruegel's painting *The Numbering at Bethlehem*, which not only depicts the arrival of Mary and Joseph at what will become the scene of Christ's birth but also transposes the census conducted by the Roman governor Quirinius (as described in Luke 2:1–5) to the Netherlands of Bruegel's sixteenth century, as a means of critiquing the bureaucracy and severity of Spanish Hapsburg rule there. In eliding the painting's critique of oppressive foreign rulership (a subject which would seem well suited to the poem's focus on suffering) and instead limiting its ekphrastic engagement to referencing the impending nativity, the poem thus emphasizes not only Christ's "dreadful martyrdom" (a phrase that appears four lines later in reference to another Bruegel painting, *The Massacre of the Innocents*) but also the attendant promise of salvation. In this instance, then, the poem subtly embodies a millenarian hope at odds with its surface stoicism. Similarly, the pointed characterization in the poem's antepenultimate line of the "expensive delicate ship" implies a degree of social critique, with the concomitant implication that things might be otherwise. While earlier, "the ploughman *may / Have heard* the splash, the forsaken cry, / But for him it was not an important failure," in the poem's final lines we are told of the ship that it "*must have seen /* Something amazing, a boy falling out of the sky" but it "Had somewhere to get to and sailed calmly on." While we might read the presence of both the ploughman and the ship as signaling that the human propensity to self-absorbed indifference transcends class disparities, the fact that the peasant farmer in Bruegel's painting only "may / Have heard" Icarus's fall, while the ship (and by extension its inhabitants) "must have seen" it—i.e., that the latter's encounter with the fall is cast in both more definite and more sensorily proximate terms—contains the suggestion that callousness is not in fact evenly distributed across humanity, but is rather amplified by affluence. While earlier the poem declines to take up the politicized elements of *The Numbering at Bethlehem*, here in its engagement with *Landscape with the Fall of Icarus*, it virtually inserts such elements, infusing the painting's *paysage moralisé* with an element of class consciousness that recalls the Auden of the late 1920s and earlier 1930s, flirtatious with Marxism. Across this difference, however, both instances find "Musée des Beaux Arts" shifting the angle of its ekphrastic engagement in order to express in its content the aspirational impetus inherent in its form, thus highlighting the extent to which one must attend to their dialectical interplay in order to grasp how thoroughly the utopian desire for a better way of living and being is woven into the poem's fabric.

Poetry and Minor Utopias

While "Musée des Beaux Arts" is not a utopian poem in a generic sense, then— i.e., it does not project a tangible vision of a more ideal world the way, say, Yeats's "Innisfree" or Auden's own "On This Island" might be seen to do—it is a utopian artifact in ways much more relevant to the tenor of contemporary utopian studies, with its emphasis on reclaiming the critical, aspirational, and transformational powers of utopia from the slough of disrepute to which it is still too often consigned. The dialectical, figurative, often implicit, yet powerfully resonant utopianism embodied in "Musée des Beaux Arts"—and, as this book hopes to illuminate, in so much of modern poetry, taking Yeats and Auden as exemplars—dovetails with the emphasis in contemporary utopian studies on "minor" or "limited" utopias: expressions of the utopian impulse that avoid the panacean logic of blueprintist approaches to instead offer fragmentary, elusive, and indeed flawed visions of melioration that are produced out of an awareness of the limits of such visions and the inevitability of such flaws. The formulation "minor utopias" originates with Jay Winter, who elaborates the term by contrast to "major utopias" characterized by "their totalitarian visions, and their commitment to the ruthless removal from the world of those malevolent elements blocking the path to a beneficent future" (4). Minor utopias, on the other hand, are "imaginings of liberation usually on a smaller scale" that "sketch out a world very different from the one we live in, but from which not all social conflict or all oppression has been eliminated" (5). Winter's work is wide-ranging, drawing examples of such minor utopias from across twentieth-century politics and culture, including much literature—but once again to the neglect of poetry. As should by now be clear, this book insists not only that poetry frequently undertakes the sorts of minor-key "imaginings of liberation" envisioned by Winter but also that the configurative dynamics that define poetry as an artform allow it to embody such imaginings in particularly nuanced and resonant ways. Anahid Nersessian proposes a similar formulation to that of "minor utopias"—and this time one whose elaboration not only includes but also depends upon poetry—in the concept of "limited utopias," which she characterizes as "uphold[ing] the practice of artmaking as a performance of non-fulfillment and the conscientious regard for earthly matter such a performance models and enacts" (8). In other words—and to adapt Nersessian's characterization into terms that will be particularly crucial to my argument in Chapter 2, on the later Yeats's utopian fetishization of states of unrequitement—the concept of limited utopia applies particularly to art that recognizes its own status as failure and, through that recognition, tacitly acknowledges that the limits of art accord with those of a material world characterized by finite resources. Though its argument centers on Romanticism, Nersessian's book *Utopia, Limited* is the only sustained work to integrate careful attention to poetic form into a theorization of utopia, and thus it serves as a crucial precursor to this study. In claiming that "the Romantics think about utopia in the same way as they think about art, as a means of capturing and thereby emancipating an infinite human potential within a finite space," Nersessian both touches upon the analogy between poetic form and social formations at the core of Auden's claim that "every good poem is very nearly a utopia" and extends it in analytical terms to imply that for the Romantics, the boundedness of form is a liberating force, akin to how planetary limits might necessitate and therefore liberate into being new sustainable modes of collectivity (19). While Nersessian's focus on a vein of environmentally oriented Romanticism lends the concept of "limited utopia" a specific ecological thrust lacking in Winter's broader and more strictly political concept of "minor utopia," both testify to a salutary trend in contemporary utopian studies toward finding ways of theorizing the aspirational impetus of cultural productions outside the exclusionary strictures of utopia as either a textual genre or a sociopolitical model. And crucially, such theorizations serve to open a conceptual space into which this study can productively intervene to stage its impelling conviction that lyric poetry, despite employing neither the narrative scope nor the prosaic directness to contribute to the utopian genre as constituted in the line from More and Bacon to Bellamy and Morris and beyond, is nonetheless an indispensable repository of utopian hope, desire, and myriad other modes of affirmative futurity that serve to continually expand our sense of the possible.

While the utopias to be found in poetry are indeed often minor and limited in the senses touched upon in Winter's and Nersessian's formulations, it should not be ignored that the careers of Yeats and Auden span what Winter has termed "the age of extremes"—a label particularly applicable to the decades from the First World War to the Stalinist era in the Soviet Union—and so their milieu is precisely the one in which the so-called major utopias most proliferated. This is one crucial reason Yeats and Auden make such fitting subjects for this study: not only does their unusual degree of political engagement mean that their work frequently embodies collective rather than just personal aspirations (a prerequisite for truly *utopian* consciousness), but their situatedness in history, literary and otherwise, means that they are confronted quite directly with the concept of utopia in ways that concretely inform their work. If, as Reeve-Tucker and Waddell suggest, "the twentieth century was a century of utopianism" (5), the period of the long twentieth century covered by this book—from Yeats's earliest poems in the 1880s to Auden's *Homage to Clio* in 1960—was particularly rich in seeing the publication of many defining works of the modern utopian and dystopian genres: Edward Bellamy's *Looking Backward* (1888), William Morris's *News from Nowhere* (1890), H. G. Wells's *A Modern Utopia* (1905), Yevgeny Zamyatin's *We* (1924), Aldous Huxley's *Brave New World* (1932), Katherine Burdekin's *Swastika Night* (1937), and George Orwell's *Nineteen Eighty-Four* (1949), along with many other less prominent examples. To this list can be added major historical and theoretical works like Mumford's *The Story of Utopias* (1922), Mannheim's *Ideology and Utopia* (1929), and Bloch's landmark works (*Geist der Utopie* (*The Spirit of Utopia*, 1918) and *Das Prinzip Hoffnung* (*The Principle of Hope*, 1938-47))—the latter of which, though they did not begin to be translated into English until the 1980s, nonetheless attest to a European climate vibrant with socially oriented aspirational thinking. The long shadows cast over Western liberal democracies by the twin ideological poles of fascism and communism—shadows which, as is well known and as this book will in places explore, often tinted Yeats's and Auden's lives and work—ensured that the cultural, intellectual, and political atmosphere of the era was animated by a manifold discourse on how society might best be organized to maximize harmony and justice while minimizing suffering and strife—i.e., the chief motive forces of utopian thinking.

Poets and the Pressure of Engagement

The poets of the era were thus often responding to a multidirectional cultural pressure to embody a collective consciousness rather than just an individual one. This highlights another reason for this book's particular focus: not only does the variety and intensity of responses to such pressure that one finds in Yeats's and Auden's work mark them out as extraordinary even among the myriad socially engaged poets of their era, but their responses are also remarkable for how often they are formulated in relation to each other, whether directly or, more often, in terms of the kind of poet each saw the other as being. Contained in Auden's assertion, in his elegy for Yeats, that "poetry makes nothing happen," for example, is a critique not just of Yeats himself but of the Romantic legacy he embodied and, to a certain extent, bequeathed (more on which later), which Auden saw as breeding auto-idolatrous illusions of worldly power in poets desperate to reclaim an ostensibly lost and yet actually chimerical cultural stature. Similarly, when in an October 1936 BBC radio broadcast, Yeats discusses Auden and his circle in terms of "their social passion, their sense of tragedy, their modernity" and remarks of them that "Some of these poets are Communists, but even in those who are not, there is an overwhelming social bitterness," it is clear within the context of Yeats's work that terms like "social passion," "modernity," and "bitterness" carry pejorative connotations in the way they contrast with the stentorian equanimity he was cultivating at this point in his career (*Later* 95). Neither is "modernity" a compliment from a poet who a year earlier had declared that "Ancient salt is best packing," nor can "passion" and "bitterness" help but ring as patronizing gestures to naïve youth from an elder statesman who had culminated a major poem just three months earlier with the Nietzschean assertion that "All things fall and are built again / And those who build them again are gay" (*Later* 213). As the context of these quotations makes clear, Yeats's and Auden's careers converge most intensely in the 1930s, both for historical reasons—Auden publishes his first (privately printed) book in 1928, Yeats dies in 1939, and both spend the decade as arguably the most prominent English-language poets of their respective generations—and because both occupy the role of public poet in a politically charged literary culture that draws them (at least discursively, for they never actually met) into each other's orbit.

The little magazine *New Verse*—which ran under the editorship of Geoffrey Grigson from 1933 to 1939, and to which Auden contributed more poems than any other publication—offers illustrative examples of the kinds of discourse that proliferated in this literary culture to urge a public, political role upon poets and the venues that published them. Samuel Hynes has amply charted how, despite Grigson's claim in its second issue that "*New Verse* has no politics" and his determination "to run an elitist, highbrow magazine that ... would avoid political commitment," the fact is that "*New Verse* was political, left-wing, and propagandist from its beginning, because the writers whom Grigson admired and wanted to publish were political" (115–16). This included, above all, Auden: Grigson claimed in the magazine's penultimate issue that "*New Verse* came into existence because of Auden," and its November 1937 issue was a special "Auden Double Number" consisting largely of essays on his work and brief testimonials (many of which are too caustic to be called tributes) from contemporaries such as George Barker, Cecil Day-Lewis, Graham Greene, and Dylan Thomas. Most of this material at least alludes to, if not discourses upon, Auden's perceived political commitments, and Yeats notably recurs as a figure of comparison. Greene, for instance, offers that "with the exception of *The Tower*, no volume of poetry has given me more excitement than *Look, Stranger*" (28–9), while Thomas, who lauds Auden as "a wide and deep poet," offers a much more pointed comparison: "[Auden] is as technically sufficient, and as potentially productive of greatness, as any poet writing in English. He makes Mr. Yeats's isolation guilty as a trance" (25). This distinction is echoed by Grigson himself in the issue's prefatory essay, which opens: "We salute in Auden (though we do not forget all that can be said against him) the first English poet for many years who is a poet all the way round. There are angles from which Mr. Eliot seems a ghost and even Mr. Yeats a gleam" (1). Though Thomas's and Grigson's language is elusive, within the context of *New Verse* in particular and the British literary climate of the 1930s in general, it is clear that their praise for Auden as "wide and deep" and "a poet all the way round" by contrast to Yeats's "isolation" (which is framed as "guilty" and "trance[like]") and his status as a comparative "gleam" is rooted in the sense that the *engagé* aura of Auden's work better meets the urgency of the times than Yeats's esoteric aestheticism. Even amidst the magazine's pervasive idolatry of the Audenesque, however, we see the man himself being held to account in ways that index the extraordinary pressure exerted upon poets within this literary milieu to position their art in sociopolitical terms. In an essay in the Auden Double Number entitled "Auden and Politics," Edgell Rickword critiques his subject in terms that will recur (most prominently in the reproachful assessments of Randall Jarrell in 1945 and Philip Larkin in 1960) throughout Auden's career:

> The lyric grace of Auden's later poems is achieved at the expense of that sensuous consciousness of social change which made his early poems such exciting discoveries. Auden is too good a poet to fall back into the simple exploration of individuality, after having originated a poetry of the social type along the lines of which there are so many fertile experiments to be made. (22)

In other words, Auden is a backslider, in serious danger of becoming bourgeois by relinquishing "poetry of the social type" in favor of "the simple exploration of individuality." Granted, Rickword was a card-carrying member of the Communist Party, and so a certain dogmatism is not unexpected. But this sentiment is echoed almost a decade later by the far less doctrinaire (though still in some senses Marxist) Jarrell, who excoriates the now-Christian Auden as a "writer [who] has saved his own soul, but has lost the whole world—has forgotten even the nature of that world" (456) and then more than a decade after that by the decidedly un-leftist Larkin, who likewise characterizes Auden's 1939 move to the United States as a retreat from the collective: "At one stroke he lost his key subject and emotion—Europe and the fear of war—and abandoned his audience together with their common dialect and concerns" (125). That Auden should face versions of this same criticism again and again, including early on in the pages of the magazine that published him most, attests to the extent of the critical pressure exerted on him by his most passionate and prominent critics to fill the role of social poet that he seemed to them to have originated, at least for his generation. Yeats, of course, had filled a similar social role for his, particularly in advancing the cause of Irish independence through his Celtic Revivalist and theater work. In awarding him the Nobel Prize for Literature in 1923 (five years before the publication of *Poems*, Auden's privately printed debut), the Swedish Academy cited "his always inspired poetry, which in a highly artistic form gives expression to the spirit of a whole nation" ("Nobel"). As the preeminent elder model of the successfully public poet for the politically minded young writers of Auden's generation, then, Yeats

NEW VERSE

Nos. 26-27   One Shilling   November, 1937

AUDEN DOUBLE NUMBER

Contributors: CHRISTOPHER ISHERWOOD, LOUIS MACNEICE, STEPHEN SPENDER, GEOFFREY GRIGSON, KENNETH ALLOTT, CECIL DAY LEWIS, HERBERT READ, EDWIN MUIR, EDGELL RICKWORD, ALLEN TATE, Etc.

THE REASON FOR THIS

WE SALUTE IN AUDEN (though we do not forget all that can be said against him) the first English poet for many years who is a poet all the way round. There are angles from which Mr. Eliot seems a ghost and even Mr. Yeats a gleam. Most authors still belong to the 1900 in which Mr. Sturge Moore, one of the spectres attendant on Mr. Yeats, said that " art seeks to reveal beauty, and that contemplation of beauty exhilarates, refines and elevates." Some others stick in those curious years when the limitations of Eliot and Pound were made into a system because their virtues were considerable and rare. But Auden does live in a new day. He is solid enough, poke him where you will, not crumbling like fudge. He is traditional, revolutionary, energetic, inquisitive, critical, and intelligent.

Some of the older living writers, Yeats, Wyndham Lewis and Eliot among them, have recognised this and committed themselves publicly (Lewis in " Blasting and Bombardiering ") in Auden's praise. Others are peevish, petty, jealous and silent. But, as this number shows, there are plenty of writers who do recognise Auden's broad power of raising ordinary speech into strong and strange incantation, and do see no reason for waiting to praise and criticise Auden until he has been dead a hundred years.

Figure 1   The cover of the November 1937 issue (the "Auden Double Number") of *New Verse*.

becomes a natural target when he is seen to retreat into insularity. Two issues after the Auden Double Number, in the March 1938 issue of *New Verse*, Grigson himself uses a review of several of Yeats's late publications as an opportunity to expand upon the earlier issue's more sidelong criticisms of him:

> The value of Yeats is nothing but the sum of his expressed moments of reality: the value of Communism, or the value of Fascism, is the sum of its working truths or realities. What is shocking about Yeats is asking us to declare only for Reality, in general, in the singular. *All things fall and are built again.* How comfortable! We have no right to listen to Yeats, no right at least to stay outside. To be free as a poet, to be free and to be allowed to have Reality in view, enjoins upon us, that, as clearly as we can with our imperfections of reason and sensibility, we must recognise, and not evade, realities of the present. (22)

In contrasting "expressed moments of reality" with "working truths or realities" and "Reality, in general, in the singular" with the "realities of the present," Grigson recapitulates the dichotomy between subjectivity and objectivity, the individual and the collective, that formed the basis of Rickword's critique of Auden in the earlier issue. Ironically, then, while Yeats is repeatedly held up as a negative example of a poet's retreat from the social world by contrast to Auden's committed engagement, at the same time the latter is already beginning to be negatively compared to his earlier self in precisely the same terms. Just as Yeats, as he moved out of the earliest phase of his career, faced repeated criticisms of his unwillingness to engage the national cause more directly by producing the kind of art that he would deride as propaganda—and was pursued throughout his career by criticisms of his failure to fulfill the public role he had earlier occupied—we can trace the same trajectory, albeit in markedly different historical and national circumstances, through Auden's career.

If Yeats and Auden can be criticized for evidencing less and less consciousness of the collective in their work as their careers evolve, how, then, can they be said to advance a poetics of utopia—which of course depends upon just such a consciousness in embodying the desire for a better way of living and being? As this book will illuminate, the received ways of mapping the two poets' career trajectories—with Yeats largely abandoning his early cultural nationalism in favor of an increasingly insular esotericism and Auden relinquishing his early communalist Freudo-Marxism in favor of a rarefied Kierkegaardian Christianity—serve to mask the extent to which, even across these significant shifts, their work continually resonates as utopian in both its persistent engagement with stances of affirmative futurity and the trans-individualistic expansiveness with which it takes up those stances. In other words, through all their various reorientations, Yeats and Auden both remain deeply *social* poets. Granted, this may be more difficult to see when the unit of sociality being addressed shifts from that of a single polity (Ireland, for example, or Europe) to something more encompassing and even cosmic in scope (such as "humanity," whether across history or under God). In a sense, the analogous shift undertaken by both poets from more specific to more universal frames of concern is a way of evading the clamorous demands from certain cultural sectors (as we see with *New Verse*) to put their art to concrete social use, and thus is a declaration of artistic independence from matters of sociopolitical utility. At the same time, such a shift is also a means of asserting poetry's ultimate importance to such matters: Yeats's late immersion in the arcana of historical cycles and Auden's post-conversion insistence on humanity's inveterate fallenness can be seen not as retreats from a poetics of utopia but higher-order enactments of it, as in both cases poetry is asserted to play a crucial role in illuminating how we might more searchingly commune with the metaphysical forces that encompass our existence—thereby embodying the desire for a better way of living and being in a way that transcends the worldly materialism and parochiality of national and other -isms.[8]

I have already discussed how poetry can be seen to embody utopian desire at the formal level, and this Schillerian sense of form as fundamentally aspirational is one aspect of the Romantic legacy that both poets inherit. A more overt aspect of that legacy, however, derives from Percy Bysshe Shelley, whom Yeats revered, and Auden—in a way that often seems a reactionary response to the former's reverence—treated mainly as an object of ridicule. If Auden's "poetry makes nothing happen" is the most renowned aphorism about poetry to emerge from the twentieth century, Shelley's "Poets are the unacknowledged legislators of the world" is surely its nineteenth-century equivalent in renown. The vast surface difference between these two statements in terms of the role they attribute to poetry and poets in shaping the world's destiny is partly explicable by the fact that Auden's chief concerns as a public intellectual throughout the first decade-plus of his career are the rise of fascism and the threat of war, and he saw clearly that for all the pacifist and anti-fascist impetus among his contemporaries, poetry was impotent in the face of these encroaching disasters. Yeats, by contrast, repeatedly toys with the idea that his work actually did contribute to altering the course of political affairs (for example in "Man and Echo," in which he wonders at his role in fostering the nationalist fervor that culminated in the 1916 Easter Rising: "Did that play of mine send out / Certain men the English shot?"), and no less a political critic than Edward Said eulogizes him as "a poet of decolonization" (84) and celebrates "[his] accomplishment in restoring a suppressed history, and rejoining the nation to it" (90). While Auden's experience of helplessness fed into his distaste for the Shelleyan exaltation of poetry's capacities, then, Yeats's political success within a cultural nationalist context (most concretely registered in his being made a senator of the Irish Free State in 1922) led him in the opposite direction. This contrast is oversimplified, however, as Auden's early work often evidences the hope that poets might indeed serve a legislative function. As late as his 1935 essay "Psychology and Art To-day," he links his own work with the notion of "parable-art, that art which shall teach man to unlearn hatred and learn love," and so his later rejection of such ambitious claims for art should be read as born of disillusionment rather than long-held conviction (*English* 341–2). Given that this disillusionment can be seen to have culminated in his elegy for Yeats, with its repudiation of its subject's Shelleyan convictions of poetry's worldly power, it is crucial that we turn to the textual root of such convictions: Shelley's 1821 *Defence of Poetry*, the source of the "legislators" claim and the most influential account of how poetry's power manifests in sociopolitical actuality.

Shelley's Utopian Poetics

Though it never employs the word "utopia," the conviction and audacity with which Shelley's *Defence* attributes to poetry an inherent futurity and accords it an indispensable role in the founding of more ideal societies makes it essentially the urtext of the utopian poetics that reverberates through Yeats's and Auden's work. Shelley begins with a crucial distinction: "Reason respects the differences, and imagination the similitudes of things" (480)—thus casting reason as a dividing and imagination as a harmonizing faculty. Poetry, he goes on to claim, "may be defined as 'the expression of the Imagination': and poetry is connate with the origin of man" (480). Positing within humanity an inherent principle of harmony, and exalting poetry as the expression of this principle, Shelley thus grants to poets—"in the most universal sense of the word"—responsibility for all that is praiseworthy in human achievement, social and political as well as artistic (481). In their narrower sense, too, poets represent a crucial force for unity, as their "vitally metaphorical" language "marks the before unapprehended relations of things, and perpetuates their apprehension" (482), thus widening our spheres of inclusivity. Later in the *Defence* he refines this formula, claiming of poetry that "It awakens and enlarges the mind itself by rendering it the receptacle of a thousand unapprehended combinations of thought" (487). This enlargement has not only aesthetic but also moral consequences; calling imagination "the great instrument of moral good," Shelley broadly asserts that "poetry strengthens that faculty which is the organ of the moral nature of man, in the same manner as exercise strengthens a limb" (487). In other words, poetry stands, in Schillerian fashion, as a chief agent of moral conditioning, so much a precondition for any more ideal society that without it, Shelley claims, any more practical means of social improvement could never have arisen:

> It exceeds all imagination to conceive of what would have been the moral condition of the world if neither Dante, Petrarch, Boccaccio, Chaucer, Shakespeare, Calderon, Lord Bacon, nor Milton, had ever existed; if Raphael and Michael Angelo had never been born; if the Hebrew poetry had never been translated; if a revival of the study of Greek literature had never taken place; if no monuments of antient [sic] sculpture had been handed down to us; and if the poetry of the religion of the antient world had been extinguished together with its belief. The human mind could never, except by the intervention of these excitements, have been awakened to the invention of the grosser sciences, and that application of analytical reasoning to the aberrations of society, which it is now attempted to exalt over the direct expression of the inventive and creative faculty itself. (502)

Did Auden have this passage specifically in mind when he hyperbolically asserted, in "The Public v. the Late Mr. William Butler Yeats," the utter lack of material difference that art has made upon the world? Whether he did or not, the contrast here is direct: Shelley sets out a catalogue of immortal poets (plus two painters, themselves "poets" according to his extended definition) whose achievements improved both our moral and (it is implied) material condition to an unimaginable degree. For it is only through the "intervention" of poetry and its "excitements" that we have been "awakened" to the possibility of improving our world through the "application of analytical reasoning"—which now, forgetting its dependence upon poetry at its very nascency, we have come to value over the creative, moral, synthetic faculty that gave it birth.

While poetry may not itself effect practical change, then, the very impulse to change—to effect affirmatively different futures—derives from it. When Shelley claims of the poet that "he beholds the future in the present, and his thoughts are the germs of the flower and the fruit of latest time," he is not attributing to poetry any literally prophetic or future-telling role, but rather emphasizing that as an art reliant upon metaphor and thus always concerned with harmony, resemblance, and similitude, poetry always implicitly looks forward to a time of greater unity: its futurity is inherent in its rootedness in trope (482). It is on this basis that Shelley sets forth the connection—hugely influential on Yeats—between poetry and the forging of nations or peoples. Praising the English poets and philosophers of his own time for "surpass[ing] beyond comparison any who have appeared since the last national struggle for religious and civil liberty," he goes on in the last paragraph of the *Defence* to more broadly eulogize the poet's role as harbinger of any potential utopia:

> The most unfailing herald, companion, and follower of the awakening of a great people to work a beneficial change in opinion or institution, is Poetry. At such periods there is an accumulation of the power of communicating and receiving intense and impassioned conceptions respecting man and nature. The persons in whom this power resides, may often, as far as regards many portions of their nature, have little apparent correspondence with that spirit of good of which they are the ministers. But even whilst they deny and abjure, they are yet compelled to serve, the Power which is seated upon the throne of their own soul. It is impossible to read the compositions of the most celebrated writers of the present day without being startled with the electric life which burns within their words. They measure the circumference and sound the depths of human nature with a comprehensive and all-penetrating spirit, and they are themselves perhaps the most sincerely astonished at its manifestations, for it is less their spirit than the spirit of the age. Poets are the hierophants of an unapprehended inspiration, the mirrors of the gigantic shadows which futurity casts upon the present, the words which express what they understand not; the trumpets which sing to battle, and feel not what they inspire: the influence which is moved not, but moves. Poets are the unacknowledged legislators of the World. (508)

Shelley's claim that poetry both prefigures and arises out of great upsurges in political awareness would be echoed continually by the early Yeats, who saw art as helping to forge the Irish people into a national consciousness while at the same time wondering whether the best art was not rather the *result* of such a consciousness—an ambiguity nicely captured in the climactic question of his 1903 essay "The Galway Plains": "Does not the greatest poetry always require a people to listen to it?" (*Early* 158). Shelley's figuration of "the spirit of good" of which poets are the often-unwitting "ministers," and of "the electric life which burns within their words" are also frequently echoed in Yeats's early cultural nationalist writings; in his 1898 essay "The Autumn of the Body," for example, he rhapsodizes on the transfigurative "energies" of the arts, which "lie dreaming of things to come," and asserts that "the arts are ... about to take upon their shoulders the burdens that have fallen from the shoulders of priests" (*Early* 140-1).

If the influence of the *Defence* on Yeats is readily attested to by his echoes of it, any such echoes to be found in Auden speak to his disdain for Shelley's grandiosity. Of the *Defence*'s famous last sentence Auden wrote: "How glad I am that the silliest remark ever made about poets, 'the unacknowledged legislators of the world,' was made by a poet whose work I detest. Sounds more like the secret police to me" (*Prose II* 348). In response, Shelley or his advocates might point to that last paragraph's repeated implicit assertion that the legislative function of poets is not just "unacknowledged" by society at large, but by the poets themselves: they may "have little apparent correspondence with that spirit of good of which they are the ministers," so that "even whilst they deny and abjure, they are yet compelled to serve, the Power which is seated upon the throne of their own soul." Indeed, as this book will show, although Auden came to explicitly disavow his legislative ambitions, his 1930s writings abound in them. And much like Yeats, the later Auden—while overtly rejecting the Shelleyan assertion of poetry's legislative potential—yet preserves some of Shelley's conviction that poetry can indeed stand in some crucial relation to our strivings after social change. This is why I have drawn the subtitle of this book from a less renowned claim in that last paragraph of Shelley's *Defence*, that poets are "the mirrors of the gigantic shadows which futurity casts upon the present": because most broadly I attempt to show throughout how Yeats and Auden did in fact effect such mirroring, reflecting in surfaces variously cracked, distorted, and otherwise fraught by their minds and times, both how loomingly persistent are our longings after better futures and how apt is poetry as a medium for refracting such longings.

The Structure of This Book

The rest of *Shadows of Futurity* consists of five body chapters—two on Yeats's career, two on Auden's, and one that reads their late work in juxtaposition—plus a Conclusion that attempts to derive from my exploration of Yeats's and Auden's various iterations of a poetics of utopia a framework through which to view modern poetry more generally as a utopian artform. I have structured the book in this way in order convey a sense of narrative arc, drawing in biographical, historical, theoretical, and artistic contexts as I trace the two poets' shifting engagements with a poetics of utopia—in terms of their direct negotiations of the concept of "utopia" as such, their forays into the utopian genre, and the way their work variously conceives of poetry as a utopian artform that can uniquely embody the desire for better ways of living and being. Though I draw extensively on both poets' published prose and letters as a means of charting their evolving thought, when it comes to the poetry, I have deliberately chosen to engage most concertedly with poems that are generally seen as central to each poet's body of work—poems that literary scholars not specifically focused on Yeats and Auden are likely to have read, that students are likely to have encountered in anthologies, and that avid readers of the two poets are likely to know intimately. I have done this in order to show that reading Yeats and Auden within the framework of utopia can renovate our understanding of their signal achievements as artists, alerting us to how thoroughly their best-known work is impelled by the conviction that poetry, as a fundamentally social medium, can potently embody the desires that fuel our search for more perfect forms of sociality. Put another way, while the status of Yeats and Auden as preeminent *political* poets has rarely been in question, the framework of utopia allows us to perceive anew not only the sheer scope and complexity of their engagements with the dilemmas of collectivity, but also the potential of poetry itself as a force for social melioration. Furthermore, this dynamic operates in reverse; that is, while utopia allows us to see Yeats and Auden in a newly brilliant light, their myriad expressions of utopian poetics allow us to glimpse new facets of the concept of utopia itself—what is at stake in it, how its meanings are contested, and why it remains urgently relevant to both literary and living history.

Chapter 1 begins with a reading of the first poem in Yeats's *Collected Poems*, "The Song of the Happy Shepherd"—a work that inaugurates what I term the dominant "pastoral utopianism" of his early poetry. Though pre-nationalist in the sense of hearkening back to a classical image of Arcadia rather than to the indigenous Celtic myths that would dominate his poetry of the 1890s, "The Song of the Happy Shepherd" nonetheless effects the key gesture of his cultural nationalist work in exhorting the reader to image a utopian future by looking to an idealized pastoral past. After briefly summarizing and mediating among a number of prominent theoretical views on both the differences between and the mutual inherency of the pastoral and utopian modes, I read several of Yeats's most renowned early lyrics—"The Madness of King Goll," "The Lake Isle of Innisfree," and "The Song of the Wandering Aengus"—alongside his essays of the period, with a view to highlighting how his early poetics aims at rendering inextricable the yearning of his solitary protagonists from the collective dream of Irish nationhood. In other words, I argue that Yeats's early poetry metonymically conflates the singular lyric voice with the voice of the Irish nation, illuminating what Adorno calls the "collective substratum" upon which lyric is founded ("Lyric Poetry" 217).

In the latter half of the chapter, I characterize this conflation of lyric and national striving as fulfilling the utopian function of "the education of desire," arguing (with support from his essays) that Yeats's early work aims to instill in its readers the yearning it itself embodies, and that in hearkening back to a Celticized pastoral Ireland, it hopes that such images might resonate so forcefully in the collective imagination as to model the nation's future unity. After clarifying how Yeats found authoritative precedent in Shelley (and particularly in the *Defence*) for this notion of poetry as a unifying force, I then engage with two camps of critical commentators on Yeats's early cultural nationalism: first, those who see in Yeats's appeal to Celtic myth an attempt to locate authentic Irishness in pre-Christian sources, and so to consolidate the precarious status of the Anglo-Irish Protestant class to which his family belonged; and second, those who find in the Celtic Twilight—no matter how historically dubious its characteristic images—a more authentic (and indeed successful) attempt to unite the Irish people by presenting a compensatory vision of a unified cultural past toward which the burgeoning nation might strive. In the chapter's final section, however, I acknowledge that by the turn of the century even Yeats was disillusioned as to the prospect of such unity, that his focus was already shifting from images of community to images of coterie, and therefore that explicit utopianism was dwindling from his aesthetic. As an index of this shift, I read his 1902 lyric "Adam's Curse," a poem that embodies both the burgeoning disdain for the middle classes that would dominate his bitter middle period and, concomitantly, his growing sense of poetry's social inefficacy.

Yeats's disdain for the middle classes lies at the center of Chapter 2, which explores how the poet's well-documented anti-materialism issues in an overt hostility toward the concept of utopia as such. For the later Yeats, utopian social reformers suffered not from an excess of idealism, but from precisely the opposite: an overweening materialism, rooted in the wrong belief that societal ills could be eradicated by political or economic means. By contrast, Yeats's cyclical view of history maintains the inevitability of social strife, and the concomitant perpetuity of our desire to overcome it—a desire that gives art (including his own) its animating impetus. His hostility to utopia arises, I argue, not from lack of sympathy with the impulse to social melioration, but with what he saw as utopians' crassly materialistic conviction that a better world can be achieved once and for all. Building from Levitas's definition of utopia as "the expression of desire for a better way of being," I argue that while Yeats sees the utopians he disdains as seeking the achievement (and therefore the end) of their reformist desires, he himself seeks (and indeed relishes) the endless perpetuation of desire. Furthermore, I contend that this stance, reflecting both his cyclical view of history and his conviction that the end of desire would mean the end of art, in fact makes him a kind of *antiutopian utopian*, an ardent desirer of better worlds whose explicit repudiation of utopianism conceals a deep sympathy with the affirmative futurity that drives it.

In elaborating this argument, I read every occurrence of the word "utopia" in Yeats's body of work, highlighting how his overwhelmingly pejorative treatment of the concept arises not only out of elitist sentiment—as many past commentators on Yeats's politics have emphasized—but also out of his conviction that the achievement of the socialist or mass-democratic utopia sought by reformers of his time would put an end to the antithetical striving out of which great art is generated. Through readings of several of Yeats's landmark later poems—"Upon a House Shaken by the Land Agitation," "September 1913," and "Nineteen Hundred and Nineteen"—as well as essays, letters, and sections of his philosophical treatise *A Vision*, I illuminate how despite his overt hostility to the concept of utopia, his work repeatedly comments upon, engages with, and indeed embodies the aspirational impulse at the concept's core. I end the chapter with a reading of Yeats's two Byzantium poems, focusing on how the poet's varied depictions of the mytho-historical city find him both acknowledging the allure of *eu*topia (in the desire to reach the good place that animates "Sailing to Byzantium") and concluding that all such desire ultimately leads to the static *ou*topian realm of art (the roiling purgatorial no-place portrayed in "Byzantium"). Yeats thus exalts art's capacity to embody the utopias he rejects in life, to afford us unachievable images of the desire on which the artistic imagination must never cease to feed.

This emphasis on desire carries over into Chapters 3 and 4, on early and later Auden respectively. The first of these highlights how the desire for unity—both social and psychological—can be seen as the central animating impetus of Auden's poetry from the beginning of his career until his move to the United States in 1939. Beginning with an examination of sections of his 1929 Berlin Journal that evidence the poet's early belief in humanity's essential dividedness—a doctrine that serves to implicitly justify the hermetic style of his early work—I then read his landmark 1927 poem "The Watershed" as a fraught embodiment of this doctrine, a text that both revels in the poet's singularity and laments his aloneness. Mapping out the poem's rootedness in Auden's nostalgic love for the Pennine coal-mining region, I read it as a reflection upon the speaker's inability not only to recapture the Edenic wholeness felt in his past encounters with the region's landscape (as many critics have emphasized), but also to relate meaningfully to the people of the region, from whom he finds himself divided by vocation and class. "The Watershed" thus poetically depicts the tripartite state of division set out in the Berlin Journal—psychological, ecological, and social—and presages Auden's attempts throughout the 1930s to conceive of a role for poetry in both envisioning and bringing about a state of unity that would heal these divisions.

As with the early Yeats, I cast Auden's quest for unity in this period as *utopian*, on the grounds that (1) it thoroughly conforms to Levitas's definition of utopia as "the expression of desire for a better way of being"; and (2) the poems that best embody this desire often employ topographical motifs that ally them with the mainstream of utopian literature deriving from More. In exploring the precise contours of Auden's desire for unity, I look at his 1930s essays "Writing" and "Psychology and Art To-day" as well as his Introduction to the 1935 anthology *The Poet's Tongue*, to highlight how over the course of his early career he moved from diagnosing our disunity (which he saw as rooted in our excessive "self-consciousness," a concept he borrows from D. H. Lawrence and Gerald Heard) to seeking to remedy it. Over the course of these writings, he casts poetry first as a symptom of our dissolution, then as refining our knowledge of good and evil, and finally as leading us to make more moral (and therefore more communally minded) choices. While becoming in his prose increasingly more hopeful of poetry's educative capacities, however, in his poetry he registers such hope far more ambivalently. Two close readings frame the second half of this chapter: first, of the 1933 sestina "Paysage Moralisé," which I read as using the repeated end-words of the sestina form to suggest the tragic perpetual cyclicity of the human quest for utopia; and second, of the 1938 sonnet sequence *In Time of War*, which goes further to suggest that the universality of such questing—the striving of fallen beings after a lost unity—may be the only thing that ever unites us. Chapter 3 thus closes by suggesting that by the end of the 1930s, Auden's growing conviction of humanity's fallenness had all but drained his work of the secular utopianism that had animated it throughout the previous decade.

Chapter 4 sets out the consequences of this, charting how Auden came to believe instead that poetry's chief extra-aesthetic role lay in illuminating the extent of our fallenness, and therefore the delusoriness of all our quests for earthly paradise. The chapter opens by examining Auden's assertion (in his 1950s essay "The Virgin and the Dynamo") that "Every good poem is very nearly a utopia" (*Dyer's* 71), reading this claim within its context as evidence that despite his pejorative treatment of the concept of utopia earlier in his career, Auden came to find it a useful way of analogizing poetry's capacity to embody our desire for more coherent, unified futures. The word *analogizing* is crucial here, however: for Auden continually warns against the mistaken belief that (as he puts it later in the same essay) "since all is well in the work of art, all is well in history" (71). Recognizing that the claim inherent in this warning—that art's potential to embody coherence in no way implies its ability to actualize it in the real world—is simply a less overt version of what has become his most famous line, "poetry makes nothing happen," I then move on to discuss both the 1939 elegy for Yeats in which the line appears and the contemporaneous essay "The Public v. the Late Mr. William Butler Yeats"—both of which engage much more ambivalently with poetry's extra-aesthetic impact than is commonly appreciated. Reading the dialogic structures of both poem and essay as working to embody opposed but by no means exclusive views of poetry's real-world efficacy, I ultimately argue that read in wider context, the elegy's contention that "poetry makes nothing happen" serves to set out what I call a *negative poetics*. In presencing nonexistent possibility both formally and (often) through its subject matter, poetry makes *nothing* a thing that happens, alerting us to the gap between utopian desire and its continually deferred fulfillment.

The second half of the chapter explores how throughout the 1940s and into the 1950s, Auden conceives of this gap in explicitly religious terms. Reading his 1941 poem "Atlantis" and his 1944 opus *The Sea and the Mirror* alongside his prose writings of the period, I show how Auden's engagement with the idea of a better world shifts from bearing a social emphasis to signaling a more strictly salvational one. According to the Christian-existentialist Auden of the early 1940s, art's meliorative function inheres in its capacity to flout what he calls "auto-idolatry"—the delusion that our existences are self-authorizing rather than dependent upon God's grace—and to illuminate our mutual fallenness. Focusing on the way these works register God as an absence rather than as an entity with any positive qualities, I highlight their embodiment of a negative poetics that illuminates not as before our perpetual distance from utopia, but rather (as Caliban puts it in the climactic speech of *The Sea and the Mirror*) "the ungarnished offended gap between what you so questionably are and what you are commanded without any question to become" (50)—in other words, between fallenness and salvation. I close the chapter with a reading of "Vespers," from Auden's 1955 sequence "Horae Canonicae," the last direct engagement with the concept of utopia in his oeuvre. Examining the poem's dialogic structure as a conversation between the "Arcadian" speaker and his "Utopian" nemesis, I suggest that, contrary to many readings of the poem that accept the Arcadian's playful hedonism as Auden's personal viewpoint, one might read it as embodying his final acknowledgement of his own propensity to utopian striving—a striving henceforth seemingly banished from his aesthetic, as the work of his final decades finds him more likely to gently revel in humanity's imperfections than thirst after their improvement.

Chapter 5, the book's final body chapter, brings Yeats and Auden together to illuminate how the disparate historical circumstances in which each poet's late work was produced give rise to distinct differences in how it theorizes and embodies poetry's capacity to adopt a utopian stance toward the possible and thereby to alter history's course. While Auden's post-Second World War work emerges out of the ideologically settled intellectual climate of what has come to be known as the "Liberal Consensus"—a milieu in which Lionel Trilling could opine in 1950 that "In the United States at this time liberalism is not only the dominant but even the sole intellectual tradition. ... [T]here are no conservative or reactionary ideas in general circulation" (xv)—Yeats died in 1939, and so his late work is produced in the fraught lead-up to the war whose arrival so irrevocably altered the course of Auden's career. In elaborating the ramifications of this difference in historical and ideological positioning, I build the chapter around a comparison of the poems from their later periods that most explicitly meditate upon the artist's role amid the specter of global conflict, Yeats's "Lapis Lazuli" and Auden's "The Shield of Achilles." While both poems employ the ekphrastic mode to address art's responsibility in relation to the violence of a world in crisis, and both dramatize the conflict between what an audience in times of such upheaval might expect of art and what the artist is willing to dispense, they adopt nearly opposite stances toward the transfigurative capacities of art—an opposition that attests to the fundamental irreconcilability of their respective utopian poetics.

After elaborating the distinct historical contexts of Yeats's and Auden's late work, the first half of the chapter centers on a reading of "Lapis Lazuli." Against a critical consensus that views the poem as fatalistic in its acceptance of perpetual strife and quietist in its aloofness from contemporary political conflicts, I argue that it instead projects a theory of art as a transhistorical repository of the signal virtue of gaiety that—despite the determinist implications of Yeats's cosmology—is ultimately cast as harboring an unquenchable glimmer of ameliorative potential. Highlighting how, in addressing the poem against an audience demanding political action, Yeats casts Auden himself (whom he regarded as a fetishist of "marching feet") as one of its veiled antagonists, I go on to elaborate how Auden was much less a poet of political action than his popular reputation at the time would suggest, tracing his complex thinking on "action" from his Freudian work of the late 1930s (in which interpersonal behaviors are often cast having political ramifications) to his essays of the 1960s, which see poetry's value as inhering precisely in its being "gratuitous"—that is, so marginal an activity as to be virtually free from the cycles of production and consumption that comprise the "serious" work of modern capitalist societies. This emphasis on poetry's gratuitousness places Auden in dialogue with his near-contemporary Adorno, for whom all art, despite its emergence out of the world as it exists, retains a utopian residue through its inextinguishable kernel of otherness from that world. Moving from a comparison of Auden's and Adorno's conceptions of art's utopian capacities into a reading of "The Shield of Achilles," I contend that the poem is a self-reflexive exemplar of Adorno's assertion of poetry's barbarity after Auschwitz—an ekphrastic artifact that, contrary to Yeats's vision in "Lapis Lazuli," casts poetry not as a repository of ameliorating virtue but instead as exercising a purely negative utopian function in giving estranging form to the disturbing discrepancy between our expectations of wholeness and reality's obdurate irreconcilability. The chapter closes with a brief comparison between Yeats's "The Statues" and Auden's "Homage to Clio," the latter of which answers the former's optimistic account of art's causal impact on history with the assertion that art's much more modest recourse—and perhaps the most authentically utopian gesture left to it—is to break history's silence.

In taking stock of the various iterations of a poetics of utopia to be found in Yeats's and Auden's work, the book's Conclusion seeks to extrapolate a framework through which modern poetry more generally can be examined as a utopian artform. Enumerating three key social conditions to which modern poets (at least in the Anglo-American sphere) commonly respond—social atomization, a dwindling audience for poetry, and a pressure to turn their work to political ends—I go on to outline the ways in which the pressure exerted by these conditions can be seen to manifest in the work of other modern poets, mapping out points of convergence and contrast between Yeats and Auden and such writers as Eliot, Stevens, Ezra Pound, Mina Loy, and D. H. Lawrence. Above all, I aim in the Conclusion to assert poetry's singularity as a utopian artform, theorizing its capacity to embody both the blueprintist and iconoclastic traditions of utopia at once and contending that the questions this book poses in relation to Yeats's and Auden's work—most essential among them, "What does this poetry aspire to?"—should be asked far more frequently of poetry, particularly in the twentieth century and beyond. We need to attend more pointedly, I argue, to poetry's pervasive utopian dimensions if we are not to lose sight of both what it can do that other arts cannot and how its singular synthetic capacities can be of use to us in a time when forms of fragmentation and disconnection—social, political, ecological—pose perhaps unprecedented threats.

Notes

1 For the five years from 2016 to 2020, a Google News search for "poetry makes nothing happen" produces an average of twenty-two results (with a low of eleven in 2017

and a high of thirty-one in 2019). Many of these occurrences treat Auden's words as an aphorism entirely free of context, while those that do contextualize it often do so misleadingly—as exemplified by the author of an August 6, 2020, article in the *Berkshire Eagle* entitled "A Primer on Poetry for the Practical Politician," who wrongly claims that "W. H. Auden, in a 1939 elegy for Yeats, dismissed his fellow poet's literary efforts for Irish independence, saying 'poetry makes nothing happen'" (Morrison). For a full analysis of the poem in question, see Chapter 4.

2   I have chosen not to take up debates on poetry's status as an aspirational artform as they arise out of non-English-language poetry both because, quite simply, this is a study of Yeats and Auden in particular—two poets whose work, as this book will make clear, sustains such debates to an extent unsurpassed by poets in any language—and because to broach the work of non-English-language poets in the glancing way that space affords here would do a disservice to that work's complexity, raising thorny questions that would necessarily be left unanswered. From the sundry body of scholarship that takes up non-English-language poetry in relation to utopia, one might particularly highlight Manus O'Dwyer's book *Memory and Utopia: The Poetry of José Ángel Valente*, Analisa DeGrave's essay "Ecoliterature and Dystopia: Gardens and Topos in Modern Latin American Poetry," and Maria Lourdes Otaegi Imaz's essay "Looking for Paradise. Utopia as a Social Issue in Basque Poetry."

3   Casanova's landmark book *The World Republic of Letters* (2004) conceives of the world of literature as one characterized by rivalry, competition, and shifts in fortune among hierarchically positioned literary "spaces"—a world in which, for example, "The classics are the privilege of the oldest literary nations, which, in elevating their foundational texts to the status of timeless works of art, have defined their literary capital as nonnational and ahistorical—a definition that corresponds exactly to the definition that they have given of literature itself" (15). In casting the development of Irish literature as a signal case study, she claims that "The distinctive quality of the Irish case resides in the fact that over a fairly short period a literary space emerged and a literary heritage was created in an exemplary way," singling out Yeats as the inaugural figure in the emergence of this "literary space" (304).

4   Sean Pryor's *W. B. Yeats, Ezra Pound, and the Poetry of Paradise* (2011) dialogues with my approach in its focus on poetry's propensity to envision ideal states of being, and further, in its investigation of the ways that poets see their work as not just depicting but formally embodying those ideal states. It is a rigorous and carefully argued study of the many formal and conceptual manifestations of both celestial and secular notions of "paradise" in Yeats's and Pound's work. Though it shares with the present study a sustained focus on a single guiding concept, it differs in having no significant focus on poetry's potential real-world impact—largely because "paradise" is primarily a spiritual concept rather than a political one. Furthermore, because "paradise" (unlike "utopia") does not name a literary genre, Pryor's study cannot redress poetry's neglect within a given generic framework as I aim to do.

5   See Barrett Watton, "Language Writing's Concrete Utopia: From Leningrad to Occupy" in Ayers et al., *Utopia: the Avant Garde, Modernism, and (Im)possible Life*, De Gruyter, 2015, pp. 99–119.

6   Given his implicit commitment to a blueprintist view of utopia, it is telling that Mao's characterization of Eliot's utopianism does not hinge on his poetry per se, but rather relies on his verse dramas, which afford the possibility of stagecraft to concretely spatialize their utopian implications. Unlike the present study, then, Mao's analysis is not particularly indebted to the impulse-oriented theorization of utopia that guides

most contemporary scholarship in the field—nor is it committed to advancing poetry in itself as a utopian artform.

7 In a chapter of *The Ideology of the Aesthetic* titled "Schiller and Hegemony," Terry Eagleton critiques the Schillerian conception of the aesthetic for being void of content, characterizing it as "nothing less than the boundless infinity of our total humanity, ruined as soon as realized" (110). As a consequence, Eagleton claims, "the aesthetic would seem less to transfigure material life than to cast a decorous veil over its chronic unregeneracy" (117). While from a Marxist perspective, then, Schiller's aesthetics is essentially ideological in its pretense of reconciling nature to reason while actually subordinating the former to the latter, within the framework of this study—and particularly in relation to the impulse-oriented view of utopia that prevails within contemporary utopian studies—the absence at the center of Schiller's conception of the aesthetic is a large part of what makes it useful, as it stands at the nascency of the utopian tradition of negative aesthetics that culminates in Adorno—a tradition that bears crucially on my analysis in this book, particularly in Chapters 4 and 5.

8 Said makes an analogous point to explain Yeats's shift from work concretely in the service of cultural nationalism to the otherworldly speculations of *A Vision*: "For Yeats the overlappings he knew existed between his Irish nationalism and the English cultural heritage that both dominated and empowered him as a writer were bound to cause an overheated tension, and it is the pressure of this urgently political and secular tension that one may speculate caused him to try to resolve it on a 'higher,' that is, nonpolitical level. Thus the deeply eccentric and aestheticized histories he produced in *A Vision* and the later quasi-religious poems are elevations of the tension to an extraworldly level" (80).

Chapter 1

"EVER NEW AND EVER ANCIENT": THE PASTORAL UTOPIAS OF EARLY YEATS

Yeats's early work does not readily dwell in the present. For the young poet of the 1880s and 1890s, the here and now registers mainly in its potentiality, glimmering in a state of latency, on the verge of awakening. While believing that the nascent Irish nation lay "bound together by imaginative possessions … and by a past of great passions" (*Early* 158), he also believed that "the arts lie dreaming of things to come" (*Early* 140), and that as a poet he could work to usher forth "that new great utterance for which the world is waiting" (*Uncollected 1* 250). Convinced that as an "imaginative artist" he inherently "belongs to the invisible life, and delivers its ever new and ever ancient revelation" (*Early* 143), this early Yeats not only embodies in his work the mythic and the millennial, the nostalgic and the hopeful, the pastoral and the utopian, but he also consistently illuminates the inextricability of these past- and future-looking registers. Early Yeats embodies, in a sense, Schiller's type of the elegiac poet, "in search of nature but as an idea and in a perfection in which it never existed"—except that one might substitute "nation" for "nature" in this formula (*On the Naïve* 49). Yeats hearkens back to a mythic Celtic construct which, he hopes, might resonate so heavily in the Irish imagination as to model the nation's future unity. The historical tenuousness of this construct posed little problem for a poet whose aesthetic depended so thoroughly, from his very earliest poems, on portraying states of unsatisfied (and largely unsatisfiable) desires. In this chapter I will focus on the world-building aspirations of Yeats's early lyric speakers who, while often striving toward a pastoral ideal that resides in the impossible gap between "good place" (*eutopia*) and "no-place" (*outopia*), implicitly make an objective of desire itself, casting it as the space of affirmative futurity that must be occupied as a precondition to any more concrete communal reform, a kind of antechamber to nationhood.

"The Song of the Happy Shepherd" as Post-Pastoral

The first poem in Yeats's *Collected Poems* as assembled under the poet's supervision in 1933—and still in all editions available today—begins with a characteristic proclamation: "The woods of Arcady are dead." As an entry into a body of work, this opening line situates us in the post-pastoral, a world in which the consolation once held out by the imaginary idylls of old now rings hollow. Like much of early Yeats, "The Song of the Happy Shepherd" teems with dead kings, faded vistas, and a general sense of yearning conveyed through a dreamlike haze—as though the fallenness of the modern world made it impossible even to wish with any real precision. Originally given the elegiac title "The Song of the Last Arcadian," the poem sets out in its opening lines a familiar Romantic opposition, lamenting the usurpation of imagination's authority by the forces of empiricism:

> The woods of Arcady are dead,
> And over is their antique joy;
> Of old the world on dreaming fed;
> Grey Truth is now her painted toy;
> Yet still she turns her restless head:
> But O, sick children of the world,
> Of all the many changing things
> In dreary dancing past us whirled,
> To the cracked tune that Chronos sings,
> Words alone are certain good. (1–10)[1]

First written in 1885, the poem exemplifies some of the more hackneyed tendencies of *fin de siècle* poetry, its buoyant four-beat line failing to adequately counterbalance the prevailing undercurrent of morbidity, the sense one gets of the young poet's reveling a little too indulgently in the approach of the century's end, of his wanting too desperately to find apocalyptic resonance in the coming new era. On the one hand, its vision of a fallen world reads like the maudlin fantasizing of an angst-ridden nineteen-year-old Anglo-Irishman still laboring under the earliest influences of his adolescent years, the moralistic Spenser and the visionary Shelley, both great forgers of compensatory myths. On the other hand, however, both its anti-materialist disdain and its concomitant faith in the evocative force of words would remain powerful motifs throughout the poet's career. Yeats never relinquished the hope—inherited from Shelley, Blake, and French Symbolists like Villiers de l'Isle-Adam—that one day the coat of transfixing gloss would be stripped from the present age's favorite "painted toy," exposing "Grey Truth" in all its colorless sterility and ushering in a new imaginative age. But how would such a revelation come about? Must the poets simply wait for their inevitable reinstatement on their rightful legislative heights? Yeats's earliest answer to these questions is contained, at least in kernel, in the provocatively absurd statement that closes the Happy Shepherd's long first sentence: "Words alone are certain good."

For a poet, of course, nothing could be better news, and so the self-servingness of this claim should perhaps lead us to dismiss it as the overreaching rhetoric of a young man anxious to claim for his vocation an importance surpassing the world of action. The subsequent lines certainly support this dismissal, as the poem goes on to flout logic in implying that because the deeds of "warring kings" survive only in books, then words must do more good than kings (11). This leads into the poem's climactic claim—and one of the more outrageous speculations in a poetic oeuvre full of them—as the speaker goes so far as to muse that "The wandering earth herself may be / A sudden flaming word" (18–19). In other words, not only do poets wield the one medium of "certain good," but the world itself may be composed of just that medium. Poets are so much like gods in this context that it seems only logical to cast the world's creator as a poet too. The narcissism here is hard to miss, but the fiery audacity of the wish for words to matter lends it an exhilarating quality despite (or perhaps because of) the megalomaniacal fantasy it embodies.

The poem's two remaining verse paragraphs play variations on the theme that words may utter forth worlds, literally and not just literarily. Claiming that "there is no truth / Saving in thine own heart," the speaker exalts dreaming over a scientific knowledge epitomized (with a hint of Whitman's Learn'd Astronomer) by the so-called "starry men," whose hearts have been drained of such truth (26–8). Then, he exhorts his hearers to tell their stories to an "echo-harbouring shell" (presumably that they may abide a while in the repeated truths of their own hearts) before repeating his claim that "words alone are certain good" (36, 43). Occurring as it does alongside an image of Romantic abandonment to one's own endlessly reverberant voice, this third occurrence of the claim pushes us to read it against the grain, as a statement of radical relativism: "certain" and "good" may just be words after all, epistemology and ethics matters of empty semantics, meaningless amid the echoes of the solitary heart, where life is really lived.

The poem's closing tableau finds this solipsism modulating into a more social longing, as the Shepherd returns us to the vacated woods of Arcadia, where he sings over the grave of a long-dead faun, envisioning the creature resurrected:

And still I dream he treads the lawn,
Walking ghostly in the dew,
Pierced by my glad singing through,
My songs of old earth's dreamy youth:
But ah! she dreams not now; dream thou!
For fair are poppies on the brow:
Dream, dream, for this is also sooth. (51–7)

This profusion of dreams can be taken in several ways. Most simply, we might see them as a means of escape, the introvert's way of coping with the desolations of the social realm. Finding Arcadia spent and joyless, the Shepherd retreats to the verdancy within himself, making explicit pastoral's origins in the desire for a social harmony only achievable under the unifying (and thereby distorting) force of the imagination. So while post-pastoral in one sense, the poem's last verse paragraph is also a recapitulation of the originary pastoral gesture—what William Empson calls "the pastoral process of putting the complex into the simple"—in this case the distillation of myriad desires and dissatisfactions into a single simple dream set in the imaginary past (22). But the poem does not end in that past; its final lines shift from description to exhortation, urging the reader to do the dreaming the aging earth no longer does, an imaginative act not just soothing but "sooth"—not just escapist but capable of generating new truths, new realities. What began, then, as a proclamation of the death of pastoral, has become by the end an illumination of its basic motives and an affirmation of the renovating potential of imaginative song. This may explain the change in title: the Shepherd finds himself happy in his status as the Last Arcadian, sensing the power of his dreamy music to help sing new idylls into being.

This all sounds awfully airy, of course, and it is. The Yeats of 1885 possessed only the vaguest of ends on which to pin his aspirations, and so they remained in a sense inchoate, the ambitious daydreams of a recent teenager. But juvenilia though it may be, "The Song of the Happy Shepherd" remains significant for more than just its status as the first piece in Yeats's *Collected Poems*. Originally the epilogue of his little-read first play, *The Island of Statues: An Arcadian Romance*, the poem stands as the one canonized remnant of the earliest stage of Yeats's writing, an imitative pastoral phase which also produced his other 1885 drama *The Seeker*—the period just before his concerns became explicitly nationalist, and his mythic subject matter distinctly Irish. Although it precedes the Celtic Twilight that would descend upon and define Yeats's work from the later 1880s to the turn of the century, as an entry point into his poetry, "The Song of the Happy Shepherd" serves to foreground how thoroughly the pastoral ethos pervades Yeats's later Celticism. But rather than continue to hearken back through English (via Greece and Rome) literary history to hold up Arcadia as the ideal inverse of an excessively rational and materialistic social order, the Yeats of the Celtic Twilight era turns instead to myths and symbols indigenous to Ireland, the elements of which come to serve as foundation for both a literary tradition and a constructed historical image of pre-Christian Ireland as itself a kind of Arcadia, a land before the triumph of "Grey Truth" over dream.

The Pastoral as a Utopian Mode

Before going any further, I should clarify my use of the term "pastoral," a designation still fraught with ambiguity. Scholarly commentary on the term can be split, broadly, into two camps: those (like Paul Alpers and Annabel Patterson) who treat pastoral as a fairly strictly delimited genre, deriving from the *Idylls* of Theocritus, which takes as its subject matter the lives of shepherds in a setting of simplicity and abundance, often called Arcadia; and those (like Empson, Paul Marinelli, and Terry Gifford) who aim more broadly to explore the partial or fragmentary manifestations of elements of this genre in works that cannot be placed strictly in the line deriving from Theocritus. These scholars—especially Marinelli and Gifford, who write theoretical surveys of the subject—concern themselves with identifying an impulse or (to reuse the term I borrowed from Marinelli earlier) an *ethos* at the heart of pastoral, and with exploring the ideological significance of this oft-iterated longing after bucolic simplicity. Crucially, both agree that the pastoral impulse embodies not only the nostalgic desire for a lost Golden Age, but also an implicit dissatisfaction with things as they are, and an attendant wish for a better future. Marinelli claims that "a note of criticism is inherent in all pastoral from the beginning of its existence" (22), while Gifford cites its "oppositional potential," maintaining that "behind the idealisation of the pastoral there is an implicit future," and more forcefully, that "at its best the pastoral will always imply that its vision of Arcadia has implications for a New Jerusalem" (35). Gifford draws the terms of this last pairing from (coincidentally) Auden, who envisioned "a characterological gulf" between "the Arcadian whose favourite daydream is of Eden, and the Utopian whose favourite daydream is of New Jerusalem" (*Dyer's* 409)—positing, in other words, the literary genres of pastoral and utopia as embodying inverse gestures, the former looking back while the latter looks ahead. Yeats himself echoes this dichotomy in his 1936 BBC radio broadcast "Modern Poetry," as he reminisces on himself and his Rhymers' Club colleagues in the 1890s: "We did not look forward or look outward, we left that to the prose writers. We thought it was in the very nature of poetry to look back, to resemble those Swedenborgian angels who are described as moving forever towards the dayspring of their youth" (*Later* 92). In fact, however, the young Yeats did a great deal of looking forward, much of it inextricable from his looking back. Late in life, increasingly reactionary and disillusioned with his past cultural nationalist goals, he felt it necessary to repudiate the future-orientation of much of his early thinking—a disavowal whose implications I will examine more closely in the next chapter. But for now, I want to further examine how the pastoral impulse often necessarily embodies the utopian one so often figured as its inverse, and eventually, how this Janus-faced hybrid mode of discourse—searching back to find the way ahead—typifies the method of Yeats's early poetry, as he looks to Ireland's Celtic past to legitimate a nascent literary movement which, he hopes, will lay the foundation for future nationhood.

Gifford is one of the few scholars to posit the inherency of the utopian within the pastoral; when the connection between the two genres does get made, it is usually cast as an opposition along the lines of Auden's. Northrop Frye's 1965 essay "The Varieties of Literary Utopia" exemplifies this tendency. Although he slips readily into a discussion of pastoral from an exploration of the "social ideal" of "the greatly simplified life" implicit in some utopian texts, Frye ultimately (and it must be said, characteristically) makes this connection the basis of a finer taxonomic distinction, contrasting the Arcadian ideal with the utopian along rural/urban lines: while the former concerns itself primarily with simplicity, abundance, and the satisfaction of what few desires remain in such an idyllic setting, the latter aims at structure, regularity, and the achievement of a happy and orderly metropolis (40–1). More recent scholars, however—wanting to recuperate the drive for social change at the root of utopian thinking—have challenged the narrowness of this urban-centered, technocratic definition, which has so often allowed for a conflation of utopia and its dystopian inverse. Ruth Levitas's *The Concept of Utopia* stands at the vanguard of this vein of utopian scholarship, which defines utopia broadly, not by appeal to its form or even its proposed function, but by its ontological source—namely, desire. "Utopia," claims Levitas, "is the expression of the desire for a better way of being" (8). As I touched upon in the Introduction, rather than being a strictly delimited literary genre defined by its formal characteristics, utopia in this view is a broad mode of expression accommodating myriad genres and aims, from the critical or pedagogical to the visionary or merely compensatory. One anthology of utopian scholarship in this expansive vein defines it as simply "social dreaming"—a formulation that appropriately foregrounds the communal nature of Levitas's "better way of being": though some utopias may take the form of private fantasies, they ultimately gesture toward a more ideal collective.[2]

Along these lines, Levitas specifically takes issue with the critical tendency to cordon off Arcadia from utopia as somehow embodying a separate species of desire. To J. C. Davis, whose 1981 book *Utopia and the Ideal Society* excludes Arcadia from the category of utopia on the basis of it being "unrealistic" by contrast to the more tough-minded organizational approach of true utopian thought, Levitas argues that as a vision of abundance, simplicity, and universal fulfillment, Arcadia implies "the radical transformation of needs, of satisfactions, and the relationship between them," thereby embodying the central utopian desire to address "the collective problem of the scarcity gap" (164). But *addressing* this gap, Levitas cautions, should not be confused with *solving* it; Arcadia cannot be disqualified from the category of utopia for being "unrealistic," because concrete applicability is not what utopia aims for: "Utopias are generally not convincing as political programmes," she claims, "nor are they necessarily intended to be; the transition to the good society is frequently not addressed, because utopia is the expression of desire, and desire may outstrip hope while not necessarily outstripping possibility" (164). Hope, in this view, involves the expectation that one's desires will be realized, while the broader concept of possibility lets those desires remain suspended in an ether of hypotheticality. But even possibility binds utopia too tightly to expectation, as Levitas later notes: "The problem of limiting utopia to the 'possible world' is that it conflates the categories of hope and desire. It limits utopia to the question 'what may I hope?' and refuses the question 'what may I dream?' ... The essential element in utopia is not hope, but desire—the desire for a better way of being" (190-1). Arcadia is utopian, then, to the extent that its evocation embodies that desire, and following this line of thinking, the pastoral (*pace* Frye and his more strictly genre-minded strand of critical opinion) always implicitly gestures to utopia's "better way."

Returning to Yeats's early poetry in light of this expansive conception of utopia, one can more readily perceive its social and even political dimension. For although Yeats's early career is often characterized as "cultural nationalist" in its aims, the chief points of evidence for this are usually marshalled from among his direct statements of purpose in published prose or private letters, or from explicitly nationalist plays like *Cathleen ni Houlihan*, rather than from the field of creative endeavor for which he remains best known—his lyric poetry. Lyric, of course, is often cast as the inverse of political discourse, a mode of resolutely individual expression which exalts the very fact of subjectivity over a public realm serving, within the space of the poem, any number of subordinate functions, from backdrop to active antagonist. In general, Yeats's early lyrics fit this description in their abiding focus on individual speakers and characters whose dreamy sensibilities lead them to revolt against the world as it exists, to long, and pine, and wish themselves away. But at the same time, these early poems also urge us to interrogate the extent to which even the most fiercely independent or woefully self-absorbed of lyric subjects weave their escapist tapestries from the loose threads of the social fabric. In other words, they prompt us to question whether dreamers are really separable from the societies that embed them. The broad definition of utopia offered by Levitas invites us to see the dream of or desire for a better way of life, no matter how individually expressed, as a social phenomenon; in other words, it invites us to see such individual aspirations as inherently linked to those of the collective. In terms of Yeats's early lyrics, this link can readily be made: for if we see the more explicit statements of cultural nationalism laid out in the prose and plays as discursively preparing a social field into which the lyrics intervene at the level of desire, the dovetailing of the pastoral and utopian in the early poems becomes a matter of more than generic significance. Put simply, while the prose and plays directly communicate the hope for a unified and independent Irish nation, the poems repeatedly embody the desire for a better way of life, a more ideal social order, a place to dwell in solace and plenty. After relinquishing the inherited pastoral imagery of shepherds and fauns (and thus truly admitting the death of Arcadia) in the mid-1880s, Yeats forges a new pastoral ideal from the myths of Ireland's Celtic past—an ideal which, taken alongside his future-oriented nationalist endeavors, becomes not only a place to be nostalgic for personally, but a place to be aspired to socially. At this point, the lyric dreaming of his motley solitaries becomes functionally inextricable from the collective dream of Irish nationhood.[3]

Celticism and Utopian Lyric

This is not to say that Yeats's shift to Irish subjects automatically makes his poems more socially efficacious, but it does lend them at least the illusion of greater engagement when compared to the Arcadian and Indian set pieces that begin *Crossways* (1889), the first section of his *Collected Poems*. Yeats came to believe that his poetry could help guide the course of the national cause by embodying local lore—that, should the Irish people come to inhabit their stories with the full force of their collective consciousness, the unity of "word" and "world" he so radically proposed in "The Song of the Happy Shepherd" could at least partly come to pass. But he also understood the ephemerality of this ideal, remaining sensitive to poetry's impotence even as he exalted its evocative force. This mingling of doubt and hope is thematized in the earliest piece in the *Collected Poems* to employ an Irish setting, "The Madness of King Goll." The eponymous king stands at the beginning of a long line of Yeatsian exiles, from Oisin to Crazy Jane to the poet himself in late poems like "The Circus Animals' Desertion": figures who find themselves trapped irreconcilably between the world as it exists and the world of fantasy their visionary insight permits them to imagine. The poem begins with Goll being driven by a sudden onset of madness from a life of battle and temporal rule to one of communion with nature—another recapitulation of the pastoral search for the atavistic Golden Age. Wandering the woods prophet-like, Goll stumbles upon a sleepy town where he finds deserted an "old tympan" (*tiompán*, an ancient Irish stringed instrument related to the dulcimer) and takes it back to the woods (55). There, the "married voices" of Goll and the tympan sing of "some inhuman misery" (58–9), tapping through art into a Platonic realm of forms transcending ephemeral human truths. As his hand passes over the instrument's "wire[s]," he finds his restlessness "quenched," the "whirling and the wandering fire" within him—the very force that drove him mad to begin with—at peace (65–7). But the poem's last few lines find the strings lying torn, and Goll ends up bound to an ambivalent wandering, having lost both worldly and otherworldly mastery, exiled in a limbo between action and art.

At every stage of Goll's journey, from kingship to prophethood to his final exile, a single-line refrain follows him, ending each of the poem's six stanzas: "*They will not hush, the leaves a-flutter around me, the beech leaves old.*" First signaling his madness, then his attunement to the woods, and finally his lapse into a failed poet's silence, the refrain manifests yet again the Romantic conviction of the purity of nature's speaking voice, the "unpremeditated art" of Shelley's skylark. Despite his debts to nearer contemporaries—Goll's madness recalls much from Browning and Tennyson, and the refrain's heavy stresses borrow the sprung rhythm of Hopkins, with its insistence on the immanent divinity of nature—Goll remains firmly rooted in the tradition of the Romantic vision-quest.[4] As an inheritor of that tradition, Yeats would spend much of his career haunted by the specter of a purer form of expression he could never quite achieve. The frustration of this is reflected in his hero's fruitless trajectory: Goll's flight from the heroic realm of epic to the idyllic one of pastoral only temporarily lends him visionary insight, and ends up being a sideways shift from one outmoded mythos to another. He finds brief peace with the tympan, but as a Celticized Aeolian harp with only Goll's madness for wind, it must lie broken by the poem's end, an emblem of the essential airlessness of his world. Nothing in Goll's story gestures outside the insular literary realms of epic and pastoral between which he madly slips, and nothing lifts it from the realm of the anecdotal to that of the visionary: his flight back to nature fails because it ultimately sheds no light on where he should go next, imparting neither wisdom for the future nor insight on the state of the civilization he forsook. The town where he finds the tympan is left "sleeping" and not returned to, despite having afforded him his one means of consolation. Whatever visions of coherence he may have glimpsed will serve only to gird his solipsism, never to benefit the collective. His solitary madness will never give way to the sociality of authentic prophethood.

Put simply, one might say that "The Madness of King Goll" portrays the pastoral impulse drained of the utopian desire so often inherent in it. Yeats depicts a mythic past without wishing for its contemporaneity. Whereas the Happy Shepherd clearly longed for the lost world of dream to reemerge in a better future, Goll's flight back to nature ultimately renders him futureless. The story of his madness is myth for myth's sake; like much late-nineteenth-century Aestheticism, it upholds the Romantic exaltation of wild nature and unbridled subjectivity while also highlighting the dangerous solipsism inherent in the cult of the visionary. On

KING GOLL.

Figure 2 Etching by Yeats's father John Butler Yeats of King Goll, which accompanied the poem's original publication (under the title "King Goll. An Irish Legend") in the British magazine *The Leisure Hour* in September 1887. Yeats himself modeled for the etching.

the one hand, Goll's madness testifies to late Romanticism's decadent exhaustion, and in this sense it presages Yeats's later characterization of his Rhymers' Club compatriots in 1890s London—Ernest Dowson, Lionel Johnson, and Arthur Symons—as "The Tragic Generation," all of whom (in Yeats's account) drifted into dissipation at being unable to cope with the yawning gap between art and the quotidian world.[5] Along these lines, then, "The Madness of King Goll" evidences the aimlessness of the pre-nationalist Yeats: incapable, as an Irishman, of fully embracing the imported creeds of Symbolism and Aestheticism, but not yet sure on what principles to construct an indigenous tradition to transcend the dwindling vitality of *l'art pour l'art*. Without the sense of purpose the national cause would lend his work, much of Yeats's earliest poetry finds him, like Goll, escaping to nowhere in particular, unsure of what to do when he arrives.

On the other hand, however, the very act of embodying an Irish myth in verse would come to serve as a first principle of the Celtic Revival, so that despite the lack of any explicit utopian thrust in Yeats's retelling, his choice of subject matter itself could be cast as a nationalist gesture, an implicit manifestation of utopian desire. Such are the terms Yeats begins to set out in his earliest prose pieces. In the first of two 1886 tributes to the recently deceased poet Sir Samuel Ferguson—his first published essays—Yeats is already assuming the cultural nationalist mantle he would wear for at least two decades, linking the myths of Ireland's deep history to its future prospects for independent nationhood:

> Sir Samuel Ferguson's special claim to our attention is that he went back to the Irish cycle, finding it, in truth, a fountain that, in the passage of centuries, was overgrown with weeds and grass, so that the very way to it was forgotten of the poets; but now that his feet have worn the pathway, many others will follow, and bring thence living waters for the healing of our nation, helping us to live the larger life of the Spirit, and lifting our souls away from their selfish joys and sorrows to be the companions of those who lived greatly among the woods and hills when the world was young. (*Uncollected 1* 82)

The movement from "weeds and grass" to "woods and hills" nicely encapsulates the pastoral impulse at the root of Yeats's thinking here. The great cycle of Irish myths represents a subterranean spring that the next generation of poets must tap, letting flow its "living waters" and returning the nation to its past verdancy. At the same time, Yeats manages to tacitly justify the misty symbolism that dominates his poetic approach throughout the 1880s and 1890s, exalting "the larger life of the Spirit" as more closely allied to this verdant past, and thereby implying that the national cause is partly (and perhaps at this stage primarily) a spiritual one. The mythic landscapes of the Celtic past serve as *paysages moralisés*, externalizations of the pure unjaded idealism of the countryside's ancestral spirit—a spirit the modern-day Irish must recapture as a precondition to actual nationhood. In his second Ferguson tribute, Yeats restates this conviction of myth's importance in providing a metaphysical foundation for the national idea, writing that "Of all the many things the past bequeaths to the future, the greatest are great legends; they are the mothers of nations. I hold it the duty of every Irish reader to study those of his own country till they are familiar as his own hands, for in them is the Celtic heart" (*Uncollected 1* 104). Here Yeats's propensity to model the future after the past, to envision utopia through the pastoral, is laid out almost diagrammatically. The specter of the unborn nation demands that the "Irish reader" reclaim their "Celtic heart," their buried ancestral inheritance. But the path of bequeathal from past directly to future that Yeats sets out here entirely elides the present and so also elides the very existence of an "Irish reader" who might perform such an act of reclamation. In this scheme the present registers as little more than a void of instability, an index of the precariousness of Irish identity, a featurelessness that Yeats grants only a glimmer of existence—primarily as the place-in-time to be escaped from.

In the earliest work in the *Collected Poems*, the *Crossways* section and the long narrative poem *The Wanderings of Oisin*, Yeats repeatedly depicts such escapes, leading his figures to worlds of myth where higher concerns of life, death, and eternity predominate, showing up the pettiness of the quotidian. Oisin rides "out from the human lands," journeying with his immortal lover Niamh to the Islands of Dancing and Victories and Forgetfulness, in a failed search for the Island of Content. *Crossways* presents us, in addition to the faded idylls of the Happy Shepherd and King Goll, with the childlike dream of flying off "To an Isle in the Water," the vision of meeting a doomed love "Down by the Salley Gardens," and the bittersweetness of "The Meditation of the Old Fisherman," the eponymous speaker of which remembers, "*When I was a boy with never a crack in my heart.*" As with the latter, many of these early poems employ refrains that capture the strange persistence, both ritualistic and obsessive, of the call to escape the world, the shining promise of elsewhere so hauntingly embodied in the song of the faeries to "The Stolen Child" they lure away:

> *Come away, O human child!*
> *To the waters and the wild*
> *With a faery, hand in hand,*
> *For the world's more full of weeping than you can understand.* (9–12)

In 1888, while correcting a manuscript for publication, Yeats wrote a letter to Katharine Tynan in which he singled out the refrain of "The Stolen Child" as typical of his early work's shortcomings: "It is almost all a flight into fairyland from the real world, and a summons to that flight … . [I]t is not the poetry of insight and knowledge, but of longing and complaint, the cry of the heart against necessity. I hope some day to alter that and write poetry of insight and knowledge" (*Letters* 63). In later years Yeats felt himself to have achieved such insight only after deliberately hardening his style, and many critics have agreed, relegating his early poetry (despite its enduring popularity) to minor status, casting its late-Romantic longing as merely an immature prelude to the more forcefully prophetic rhetoric of much of the later work. But I would argue that Yeats's early poetry—written by a young man not yet grown into the stentorian voice of authority that so compellingly animates such later rhetorical performances as "Easter, 1916," "The Second Coming," and "Under Ben Bulben"—communicates all the more powerfully the following twinned propositions: first, that every lyric utterance is rooted at its nascency in the basic force of desire; and second, that this same force of desire also lies at the root of every impulse for social change. To rephrase a point I made above: in Yeats's early poetry, lyric desire is rendered inextricable from utopian desire. In the cultural nationalist contexts of late-nineteenth-century Ireland in general and Yeats's body of writing in particular, the tempting call to escape to fairyland unavoidably carries social resonance as a poetic iteration of the imperative Yeats issued in his second Ferguson essay, to learn the "Celtic heart" through the legends of the land.

Yeats, Shelley, and the Poetry of Hope

But how did Yeats conceive of poetry's role in this educative process? Could the mere embodiment of utopian desire in poetry work to instill this desire societally? Phillip Marcus has elaborated at length upon what he terms Yeats's aesthetic of "artistic power," identifying its earliest roots in the Irish bardic tradition, then in Shelley and Blake, and finally in the Oscar Wilde of "The Decay of Lying"—with his claim that "Life is Art's best, Art's only pupil" (qtd. in Marcus 30).[6] For the young poet of the 1880s, however, the majority of these influences had either not yet been encountered or not yet fully felt, and Shelley alone remained the first word on poetry's ultimate aims and potentials. If, as I have argued, Yeats's early poetry presents lyric and utopian desire as inextricable, Shelley stands as the predecessor who not only most fervently expresses this inextricability but goes further in imputing to poetry a formative social role.

It would be difficult to overstate the influence of Shelley's exalted view of poetry on Yeats's early career. In his *Reveries over Childhood and Youth* Yeats tells us that by the age of eighteen he had made *Prometheus Unbound* his "sacred book" (95), and in his essay "The Philosophy of Shelley's Poetry," begun in 1899 when he was thirty-four, he amplifies that earlier judgment, claiming that "it [*Prometheus*] seems me to have an even more certain place than I had thought, among the sacred books of the world" (51). We know from the latter essay that the eschatological elements of Shelley's work particularly appealed to Yeats, as he compares the prophetic faith embodied in *Prometheus* to the ancient faith of the "country people" in the west of Ireland, which according to him held that a battle would be fought on Slieve-dan-Orr, the Golden Mountain, to usher in a thousand years of peace. (This is the subject of Yeats's oblique lyric "The Valley of the Black Pig," written around the same time as the Shelley essay.) For the Yeats of 1900, already well embarked on his project of cultural nationalism, Shelley's vision of "Man, oh, not men! a chain of linked thought, / Of love and might to be divided not" (*Prometheus* IV.394–5) represented a practical end to be actively sought. This maturing Yeats interpreted Shelley in a way that lent authoritative support to his notion that Ireland might be molded into unity through exposure to a calculatedly national literature. Writing of Shelley's conviction that the path to liberty lay through beauty, Yeats claims: "He does not believe that the reformation of society can bring this beauty, this divine order, among men without the regeneration of the hearts of men" (54).

Even by the time of his 1898 essay "The Autumn of the Body," Yeats was convinced that the path to such a regeneration lay through the arts, and that it was the artist's responsibility to shepherd the people out of the petty materialism of the present into a future unified by ideals: "The arts are, I believe, about to take upon their shoulders the burdens that have fallen from the shoulders of priests, and lead us back upon our journey by filling our thoughts with the essences of things, and not with things" (141–2). In keeping with his indebtedness to Symbolist rhetoric at this stage, he remains characteristically vague as to the nature of these "essences," though one can point to his insistence on the foundational importance of Celtic myth as evidence of his meaning. He reaffirms this Shelleyan analogy between artists and priests in his 1901 essay "Ireland and the Arts," in which he writes that "We who care deeply about the arts find ourselves the priesthood of an almost forgotten faith, and we must, I think, if we would win the people again, take upon ourselves the method and fervour of a priesthood" (150). In specifying what is to be achieved by this priestly winning of the people, Yeats appeals to the prestige of ancientness to legitimate his vision for the still-nascent Irish state: "I would have Ireland recreate the ancient arts, the arts as they were understood in Judea, in India, in Scandinavia, in Greece and Rome, in every ancient land; as they were understood when they moved a whole people and not a few people who have grown up in a leisured class and made this understanding their business" (152). In other words, by the turn of the century Yeats sees the arts—and in writing of "the arts" he always gestures specifically to poetry—as capable of unifying the masses, of forging a people out of disparate individuals, and therefore of laying the foundations of nationhood.

The Yeats of the 1880s—the escapist Yeats of the Happy Shepherd, King Goll, and the Stolen Child—had only just begun to phrase his hopes for poetry in such explicitly nationalistic terms. Yet even in this nascent nationalist phase, he proceeds upon the assumption that poetry that holds out the promise of alternate realities, however futile their pursuit may seem, can somehow work to bring those realities about. This assumption no doubt derives in large part from Shelley's exalted conception (present in much of his work but laid out most forcefully in his *Defence of Poetry*) of poets as not only "unacknowledged legislators" (508), but more specifically as "the institutors of laws, the founders of civil society, and the inventors of the arts of life, and the teachers, who draw into a certain propinquity with the beautiful and the true that partial apprehension of the agencies of the invisible world which is called religion" (482). The terms of this formulation bear examining more closely. Tacit throughout Shelley's *Defence* is a Schillerian analogy between poetic form and social formations, as though the beauty woven out of metrical language, in its unity and resolute musicality, might present a model of the harmoniousness we should strive for in our societies. Although Shelley remains vague as to how specifically poetry institutes laws, founds civil societies, and reveals the timeless beauty inherent in religion, this does not detract from his essay's importance within a utopian framework. Most crucially, his stated conviction that poetry does in fact do these things indicates his ardent desire that poetry *should* have such a profound impact on political, social, and spiritual life. Looked at in this way, Shelley's *Defence* stands not so much as a coherent descriptive theory as a set of aspirations, an exemplary codification of the central role played by desire in both prodding the imagination to poetic expression and reforming communal institutions. If poetry, as Shelley claims in one of his many formulations of the idea, "enlarges the circumference of the imagination by replenishing it with thoughts of ever new delight," it embodies the potential to do no less than renovate our perceptions, and thereby to renovate the world (487).

But in Shelley's essay, the precise nature of these perceptions matters little: as long as they are "new" or "unapprehended," they widen our circle of love, and so act as a unifying force. Yeats's early work arises out of this same conception of poetry's potential. The call to escape, especially escape to impossible lands, does indeed represent "the cry of the heart against necessity," but not necessarily in the impotent sense of "longing and complaint" that Yeats so condemned in himself. On the contrary, such a cry can sound a tragic awareness of the shortcomings of the present world, an implicit recognition of the Marxist insight that the realm of freedom begins only where that of necessity ends. The poems of *Crossways* (and to some extent of *The Rose* and *The Wind among the Reeds*), in longing for past idylls of beauty and harmony, register the strength of desire at the center of the young poet's impetus to write, even when that desire has only childish faery visions to strive toward. Yeats's early poetry—with its endless urging to escapes seemingly doomed to failure—obeys the injunction of Shelley's Demogorgon in the moving final speech of *Prometheus Unbound*: "to hope, till Hope creates / From its own wreck the thing it contemplates" (IV.573-4).

This last quotation points once again to the relationship, so crucial to understanding Yeats's cultural nationalism, between desire and hope. According to Levitas (and common understandings of the concept), hope can be roughly defined as desire bolstered by the force of expectation, or more firmly, by the reasonable belief that what is desired may actually come to pass. But as I discussed earlier, Levitas finds hope too limiting a concept by which to define utopia, and thus links it to desire instead. In terms of Yeats's early poetry, this expansive definition allows even its most outlandish dreams of other worlds to qualify as utopian, without regard for their achievability; their desirous origins suffice. As the intervening discussion has made clear, however, Yeats increasingly came to see his poetry's engagement with the pastoralisms of Celtic myth as actually working in the service of the Irish cause, helping to lay down the nation's imaginative substratum. Though still rooted most firmly in desire, his aesthetic begins to be tinged with the expectation intrinsic to hope—a tendency for which he found an authoritative precedent in Shelley.

Put simply, Yeats inherited from Shelley a conception of poetry as a potentially revelatory manifestation of hope: a combination of desire and expectation, the forces of affirmative futurity through which the world is changed. As the earliest work in Yeats's canon, the poems of *Crossways* embody this hope at its initial inchoate stage as pure desire, a wishfulness with only the vaguest of concrete ends. Moving into the poems of *The Rose* (1893) and *The Wind among the Reeds* (1899), however, we can see that desire begin to take on the more explicitly nationalist orientation of his plays and prose writings of the period, and thereby to engage more directly with hope. Yeats's active involvement in nationalist causes deepened throughout the late 1880s and especially into the 1890s, as the Irish cultural renaissance initiated by him and his circle attempted to fill the vacuum left by the death of the pro-Home Rule leader Charles Stewart Parnell in 1891. This renaissance came to be known as the Celtic Twilight, a name that suits both the work's prevailing pastoralism—of a mythic past grasped at through a haze—and its transfigured subject matter. Whereas the poems of *Crossways* paraded mythic figures from the Greek and Indian traditions alongside King Goll and the child-stealing faeries of Irish lore, the myriad heroes that populate this later work remain exclusively Irish in provenance: Cuchulain, Fergus, the Wandering Aengus, Cathleen Ni Houlihan, and the wind-dwelling Sidhe. This same shift is reflected in the poems' geographies: the call to escape remains paramount, but the lands to be escaped to become more present and earth-bound—and like the characters that inhabit them, more explicitly Irish.

Innisfree and the Education of Desire

The most famous of Yeats's nineteenth-century poems, "The Lake Isle of Innisfree" stands as perhaps the earliest work to register this shift. In the section of his autobiography titled *Four Years 1887–1891*, Yeats gives an evocative account of the poem's genesis in London in 1890:

> I had still the ambition, formed in Sligo in my teens, of living in imitation of Thoreau on Innisfree, a little island in Lough Gill, and when walking through Fleet Street very homesick I heard a little tinkle of water and saw a fountain in a shop-window which balanced a little ball upon its jet, and began to remember lake water. From the sudden remembrance came my poem "Innisfree," my first lyric with anything in its rhythm of my own music. (*Autobiographies* 138)

This passage charts, in progressing from ambition to image to remembrance and finally to composition, one of the habitual movements of Yeats's aesthetic in this period. His visions of the future (ambitions) often find emblems in the present (images), which evoke the glories of a mythic past (remembrances). Typically, though, the present setting—in this case central London, the colonial metropole—functions as little more than the place to be escaped from: the image in the shop window serves merely to launch his memoried ambition, his utopian longing after pastoral bliss. Or to put this in a new way: the early Yeats, in aspiring to escape to so many Arcadias, Indias, or Irelands, comes to inhabit a curious epistemological position, and one he never fully abandons: he is nostalgic for the future.[7] In the very earliest work, this future nostalgia manifests itself as the repeated call to escape to some mythic pastoral idyll, to live out the dream of communion with nature and its spirits, free to dance and sing the pagan way, without the possibility of censure or the looming responsibilities of adulthood. But as a late Romantic brooding toward the new millennium, even the teenage Yeats understood the futility, if not the silliness, of this vision. In the poems of *The Rose*, we find a Yeats who has more fully embraced Shelley's characterization of poets as "the mirrors of the gigantic shadows which futurity casts upon the present" (508), as possessing what George Bornstein calls "a vision of the ideal order on which society should be patterned" (63). And so his emphasis begins to shift, as the desire to escape to another world becomes alloyed with the more explicitly utopian hope of altering the future one—with at first only the fuzziest of boundaries between these two aspirations. It is this shift that "The Lake Isle of Innisfree" evidences.

Hazard Adams singles the poem out as "a startling statement ... because the poet suddenly speaks out strongly and directly and because for the first time we sense that he is speaking from a real place" (54). In the terms of my discussion, this sudden placefulness is crucial not only in locating the poet himself, but in spatializing the object of his utopian desire, in putting the *topos* back in utopia:

> I will arise and go now, and go to Innisfree,
> And a small cabin build there, of clay and wattles made:
> Nine bean rows will I have there, a hive for the honey bee,
> And live alone in the bee-loud glade. (1–4)

"The Lake Isle of Innisfree" stands as the most traditionally utopian of Yeats's early poems, embodying not only utopia's aspirational basis in desire but also its status as a literal place one might travel to (and most crucially, an island, which links it to the utopian lineage beginning with More). On the other hand, it could seem odd to classify the poem as "utopian" at all, for though it undoubtedly embodies the desire for a better way of being (to an extent that it has often been cast as the paradigmatic utterance of the early "escapist" Yeats), the "better way" it envisions may seem too resoundingly solitary to be properly utopian. The speaker's wish to "live alone in the bee-loud glade" reads like an assertion of the lush possibilities of seclusion (those insistent Ls look so much like 1s), a repudiation of collective life. And yet the poem remains so obviously dependent for its effect on the implied presence of the very collective it threatens to abandon. "I will arise and go now" signals not only a speaker just about to leave, but a poet repeatedly vowing to relinquish the very audience upon which his lyric status depends. By the time he reiterates that he "will arise and go now" at the beginning of the third quatrain, the promise sounds convictionless, with the word "now" hollowed of its performative force, serving only as a rhetorical instantaneity, a platform upon which the poet can proclaim his dissatisfaction with the urban world of "roadway[s]" and "pavements grey" (11). But this spatial and temporal extension of "now" from the realm of the immediate moment to a more encompassing sense of situation or milieu is crucial to the poem's status as utopian, for with this extension of "now" comes a corresponding vagueness in the nature of the circumstances revolted against, and thus an implicit invitation to share in the poet's dissatisfaction and to desire with him the peace we all (it is implied) lack. This dynamic recalls Adorno's claim that the modern lyric utterance, so often predicated upon solitude, is nonetheless founded in "a collective substratum" ("Lyric" 217). "From a condition of unrestrained individuation," Adorno claims, "the lyric work strives for, awaits the realm of the general" (214). We can see this striving at work in Yeats, whose poetics so often depends on a metonymic blending of individual desires with those of an implied collective.

In "Innisfree" in particular—besides the speaker's rhetorical extension of the realm of "now"—this blending involves both spatial and temporalizing gestures. Spatially, the speaker's dream destination is not just an island, but an island in Ireland, a smaller gem within the Emerald Isle. This matryoshka-like spatial nesting works to emphasize both the poem's Romantic inheritance (by setting doubly definite boundaries around the speaker's solitude) and the metonymic substitution at its center: Innisfree *is* Ireland. This works both with the circumstances of the poem's composition and in the wider context of Yeats's early cultural nationalism, so often rooted in the myth of a pastoral Ireland whose loss lies rooted in "the deep heart's core" of all true Irish—notice the definite article "the" rather than the possessive pronoun "my"—who must aspire together to return there. In later years Yeats criticized several of his compositional choices in the poem, particularly the "conventional archaism" of "I will arise and go now" and the syntactic inversion of "pavements grey" (*Autobiographies* 140). But the antiquated tone produced by such choices serves to highlight the temporal paradox that haunts the speaker's aspirations: *In the future*, he seems to say, *I will go to the past*. In displacing his pastoral utopia in both space and time, the poet of "Innisfree" dooms himself to dwell in the elastic "now" of a desire with no prospect of fulfillment, a kind of utopic purgatory, a glorious falling short that even finds its formal embodiment in each quatrain's truncated last line. This exemplifies in structural terms Jahan Ramazani's observation that "Yeats's nationalism ironizes itself in the knowledge that fulfillment would come at a great cost to a poetry built on melancholic desire" (*Hybrid* 30). In other words, while national goals themselves remain paramount, Yeats builds into his poetics the implicit concession that (contrary to Shelley) art cannot reasonably expect to directly alter social institutions. By so compellingly expressing desire, however, it can hope to condition the desires of its audience. Ramazani neatly summarizes the dependence of Yeats's cultural nationalist aesthetic on this virtual fetishization of desire: "Desire," he writes, "is the basic unit of the communal imaginary, without which there can be no national aspiration or hope. Without the constitutive force of culture giving force to dreams, 'the indomitable Irishry' would fall under domination once again" (29). Ramazani's formulation here gestures toward the manner in which, in early Yeats, individual desire comes to metonymically embody national hope. By so often expressing their desire to reinhabit a lost pastoral Ireland, Yeats's lyric speakers model such an idyll as the ideal after which would-be nationalists must (rather paradoxically) strive. The "lake water lapping" heard in the heart of the yearning poet posits an analogous echo in the chests of all true Irish, an uncanny call emanating from past and future at once.

In light of how it embodies all these aspects of Yeats's early aesthetics—its simultaneous call to past and future, its engagement with the inherency of the utopian within the pastoral, and its implicit awareness that to fail may be inevitable or even itself desirable—the curious prominence of "Innisfree" amid Yeats's canon comes to seem more fully justified. Coming at a point in the young poet's career at which he stood poised almost equally between an artistic preoccupation with the lost world of myth and an increasing determination to alter the future course of the real Ireland of his time, it aptly conveys this ambivalence. As a Romantic stranded in modernity—a pose he would never fully relinquish—Yeats must, to remain relevant, constantly seek ways to highlight the utopian element within his pastoral nostalgia, and to infuse his desire with the force of expectation that sets it glimmering with hope. In casting Innisfree as a real island, distant in space rather than time from the present of himself and his readers, he imbues his longing with a sense of achievability. At the same time, however, the archaic tinge of his language and the way the stanzas truncate imply that part of what the speaker harks back to may in fact be irrecoverable. Believing, with Blake, that "all art is a labour to bring again the Golden Age," Yeats constantly seeks not *in*novation, but *re*novation (*Early* 123). Never fully modern, he accepts Ezra Pound's signal modernist directive only with a crucial amendment, perhaps implicit in it all along: "Make it new, again."[8]

One might reasonably assert that the object of this renovating impulse in early Yeats is not (as Pound would have it) poetic expression itself, nor even (as my discussion so far would imply) the Irish nation, but rather the minds of his readers. One might say the early poetry aims primarily at what Levitas has called "the education of desire" (124). This is a crucial term for understanding Yeats's early aesthetics. As I have discussed, Levitas's expansive definition of utopia as "the expression of desire for a better way of being" precludes any definition in terms of ends or functions—though as she herself points out this does not therefore preclude the *existence* of such functions. In expressing desire so powerfully, utopian texts can have the effect of educating the desires of their audiences, "encouraging the sense that it does not have to be like this, it could be otherwise" (124). That Yeats hoped his poetry would operate this way, shaping the minds of his readers, is obvious: I have already highlighted the Shelleyan grandiosity with which he conceived of the poet's role in forging a culture—and indeed, one might see the phrase "the education of desire" as itself an incisive clarification of how precisely Shelley's legislator-poets might go about enacting their social visions. In *Four Years 1887–1891*, Yeats delivers his most direct and forceful statement of poetry's educating and unifying potential. It is a passage worth quoting at length:

> Might I not, with health and good luck to aid me, create some new *Prometheus Unbound*; Patrick or Columcille, Oisin or Finn, in Prometheus' stead; and, instead of Caucasus, Cro-Patrick or Ben Bulben? Have not all races had their first unity from a mythology that marries them to rock and hill? We had in Ireland imaginative stories, which the uneducated classes knew and even sang, and might we not make these stories current among the educated classes, rediscovering for the work's sake what I have called "the applied arts of literature," the association of literature, that is, with music, speech, and dance; and at last, it might be, so deepen the political passion of the nation that all, artist and poet, craftsman and day-labourer would accept a common design? (166-7)

This lays out the dynamics of "the education of desire" almost programmatically: "imaginative stories," disseminated widely enough, will "so deepen the political passion of the nation" that all will accept "a common design," fulfilling at last the elusive, shining, ill-defined promise of "unity." The mythmaking impulses of Shelley and Blake here combine with the more bluntly manipulative goals of propaganda—a concept which, though he frequently railed against it late in life, the younger Yeats was not at all averse to deploying in a positive light. This early attitude is captured in an 1897 letter to a journalist profiling him for the *Bookman*: "I shall look forward to your article with great interest. If you find it hard to fill up you might say something of my work as a propagandist of Celtic ideas among the Irish people. I have never written simply as a poet but always as a poet whose poems are an action as well as a thought" (*Collected Letters* August 5, 1897). This insistence upon poetry as an "action" evidences Yeats's intense anxiety that his life's work should contribute, however ephemerally, to the national cause—even at the cost of sacrificing its purity as conceived of by his Symbolist and Aestheticist inheritance. Ideally, however, Yeats sought in his poetry to achieve a seamlessness between the expression of desire and the education of it, to propagandize covertly, subtly transfiguring individual desire into national hope. For Terry Eagleton, Yeats stands as a representative of the view that "symbolist poetry can be nationalist too, since the purity, unity and autonomy of the work of art can be seen to mirror the ideal qualities of nationhood" (*Heathcliff* 240). According to this logic, then, poetry can educate the desires of its readers not just through its mythic subject matter, but (echoes of Shelley again) through the very coherence of its form.

Yeats's Aesthetics of Desire: Critical Controversies

Many critics have pointed out the strong element of false consciousness inherent in Yeats's cultural nationalist aesthetic, particularly in its escapist willingness to turn away from the fractious present to focus instead on the myths of the past. In addition to condemning the general element of (to borrow a phrase from Ramazani) "aestheticist fantasy" in the idea that poetry can meaningfully influence social formations, several prominent critics have pointed to the rootedness of Yeats's aesthetic in the changing position within Irish society of the class from which he emerged (*Hybrid* 28). R. F. Foster highlights the degree to which Yeats's Celticism (and that of the Revival in general) cannot be understood without reference to his Anglo-Irishness and the increasing marginalization of the Anglo-Irish with the gradual rise to prominence of a Catholic middle class. In Foster's view, the Anglo-Irish architects of the Revival appeal to Celtic myth as a way of locating the roots of true Irish identity prior to Catholicism, to reassert their own precarious class identity. Yeats's frequent recourse to the pastoral mode, then, represents not just the utopian desire for a more poetically coherent collective but, more historically, it registers his nostalgia for "the long-lost world of social dominance"—the elitist "race memory" of a dwindling aristocracy (228, 232). Along similar lines, Eagleton claims that the Revivalists sought in art an "Archimedean point" from which "they could transcend the social, ethnic and religious differences which estranged them from the majority of the common people, and so buttress their own position as a declining breed" (*Heathcliff* 245). At their most extreme, such views drain the aesthetics of the Celtic Revival of much of their utopian content, attributing their appeal to pastoral myth not to an authentic longing, however impractical, for societal unity, but instead to a desperate bid to restore the lost class power of the Anglo-Irish minority. While the latter motivation certainly resounds clearly through Yeats's later work, it is virtually absent from (or at least heavily repressed in) the early work I have been discussing here.

Conversely, other critics have emphasized the more authentically national aspect of Yeats's aesthetic, seeing in his appeal to Celtic myth a decolonizing attempt to reclaim Ireland for the Irish, a maneuver rooted in identarian striving. Rather than focus on the delusoriness of Yeats's appeals to the mythic past, such critics have chosen to judge Yeats more along the Shelleyan lines he himself followed, crediting him with actually having succeeded in using his art to forward social goals. Again, Ramazani—while acknowledging that the full effect of Yeats's poetry depends on its desires remaining unfulfilled or even unfulfillable—recognizes the crucial role his work played in presenting the Irish a new liberatory image of themselves: "Since *Cathleen Ni Houlihan* helped to inspire the Easter rebels to martyrdom and his early nationalist poetry and activism helped to foment rioting and resistance to British imperialism, Yeats's art should be credited with being partly formative of the postcolonial nation" (28). Edward Said goes further, casting him as one of the "great nationalist artists of decolonization" (73) and claiming that "Yeats's poetry joins his people to its history" through its assumption that "the narrative and density of personal experience are equivalent to the experience of his people" (92). Declan Kiberd, meanwhile, counts Yeats prominently among those whose art helped "invent" Ireland, and finds in his utopian escapism an ultimately noble purpose: "Art in this context might be seen as man's constant effort to create for himself a different order of reality from that which is given to him … Fictions, though they treat of the non-existent, by that very virtue help people make sense of the world around them" (118). Like Ramazani and Said, Kiberd here emphasizes the effects of Yeats's poetry upon its (particularly *national*) audience, and more fundamentally, the role of Yeats's art in helping to constitute Ireland as a nation—on however fictitious, mythical, or symbolic a ground.

To summarize: two main strands of critical opinion proliferate with regard to Yeats's cultural nationalist aesthetic. The more condemnatory one focuses on Yeats's ignoble motives for attempting to forge an image of Ireland through its Celtic myths: his class insecurities, his inveterate idealism, his neo-Romantic readiness to favor the metaphysical over the material realm. From this point of view Yeats's pastoral utopianism adds up to little more than false consciousness and empty escapism—the poet's easy retreat into a world of his own making. To unify a nation through symbols does little to resolve the cultural, economic, and religious disparities within that nation, and may just work to obscure them in the interests of a status quo. For the more laudatory critics, on the other hand, Yeats's utopianism serves more as invitation than escape. The bygone pastoral worlds he conjures serve to highlight the strife and disunity of his own times, and in the historical context of Ireland's national struggles, present a compensatory vision toward which the nascent nation might aspire. Even when Yeats's early poems lack the explicitly political vision his essays and plays present, they viscerally embody the desire that drives not just the social dreaming of utopia, but all efforts toward a better collective.

One might see the two aforementioned strands of critical opinion on Yeats's cultural nationalism as roughly corresponding to two opposed outlooks on the relation of poetry (and particularly lyric poetry) to the social realm. One side emphasizes above all the historically specific subjectivity of the lyric voice, while the other stresses the communal thrust of lyric, its objectivization of ostensibly individual emotion. Or to inflect this dichotomy in a way more specifically related to Yeats's early work, one might reassert the distinction between the *expression* of desire and its *education*—a distinction that highlights the inextricability of the individual and communal resonances of early Yeatsian lyric. As I have been arguing, Yeats's speakers express certain longings (often directed toward a Celticized pastoral idyll) in order to model the ends toward which the Irish nation might strive, thus attempting a conflation of individual and communal desire. That such desire takes as its object a vague mystical ideal with little substantive content speaks not only to the young poet's anti-empirical predilections, but also to the ephemerality of nationhood itself.[9]

The Cultural Nationalist Dream Vision of "The Song of the Wandering Aengus"

This ephemerality is memorably personified in "The Song of the Wandering Aengus," from the 1899 volume *The Wind among the Reeds*. The poem presents Yeats's take on the Gaelic *aisling* lyric, wherein a magical woman embodying the nation appears in a vision to the dazzled speaker:

> I went out to the hazel wood,
> Because a fire was in my head,
> And cut and peeled a hazel wand,
> And hooked a berry to a thread;
> And when white moths were on the wing,
> And moth-like stars were flickering out,
> I dropped the berry in a stream
> And caught a little silver trout.
>
> When I had laid it on the floor
> I went to blow the fire aflame,
> But something rustled on the floor,
> And some one called me by my name:
> It had become a glimmering girl

> With apple blossom in her hair
> Who called me by my name and ran
> And faded through the brightening air.
>
> Though I am old with wandering
> Through hollow lands and hilly lands,
> I will find out where she has gone,
> And kiss her lips and take her hands;
> And walk among long dappled grass,
> And pluck till time and times are done
> The silver apples of the moon,
> The golden apples of the sun. (1–24)

Along with "Innisfree," this poem best encapsulates the affective conflation of individual desire and national hope upon which Yeats's early poetry relies. *Aisling* is the Irish word for "dream," and at its seventeenth-century origins the genre had more in common with the Chaucerian dream vision than the sort of mythopoetic lyric Yeats creates here. In these earlier examples of the genre, the poet figure would fall asleep and be visited by a beautiful woman (called the *spéirbhean*, or "sky-walker," and usually identified as Ireland herself) who would recount her many sufferings and shifts of fortune. Bríona Nic Dhiarmada notes that the seventeenth-century *aisling* marked the entry of utopian longing into Irish-language literature, and that this longing arose out of the collapse of the Gaelic polity in Ireland as a result of the Tudor conquests. The *aisling*'s feminized Ireland figure often claimed to be awaiting the return of her lover, an event metaphorically identified with the restoration of the Stuart monarchy, and so the genre embodied very specific political circumstances (Nic Dhiarmada 365). By contrast, and in keeping with Yeats's early pastoral utopianism, his adaptation of the *aisling* voids it of any specific political referent; the Catholic slant is removed, of course, but even the magical girl's identification with Ireland is muted, left implied only by the residue of generic convention that clings to the narrative shape of Yeats's paganized update. As a result, the poem becomes more about the pursuit of an ideal than the lamenting of its loss: the speaker quests after a girl who, though her potential symbolic function remains implicit in the genre's tradition, slips free of firm identification with the Irish essence. Rather than allegorizing the traumas of the colonized nation, then, the poem acknowledges that no such nation yet exists: it still must be sought, like quarry, and possessed. The poem ends, as so many of Yeats's early lyrics do, suspended in the future tense. Diffusing the traditionally nationalist elements of the *aisling* from the girl herself into the poem's Celticized landscape of hazel woods, moth-like stars, hills, hollows, and dappled grass, the poet creates a pastoral backdrop that serves to amplify this trajectory of desire and pursuit.

In his explanatory note on the poem, Yeats quotes the accounts of various Galway peasants regarding "the spirits that are in Ireland," a hodgepodge of mystical hearsay, strange sightings, and sudden disappearances, all involving shape-shifting spirits masquerading as women. Toward the end of his note, however, Yeats somewhat undermines this assertion of the Irishness of the poem's subject matter when he admits that, "the poem was suggested to me by a Greek folk song; but the folk belief of Greece is very like that of Ireland, and I certainly thought, when I wrote it, of Ireland" (*Collected Poems* 806). Yeats casts the poem, then, as rooted not only in the living pastoral of western Irish peasant lore, but in the parallel tradition of Greece, the cradle of pastoral and thus the birthplace of the very notion of a Golden Age. His point is that Ireland and Greece both possess an autochthonous idealism, an inborn unwillingness to abide in the material status quo. Indeed, beneath his comparison lies the implicit assertion that those countries with vital folk traditions hold the key to unlocking a new social order—that the glimpses of peasants into the supernatural realm work to expand the horizons of possibility toward worlds of concord and fulfillment as yet only dreamt of by most.

Throughout the 1890s, as anticipation of the approaching new century built to a millennial pitch, Yeats set forth an ambitious vision of Ireland's potentially revelatory role. As early as 1892, Yeats had speculated in his essay "Hopes and Fears for Irish Literature" that "If we can take that history and those legends and turn them into dramas, poems, and stories full of the living soul of the present, and make them massive with conviction and profound with reverie, we may deliver that new great utterance for which the world is waiting" (*Uncollected 1* 250). By his 1897 essay "The Celtic Element in Literature"—with his own place in the burgeoning movement much more secure—he continued to mine this millennial vein, casting the Irish revival as crucial in issuing forth "a new fountain of legends," which "may well give the opening century its most memorable symbols" (137–8). The literature of Ireland, Yeats hoped, would mark the culmination of the counter-movement against the dominant rationalism and materialism of the eighteenth and nineteenth centuries, helping to restore art to its rightful authority, a place akin to religion in the people's hearts. The Symbolist movement and its influence throughout Europe had set the pendulum swinging back in this direction, but in its overriding concern with pure linguistic evocativeness it lacked the practicality and authentic sense of struggle that enriched the Irish context. For Yeats, Irish literature's great potential at the turn of the century lay in its combination of idealism and authenticity, or more properly, in the authenticity of its idealism: the otherworldly longings of Irish poets carried greater resonance both because Ireland really did have a lost Golden Age to appeal to, and because the stories of that past tradition positively teemed with other, better worlds.

"The Song of the Wandering Aengus" depicts just such a better world—not only in its Celticized landscape, but also in the degree to which the eponymous singer exercises his creative agency to alter that landscape. The most significant (and typically Yeatsian) alteration Yeats effects upon the *aisling* genre involves this shift in the speaker's status from passive dreamer to active creator, possessed by the force of inspiration: "I went out to the hazel wood / Because *a fire was in my head.*" Aengus, variously characterized by Yeats and his critics as "the Irish god of love," "the eternal male principle," and "the Irish Apollo, the god of poetry," occupies all of the above roles in the poem, both as a lyric lover seeking unity with a mate of his own conjuration, and more implicitly as an ardent nationalist seeking to unify the image of the Irish nation as he conceives it with its manifestation in reality.[10] Seen in these terms, the Ireland-girl becomes another embodiment of the poet's pursuit of a mutually foundational relationship between word and world: the bard is born of an Ireland that he then tries to reshape to the sympathies of his art. While it would be too much to read "The Song of the Wandering Aengus" as strict allegory, the dynamic it sets out of inspiration, creation, and pursuit does analogize the dynamic of Yeats's early cultural nationalism. Born Irish and yet, as an Anglo-Irish Protestant, fundamentally apart, he sets out to retell Ireland's stories to itself, to image a new nation and (perhaps most importantly) a new national audience for his art—to aestheticize a clergy-dominated Ireland, transfiguring Christianity's apple of sin into the paganized (and thereby more authentically Celtic) "golden apples of the sun." But the idiosyncrasy of his vision for Ireland—particularly its dependence upon the myths and symbols of a premodern Celticism of dubious historicity—meant that Yeats increasingly found himself, like Aengus, out of step with the entity he helped bring into being, repeatedly confronting the disparity his poems had worked so hard to efface, between the desires embodied in his own lyric utterances and those of the nation at large.

"Adam's Curse" and Anti-Utopia

After the turn of the century, the pastoral impetus animating so much of Yeats's early work gradually dissipates, with idyllic landscapes giving over prominence to the more insular spaces that typify his later work: country houses, galleries, solitary towers, and myriad visionary mindscapes. This spatial contraction entails a concomitant reining in of lyric desire, as Yeats's speakers increasingly express their individuality more specifically, rather than dwelling in the mythic haze that once allowed personal and communal aspirations to blur together. Put another way, Yeats's speakers come more and more to express opinions rather than tell tales, making his poetry increasingly resistant to the allegorization upon which his cultural nationalist aesthetic depends. This means, of course, that at some point Yeats's poetry almost stops being *utopian*, forsaking its investment in a better way of life for the collective and instead assuming toward the mass of the Irish people an aristocratic hauteur often verging on disdain. Indeed, the word "utopia" never appears in Yeats's writings until the 1920s—long after most explicit traces of utopianism had been vanquished from his work—and only ever derogatorily. He increasingly repudiated, too, the Shelleyan conviction of poetry's formative social role, as he came to see the inexorable cycles of history itself as the driving force of historical change, and thus to regard most projects for sociopolitical reform as contemptible in their futility. The wider implications of these three shifts in Yeats's work—the repudiation of utopian desire, the evaporation of the pastoral ethos, and the increasing insularity of his lyric spaces—will be traced in the next chapter's exploration of what I term Yeats's "anti-utopian utopianism." For now, however, I want to focus on one final poem, from just after the turn of the century, which portrays this anti-utopian Yeats in his nascency.

As the predominant narrative of his career has it, the years just after 1900 found Yeats feeling more and more keenly the bitterness of having failed to shape the tastes of the Irish public to his satisfaction. *The Wind among the Reeds* would stand as his last full-length collection of poetry for eleven years, until *The Green Helmet and Other Poems* in 1910, as the first decade of the new century found him focusing his energies primarily on drama, both authoring his own plays and working to administrate the burgeoning Abbey Theatre. Among the poems he did produce in this interim period, "Adam's Curse"—published in the 1903 mini-volume *In the Seven Woods*—has been accorded the most esteemed place in his canon. Part love poem and part *ars poetica*, it starkly diverges from earlier work in both its plainspokenness and its clear-eyed vision of poetry's less-than-exalted place in contemporary society. The poem's first few lines recall a summer evening spent discussing poetry with Maud Gonne and her sister, before the speaker quotes himself:

I said, 'A line will take us hours maybe;
Yet if it does not seem a moment's thought,
Our stitching and unstitching has been naught.
Better go down upon your marrow-bones
And scrub a kitchen pavement, or break stones
Like an old pauper, in all kinds of weather;
For to articulate sweet sounds together
Is to work harder than all these, and yet
Be thought an idler by the noisy set
Of bankers, schoolmasters, and clergymen
The martyrs call the world'. (4–14)

Several new notes are struck here. First, poetry is work: its effects may still transcend the quotidian—indeed, later stanzas link it to the surpassing labors of beauty and love—but its creation entails drudgery. Second, Yeats's claim that a well-made poem must "seem a moment's thought," finds him both repudiating the deliberate ornateness of much of his earlier poetry, and celebrating the aristocratic ideal of *sprezzatura*, whereby (as Baldassare Castiglione puts it in his sixteenth-century *Book of the Courtier*) "true art is what does not seem to be art" and "to reveal intense application and skill robs everything of grace" (67). The poet may "work harder" than any manual laborer, but his cultural status depends on his giving no evidence of it—on never sweating in public.

Castiglione's text and the ideals it celebrates came to exert an increasing influence on Yeats, with its depiction of the court at Urbino as a haven of refinement, harmony, and civilized conversation effectively coming to supplant the mythopoetic vision of a lost pastoral Ireland as the social ideal toward which his poetry strove.[11] Though he would continue to occasionally hark back to the idyllic countryside—in "The Wild Swans at Coole," for example—by and large the images he deploys no longer aspire to Celtic folkiness, but rather appeal to a more specifically Anglo-Irish sense of loss: as in "The Wild Swans," the Big House and its hallowed grounds often figure prominently in the later Yeats's infrequent appeals to the pastoral ethos.

As a transitional poem, however, "Adam's Curse" finds Yeats's burgeoning enthusiasm for the trappings of aristocracy partly tempered by a sense of loyalty to his solitary vocation as poet; he might share with Castiglione and his Anglo-Irish inheritors a disdain for the bourgeois materialism of the "bankers, schoolmasters, and clergymen / The martyrs call the world," but the poem hinges on an ambivalence that suggests his unreadiness to fully ally himself with his ancestral class just yet. After all, while on the one hand he asserts that a poet must not betray his labor, on the other he gives the game away, affirming that poetry is in fact hard work, akin to "scrub[bing] a kitchen pavement, or break[ing] stones." This contradictory stance that the speaker takes with regard to the poet's relation to society—wanting to affirm his place among the mass of laborers, yet needing to assert his exceptional status as artist—is recapitulated in the poem's second half, this time in relation to love. When Gonne's sister implicitly compares women to poets, saying "we must labour to be beautiful," the poet responds:

> I said, 'It's certain there is no fine thing
> Since Adam's fall but needs much labouring.
> There have been lovers who thought love should be
> So much compounded of high courtesy
> That they would sigh and quote with learned looks
> Precedents out of beautiful old books;
> Yet now it seems an idle trade enough'.
>
> We sat grown quiet in the name of love;
> We saw the last embers of the daylight die,
> And in the trembling blue-green of the sky
> A moon, worn as if it had been a shell
> Washed by time's waters as they rose and fell
> About the stars and broke in days and years. (21–33)

The first of these stanzas hinges on the contrast between love as on the one hand "compounded by high courtesy," and on the other as "idle trade enough." Love was once, Yeats implies, one of those "fine thing[s]" requiring "much labouring" to come to fruition. Again, one doubts the extent to which Yeats had internalized his own doctrine of *sprezzatura* here, as in addition to emphasizing the fact of love's labor, he depicts the lovers themselves as "sigh[ing] and quot[ing] with learned looks"—betraying rather more of their exertion than would likely be permitted by the tenets of courtly nonchalance.

The transition to the next stanza embodies a similar ambivalence; though modern love has just been characterized as "an idle trade," the first line past the gap finds the three companions hushed in a kind of pagan awe: "We sat grown silent in the name of love." Though not capitalized here, love is nonetheless accorded "name[d]" status and so virtually personified, an indication that the three still hold love in the deific esteem it warranted in premodern, precommercial times. Rather than express desire or even hope for the possible return of such times, however, the rest of the poem conveys a resigned despondency. The image of the moon "worn as if it had been a shell" recalls the "echo-harbouring shell" of "The Song of the Happy Shepherd," though rather than resonate with the heart's regenerative desires, carrying forward the singer's hopes for renewal, the shell here ends up "hollow," filled only by silence. Viewed from a wider perspective, "Adam's Curse" marks a major point at which we can see Yeats unrooting his aesthetics from the pastoral utopianism I have been delineating throughout this chapter, as a new note of inconsolability enters his tone, especially acute in the oddly tensed final lines:

> I had a thought for no one's but your ears:
> That you were beautiful, and that I strove
> To love you in the old high way of love;
> That it had all seemed happy, and yet we'd grown
> As weary-hearted as that hollow moon. (34–8)

By affirming the pastness of his pursuit of Maud Gonne—always herself an emblem of the once and future nation—the poet relinquishes his usual stance of future nostalgia for a plainer form of nostalgia, void of fervency, a bland disappointment at the passing of the past, an acquiescence at its irrecoverability. Something important is over: though he "strove" and "it had all seemed happy," the poet strands himself and his companions in the past perfect, "weary-hearted," facing sadly backward without any prospect of hope's future turn.

Notes

1. All quotations from Yeats's poems in this book are drawn from *The Collected Poems of W. B. Yeats*, Revised Second Edition.
2. For the formulation "social dreaming," see Tom Moylan and Raffaella Baccolini's edited volume *Utopia Method Vision: The Use Value of Social Dreaming* (Peter Lang, 2007).
3. Theodor Adorno's essay "Lyric Poetry and Society" informs my analysis throughout this chapter, both positively—in its insistence that all lyric poetry is essentially social, that "all individual lyric poetry is indeed grounded in a collective substratum"—and negatively—in its condemnation of Romanticism as artificially "transfusing the collective into the individual," and thus producing "a technical illusion of generality" rather than an authentically social utterance (217). Adorno's essay is thus useful both in contextualizing Yeats's early lyrics within the explicitly communal context of his cultural nationalism, and in illuminating the Romantic tenuousness of Yeats's attempt to conflate the lyric desires of his individual speakers with the Irish nation's quest for self-determination.
4. My terminology here owes a good deal to Harold Bloom, who situates Yeats so firmly in the Romantic tradition that his magisterial 1970 study proceeds upon the

idiosyncratic premises that "Yeats's most typical poem is a dramatic lyric that behaves as though it were a fragment in a mythological romance, as though the poet himself as quest-hero undertook continually an odyssey of the spirit," and that "the single poem that most affected his life and art … is Shelley's *Alastor*" (7–8). Though my own critical outlook places greater emphasis upon historical factors as opposed to the strictly literary-historical lineage in which Bloom places Yeats, I do find his readings of the pre-nationalist poetry convincing, particularly in the way they emphasize the poet as a figure driven to quest after an ephemeral coherence with at best a spectral connection to concrete social and political aims.

5   See *The Trembling of the Veil*. Book IV. The Tragic Generation, in Yeats's *Autobiographies*, which attributes the decline of especially Dowson and Johnson not just to their dissolute lifestyles, but to the fruitless striving after spiritual fulfillment of which those lifestyles were a symptom.

6   Marcus's 1992 book *Yeats and Artistic Power* builds its reading of Yeats's early career on the premise that because he felt himself unsuited or unable to produce work with immediate political relevance to the Irish cause, Yeats developed an aesthetic that "provided the compensatory thought that the real forces behind the great political events of the day might not in fact be the obvious ones" (10). Marcus focuses largely on Yeats's bardic inspiration in the development of this aesthetic, and on his evolving conception of his own political power as an artist. While my emphasis remains more on Yeats's lyrics as utopian creations than on the creator himself, and more on the expression and education of desire than the assertion of power, I find Marcus's study valuable in the way it shares my concern with how Yeats conceived of the political efficacy of his aesthetic.

7   Unbeknownst to me when I wrote this chapter, Edward Mendelson characterizes utopianism as "nostalgia for the future" in condemning Auden's "Spain" and the "Commentary" to *In Time of War* "not as public poems but as utopian poems"—poems that "envision a world only imagination can build" (*Early* 202). Thus Mendelson joins the chorus of modern critics who dismiss utopia as unproductive dreaming rather than seeing it (as I do) as a potentially productive manifestation of desire.

8   Declan Kiberd cuts to the nostalgic core of Yeats's myth of Innisfree with the following anecdote:

> The more he sought to recapture the dream, the more it seemed to elude him. When the much older man finally brought his newly-wed English wife on a boat-trip across Lough Gill, he failed ignominiously to locate, much less land on, the lake isle of Innisfree: a sign, perhaps, that the past in that simple-minded version was not easily recoverable. (102–3)

9   The classic statement of the ephemerality of nationhood is of course Benedict Anderson's 1983 book *Imagined Communities*, which claims of the nation: "It is *imagined* because the members of even the smallest nation will never know most of their fellow-members, meet them, or even hear of them, yet in the minds of each lives the image of their communion" (6). Compare Yeats, in his 1909 journal: "One cannot love a nation struggling to realize itself without an idea of the nation as a whole being present in one's mind. One could always appeal to it in the minds of others" (*Memoirs* 180). Of Yeats's critics, Eagleton has most forcefully asserted the aesthetic roots of nationalism, claiming in this discussion of the Celtic Revival that "the kind of fulfillment one reaps from belonging to a community of national sentiment is akin to the pleasure the Kantian subject derives from the *sensus communis* of aesthetic taste"

(*Heathcliff* 232). This analogy is absolutely crucial to Yeats's cultural nationalism, which strives to reverse the causality of Eagleton's formulation, attempting to build Irish national sentiment by drawing on an ostensibly shared symbolism, working to blur the distinction between aesthetic and political consensus.

10 The first characterization of Aengus ("the Irish god of love") comes from the footnotes of Volume 2 of Intelex's electronic edition of *The Collected Letters of W. B. Yeats*, where it occurs three times. The second ("the eternal male principle") comes from the same footnotes, but is a quotation from Yeats himself, in an unpublished mystical manuscript on "The Initiation of the Sword" held in the National Library of Ireland. The third of Aengus's epithets ("the Irish Apollo, the god of poetry") is from Helen Vendler, *Secret* p. 105.

11 It is not entirely clear when Yeats read Castiglione's work. In her book *Yeats and Castiglione: Poet and Courtier*, Corinna Salvadori—drawing on Yeats's account in his autobiographical 1922 essay "The Bounty of Sweden"—claims that Lady Gregory introduced *The Book of the Courtier* to the poet in 1903. Since "Adam's Curse" is usually thought to have been composed in 1902, this would mean that Yeats's exposition of *sprezzatura* in the poem actually precedes his encounter with the concept in the Italian original. Salvadori concludes, therefore, "that the Italian work gave Yeats nothing new in this respect but helped him, rather, to develop and define something he had already conceived" (40). I have nonetheless felt it necessary to emphasize Castiglione in discussing "Adam's Curse" both because of the exactitude of the correspondence between his and Yeats's conceptions of *sprezzatura*, and because he did in fact become, in the years after Yeats read him, one of the poet's most cited authors.

Chapter 2

"HISTORY IS VERY SIMPLE": DESIRE AND THE MEANINGS OF UTOPIA IN LATER YEATS

The prominent pejorative view of utopia sees it as signifying an unrealizable—and therefore implicitly pointless—ideal.[1] To a certain extent, as we will see, the later Yeats shared this view of utopia; living in an era that abounded in projects and stances liable to be characterized as "utopian," he disdained the majority of these for what he saw as their excessive materialism, for harboring the conviction that societal ills could be eradicated by political or economic means. Consequently, he would never (contrary to today's colloquial usage) have dismissed such utopians as "idealists"—a label he frequently applied to himself with pride, and which registered his belief that subjective states of mind and feeling figure at least as prominently as material conditions in altering the course of history. As much as he would have repudiated the label, this makes Yeats a utopian according to theorizers of the concept in both our time and his own. This chapter engages with the Yeats of the later work as an anti-utopian utopian, an ambivalent desirer of better worlds who at the same time repudiates his era's most earnest attempts to construct such worlds, a poet whose work uniquely illuminates the grounds upon which the term "utopia"—and the artist's relationship to the dreams of social harmony it embodies—has been and continues to be contested. I begin with a brief account of the most prominent theorization during his own lifetime of Yeats as a utopian artist, before going on to trace the development of his anti-utopian utopian poetics over the course of his later career, a period during which he comes to conceive of poetry as generated out of not only the confrontation between just such opposing dispensations (i.e., "anti-utopian utopian") but also the perpetuation of desire, however futile. Often envisioning the fulfillment of desire in terms of a state of stasis that would be anathema to the artistic impulse, Yeats thus equates the dawn of utopia with the death of art—an equation that lends impetus to his own conception of history's cyclicity, as it virtually mandates the ceaselessness of desire that, for the poet, is the only authentic manifestation of affirmative futurity.

The Story of Utopias *and Yeats as a Eutopian Artist*

Published in modernism's *annus mirabilis* of 1922, the historian and sociologist Lewis Mumford's *The Story of Utopias* surveys the history of utopian thought from a disillusioned vantage. In taking stock of prominent literary utopias from Plato to Morris, Mumford finds them too often rooted not in the facts of culture and geography upon which any new societal order must be founded, but rather in the boundlessness of authorial fancy; even where their blueprints are richest in practical details, "their projections have nevertheless literally been up in the air, since they did not usually arise out of any real environment presented" (185). Similarly, contemporary political creeds informed by the utopian desire to "effect a change in the economic order"—the mostly leftist movements that Mumford labels "partisan utopias"—too often view personal relations in purely transactional terms, neglecting the "social inheritance" that binds us as human beings, those shared faculties of imagination, reason, and ingenuity that run beneath any "irrelevant partisanisms" that might divide us (182).

Thus condemning the bulk of extant literary and political utopias as impracticable, Mumford moves to theorize how utopian thought might contribute more concretely to his oft-iterated though rather hazy liberal humanist vision of "the greater good." His key rhetorical gesture in laying the conceptual foundations for such a theorization is to divide the word "utopia" into its two punned-upon cognates, *outopia* and *eutopia*, no-place and good place. Favoring (of course) the latter, Mumford exalts humanity's "will-to-eutopia" as the sole force preventing our societies from sinking into a kind of late-imperial dissolution. In attempting to identify the key manifestations of this eutopian thrust, Mumford turns first to the sciences, which, although they have developed endless means of transforming the physical world, have often seemed unguided by an ethical vision in their application. "Indeed," he writes, "scientific knowledge has not merely heightened the possibilities of life in the modern world: it has lowered the depths. When science is not touched by a sense of values it works—as it fairly consistently has worked during the past century—towards a complete dehumanization of the social order" (192). The "sense of values" Mumford prescribes entails scientists applying the impersonal breadth of their knowledge ("that vast over-world of scientific effort which is the product of no single place or people or time") to the concrete improvement of local communities. The balancing of an encyclopedic trans-historical erudition with the desire to bring this learning minutely to bear on specific geographical regions stands for Mumford as the key to actualizing the eutopian impulse and bringing the good place down to earth.

But how precisely does Mumford believe that our communities might be improved? As so often throughout the theoretical sections of his treatise, he remains vague on this point, repeatedly referencing "the good life" without ever detailing its contours. He comes closest to specificity when he elaborates his vision of the eutopian citizen, contrasting this ideal being with the rootless denizens of modern cities: "The inhabitants of our eutopias will have a familiarity with their local environment and its resources, and a sense of historic continuity, which those who dwell within the paper world of Megalopolis and who touch their environment mainly through the newspaper and the printed book, have completely lost" (212). This concept of the "local" is central to the climactic chapters of *The Story of Utopias*; but far from recommending an insular parochialism, Mumford demands that our local foci be enriched, both vertically and horizontally, by the "sense of historic continuity" that perceives both the depth of tradition that abides in any given place, and the way that each rich locale is woven into the wider tapestry of human history. (In this Mumford stands as an implicit early formulator of the progressive exhortation to "think globally, act locally.") In Mumford's view, the impetus for this local-historical mode of citizenship must come from the arts, which, though they have gradually loosened their once-inextricable ties to one another and to the community, still hold the capacity "to equip us with patterns, with images and ideals, by means of which we might react creatively upon our environment" (201). Artists, therefore, when fully embracing their "proper relation to the community," work to generate the images after which eutopias are modeled (204).

As his one archetypal example of the properly eutopian artist, Mumford offers W. B. Yeats, citing the poet's cultural nationalist hope that the imaginative arts might "so deepen the political passion of the nation that all, artist and poet, craftsman and day laborer, would accept a common design" (qtd. on 205). The text Mumford cites from, *Four Years*, finds Yeats reflecting on his very early career, from 1887 to 1891, when the "common design" he aspired toward would have been very different from that which he upheld by the time he wrote the text in the early 1920s, when his thinking was becoming increasingly hierarchical. Nonetheless, while Yeats's definition of national "unity" may have changed from the more holistic vision of the Celtic Revival years, his belief that art's atavistic reservoir of images might work to produce such a unity never did, and this is what Mumford exalts. While not discounting the value of purely aesthetic experience, Mumford emphasizes the didactic force of such images, going so far as to assert that "Pure art is inevitably propaganda. I mean by this that it is meant to be propagated, and that in so far as it fails to impregnate the community in which it exists with its ideas and images, in so far as the community is not changed for better or worse by its existence, its claims are spurious" (203). In this view, "pure art" proves itself by its power to plant seeds of change among its audience. That Yeats strove to create such transfigurative art throughout his poetic career is not in doubt; in his 1897 essay "The Celtic Element in Literature" he speculates: "It may be the arts are founded on the life beyond the world, and that they must cry in the ears of our penury until the world has been consumed and become a vision" (*Early* 136). As I explored in the previous chapter, this stance undergirds the early poetry, with its overwhelming focus on desire and its education. But even by the time of his 1939 tract *On the Boiler*, written in the final months of his life, he acknowledges his altered vision of the arts' imperatives while clearly remaining convinced of their proliferative force:

> In my savage youth I was accustomed to say that no man should be permitted to open his mouth in Parliament until he had sung or written his *Utopia*, for

lacking that we could not know where he was taking us, and I still think that artists of all kinds should once again praise or represent great or happy people. (*Later* 249–50)

The imaging of states to which we might aspire remains for Yeats one of the artist's chief roles, despite the fact that he has abandoned the cultural nationalist aspirations of his younger self in favor of a Nietzschean exaltation of the dynamic individual. His youth was "savage" because in it he believed that political reorganization held the promise of social harmony, whereas his later years are marked by the conviction that disharmony is in fact inevitable, and that the key to happiness lies in aesthetic self-cultivation. In other words, he comes to favor states of being over nation-states; the communal "good place" largely gives way, as he ages, to the more exclusive "good life."

An Anti-Utopian Utopianism?

The aristocratic proclivities of the later Yeats set him at odds not only with Mumford, whose conception of the good life is always a societal rather than an individual one, but with the earlier version of himself Mumford praises: the young eutopian whose dreams of Irish harmony, though never fully extinguished, come to the older poet to seem naïve in their neglect of the inevitability of conflict and suffering, their lack of the "Vision of Evil" so crucial to his later thought. Yeats came to perceive the same lack in figures like Shelley and Morris whom he had spent his youth admiring, finding behind their reformist fervor an excessively optimistic view of human nature and historical progress. This disillusionment is memorably conveyed in "Nineteen Hundred and Nineteen," as the speaker meditates on the ravages of the Irish Civil War:

> O but we dreamed to mend
> Whatever mischief seemed
> To afflict mankind, but now
> That winds of winter blow
> Learn that we were crack-pated when we dreamed. (84–8)

One might wonder whether such repudiations of past social dreams, common throughout the later Yeats, render Mumford's characterization of him as quintessentially eutopian more or less obsolete. For while the Yeats of the early 1920s maintains his early-held belief that "nations, races and individual men are unified by an image, or a bundle of related images," his thought is already emphasizing the absolute precariousness of all such unities and the inevitability of their dissolution (*Autobiographies* 167). One of the central formulations of the first edition of *A Vision* published in 1925—and a motif that recurs time and again throughout the last two decades of his career—is the image of "all things dying each other's life, living each other's death" (*A Vision* 1925 152). The cyclical model of historical change as laid out in *A Vision* and upheld by Yeats throughout the rest of his career seems inimical to the eutopian pursuit of the good life, positing as it does the inevitability of perpetual strife. "History is very simple," he wrote in a letter of 1933, "the rule of the many, then the rule of the few, day and night, night and day" (*Letters* 812). This image of endless class upheaval stands as a rebuttal not only to utopians of a Marxist stripe, who await the synthetic resolution of such antinomies in the permanent peace of communism, but even to moderate eutopians like Mumford himself, who—though sharing Yeats's disdain for the delusion that any such harmonious stasis might be reached—still clearly believed that humanity might progress, not just technologically but morally. The later Yeats would have scoffed at Anatole France's assertion, quoted approvingly by Mumford, that "utopia is the principle of all progress, and the essay into a better future" (27). Indeed, the distinction Mumford draws between his own brand of locally rooted, historically informed *eu*topianism and the abstract, unhinged *u*topianism of those he critiques (from contemporary socialists back to Plato, their virtual ideological opposite) would likely have struck the *Vision*-era Yeats as virtually meaningless. To the extent that they hold out the possibility for lasting social betterment, all are insupportable.

And yet Yeats's later work cannot be simply characterized as anti-utopian in stance. Granted, Yeats himself only ever used the word pejoratively, associating it not only with futile political projects, but more broadly with the rationalist materialism that lay behind such projects, the modern tendency to believe that a perfect societal order could be achieved through the right calibration of political and economic factors. For him socialists were susceptible not to the charge of idealism but to that of excessive materialism. Throughout his life he proudly considered himself an idealist at odds with "the filthy modern tide"—the leveling, democratic dispensation of which the calculating plots of utopians represented the apogee. Of course, many have criticized utopian thought along the same lines; the tendency to characterize the totalitarian regimes of twentieth-century Europe as utopias gone wrong has given rise to the widespread perception that all utopias are ultimately dystopias, or will be revealed as such the moment their strictly mediated internal coherencies come under threat. But in fact this criticism applies only to one branch of utopian thought, the hyper-rationalist, engineering strain characterized by Russell Jacoby as "blueprint utopianism," a designation under which might fall the central tradition of the utopian novel from More through Bellamy and Morris to Huxley's *Island*, works that map out their ideal futures down to the minutiae of domestic arrangements, systems of education and commerce, and even the improved physical attributes of their fortunate inhabitants.[2] As Jacoby notes, however, in their very detailedness, such blueprints can "not only appear repressive, they also rapidly become dated ... History soon eclipses them" (32).

As I discussed in the Introduction, however, there exists another strain of utopianism, running parallel to that of the blueprinters, which, rather than specifying the final detailed shape the perfect society will take, abides instead in the very impulse that gives rise to social reform. Its emphasis is not strictly practical, but aspirational; utopia is not a place, but a stance—what Ernst Bloch (whom

Jacoby places at the center of this "iconoclastic" utopianism) calls "anticipatory consciousness." It is out of this tradition, which works to refute the notion of utopia as a literary genre strictly concerned with the modeling of good- or no-places, that Ruth Levitas derives her expansive definition of utopia as "the expression of the desire for a better way of being" (8). According to Levitas, "this definition goes beyond that of an alternative world, possible or otherwise" because "the pursuit of a better way of being does not always involve the alteration of external conditions, but may mean the pursuance of spiritual or psychological states" (191). As I elaborated in the previous chapter, according to Levitas's definition, Yeats is certainly a utopian thinker—and not just in his early work, with its hazy longings after ideal islands and the nymphean women that embody them, but also in the aristocratic emphases of much of his middle- and later-period work, with its Big Houses and towers. Paradoxically, it is in his confrontations after the turn of the century with what he saw as the crassly materialist utopianism of mass democratic movements—with the kind of "blueprint utopias" decried by Mumford and Jacoby—that his own aesthetics of aspiration, of utopia as desire, emerges most fully. This is not only to say that Yeats is anti-utopian according to one definition while being quintessentially utopian according to another, vastly different one. More compellingly, it is to claim that the later Yeats's most distinctly utopian sentiments take shape dialectically, in the teeth of his explicit anti-utopianism. For Yeats, those he labels 'utopian' seek the obsolescence of desire, the impossible stamping out of want in the establishment of a permanent socialistic stasis. He responds by asserting the endlessness of desire, thus embodying a paradoxical brand of idealism—one that aspires toward perfection without the deluded hope of its achievement, convinced that to arrive at an ideal is to shatter it.[3]

The Gore-Booth Sisters' Utopian Betrayal

The word "utopia" appears in Yeats's actual poetry only once, in the 1927 elegy "In Memory of Eva Gore-Booth and Con Markievicz," but its usage there typifies his animosity toward the concept. Looking back on his years of rocky acquaintanceship with the two sisters, Yeats blames the falling away of their youthful beauty on the withering influence of the political causes to which they came to devote much of their lives. After a caustic depiction of the elder sister Constance "drag[ging] out the years / Conspiring among the ignorant," he writes of Eva:

> I know not what the younger dreams—
> Some vague Utopia—and she seems,
> When withered old and skeleton-gaunt,
> An image of such politics. (10–13)

In actuality, Eva Gore-Booth's politics could hardly be called utopian, at least in the dismissive sense Yeats intends; most of her activism served the suffragette movement, as she worked tirelessly with her partner Esther Roper to better the lives of England's urban women, taking up unconventional and often thankless causes: the unionization of Manchester barmaids, of performing gymnasts, and of the flower sellers at Oxford Circus. She spoke at rallies, wrote tracts, and brought to the women's movement (in the words of her biographer Gifford Lewis) "something of the burning sense of injustice which was entirely new in the humdrum round of British suffrage societies" (3). Only a man as deeply cynical about concrete political action as the later Yeats could accuse her goals of vagueness, though the history of his relationship with the Gore-Booths suggests that the criticism has much earlier roots, and that its upshot is at least as much aesthetic as political.[4]

Yeats became aware of the Gore-Booth sisters long before he actually met them. His childhood walks in Sligo had often furnished him glimpses of their ancestral grounds, a weave of trees and lanes presided over by the austere neoclassical mansion called Lissadell. As an established Ascendancy family, the Gore-Booths stood as full-fledged representatives of a Protestant aristocratic class to which Yeats's own "merchant people" could never gain access. So, when his rising literary fame led him to their drawing room in late 1894, he could feel he had arrived somewhere: not quite utopia, but a place rather more rarefied than his usual social circles at the time. That November Yeats stayed a few days at Lissadell, which he found "an exceedingly impressive house inside with a great sitting room as high as a church & all things in good taste" (*Letters* 239). He discovered among the family and the local community both an audience for and a source of old Irish stories; he lectured on fairy lore to local parishioners, and the Gore-Booths brought him to a local tenant "who poured out quantities of tales" (*Letters* 240). Yeats found Eva particularly congenial, as both eager listener and aspiring poet herself, noting in a letter to his sister that "Miss Eva Gore-Booth shows some promise as a writer of verse. Her work is very formless as yet but it is full of telling little phrases" (*Letters* 240–1). Five months later he wrote to his novelist friend Olivia Shakespear about Eva:

> She has some literary talent, and much literary ambition, and has met no literary people. I have told her about you and, if the chance arise, would like you to meet her. I am always ransacking Ireland for people to set writing at Irish things. She does not know that she is the last victim—but is deep in some books of Irish legends I sent her—and may take fire. She needs however, like all Irish literary people, a proper respect for craftsmanship and that she must get in England. (*Letters* 256–7)

Setting aside the Ascendancy smugness of the claim that one would need to get in England the proper craftsmanship to write about "Irish things" (also a common theme in Yeats's essays of the period), we can see here Yeats's paternalistic stance toward Eva's literary education—introducing her to the right people, lending her books, and setting her artistic priorities. Given that Yeats later admitted being attracted enough to Eva's "gazelle-like beauty" that he actually considered proposing marriage to her, one might see mixed motives in his encouragement of her poetry (*Memoirs* 78–9). No doubt her apparent formlessness and inexperience made her seem malleable to Yeats, fresh to be turned to his own cultural nationalist hopes.

As it turned out, Eva Gore-Booth did end up in England, but not to roam in literary circles learning the "respect for craftsmanship" Yeats prescribed. Instead, she emigrated for love. In the summer of 1895, while sojourning in Italy for a misdiagnosed case of consumption, Gore-Booth met Esther Roper, a university graduate and suffragist who would become her partner for life. By 1897 the pair had set up house in Roper's home city of Manchester, where they worked together for women's causes, with Eva continuing to write poetry at a prolific rate and publishing her first book, *Poems*, in 1898. In a letter to Gore-Booth about the book, Yeats praised it as "full of poetical fealing" [sic] and showing "very great promise," while issuing a caution that, though standard advice from Yeats to any poet at the time, typifies his stance toward the Gore-Booth sisters in particular: "Avoid every touch of rhetoric every tendency to teach [sic]" (*Collected Letters* December 26, 1898). Eva of course ignored this advice, in both her life and her poetry. In the nine more books of verse she published, one encounters—in addition to much of the sort of delicate lyric Yeats singled out for praise—much passionate didacticizing, on subjects ranging from women's rights to urban alienation to the evils of war. She adapted many Irish tales as well, though not in the way Yeats would have done, de-emphasizing the Romantic individualism of heroes like Oisin and Cuchulain and giving center stage to the close relationships among the women characters left peripheral in most accounts.[5]

All this—her involvement in labor issues, her particular compassion for women's rights, and her willingness to preach these causes through literature—lies behind Yeats's dismissal, all those years later, of Eva's "vague Utopia." Nor can this stance toward Eva be separated from his much more thoroughly documented relationship with her sister Constance, who as Countess Markiewicz spent decades in the Irish public eye. After serving as second-in-command of a unit of the Irish Citizen's Army that held Dublin's St. Stephen's Green against the British during the Easter Rising of 1916, she was sentenced to death—a term lowered to life and then remanded entirely the following year. Upon her free return, she became the first woman in the world to be elected as a Member of Parliament and served as Minister of Labour in the first Dáil (Assembly of the Irish Republic) from 1919 to 1922. Yeats watched Constance closely throughout this period of turmoil, remembering her role in the Easter Rising in both "On a Political Prisoner"— where he invokes "the years before her mind / Became a bitter, an abstract thing"— and, most famously, "Easter, 1916":

> That woman's days were spent
> In ignorant good-will,
> Her nights in argument
> Until her voice grew shrill.
> What voice more sweet than hers
> When, young and beautiful,
> She rode to harriers? (17–23)

As in the elegy of ten years later, Yeats's criticisms of Constance here hinge on his memory of her past beauty and dignity, now warped into hysteria. And indeed, the few mentions of the Gore-Booths in Yeats's letters and journals after the turn of the century imply a similarly misogynistic narrative of decline: the story of the fall of two sisters ("Two girls in silk kimonos, both / Beautiful, one a gazelle") from the pristine realm of the aesthetic to the maculate one of political action.

In the first draft of his memoirs written in the early 1920s, Yeats recalls that "Con Gore-Booth all through my later boyhood had been romantic to me … She had often passed me on horseback, going or coming from hunt, and was acknowledged beauty of the country" (*Memoirs* 77–8). As he had done in "Easter, 1916," Yeats emphasizes Constance's aristocratic pedigree in depicting her at the hunt, further evidence that his admiration was for her class as much her beauty. That this and all traces of the Gore-Booths came to be expunged from the final published *Autobiographies* illustrates the degree to which their commitment to radical political causes disturbed him, not so much for the supposed utopias they pursued—neither of which, Irish revolution or female equality, specifically offended Yeats—but rather (as the nostalgic tone of his remembrances repeatedly suggests) for the good place they abandoned. Increasingly after the turn of the century, Yeats idealized the aristocracy as a preserve of aesthetic purity, seeing the rituals of class as one of beauty's principal manifestations:

> Three types of men have made all beautiful things. Aristocracies have made beautiful manners, because their place in the world puts them above the fear of life, and the countrymen have made beautiful stories and beliefs, because they have nothing to lose and so do not fear, and the artists have made all the rest, because Providence has filled them with recklessness. (*Early* 183)

The urban working and middle classes' conspicuous absence from this picture makes perfect sense given Yeats's emphasis on fear. For if the making of beautiful things requires fearlessness, then the average city-dweller—living amidst an ever-shifting grid of concrete, crowds, and credit—must find such making next to impossible. There is more than a hint of Platonic idealism here, as caught up in crass material concerns, the urban classes neglect the timeless forms of beauty. What binds Yeats's sacred trinity of aristocrat, peasant, and artist is an almost metaphysical reverence for tradition, a sense that the manners, stories, and creations of past ancestors represent not just an inheritance but a refuge—a sphere of legitimacy, dignity, and purity in which to escape the uncertain taint of the masses. That Eva and Constance Gore-Booth should willingly choose to leave this place of safety, to give up the sanctity of Lissadell for the vulgarity of crowded cities—and by analogy, to abandon art for action—was incomprehensible to Yeats.[6]

The Protestant Big House as Aesthetic Utopia

The above analogy is crucial here: for it is as an *artist* that Yeats comes to admire the peace and comfort of aristocratic life. In this period Yeats's earlier utopian hopes contract from their wider societal scope to focus instead on the pristine microcosms of the Renaissance court as depicted by Castiglione and its contemporary analogue in courtesy, the Protestant Big House, epitomized by Coole, the County Galway estate of his artistic collaborator and patron Lady Augusta Gregory. The single poem that best illuminates Yeats's aesthetic motives for this contraction is "Upon a House Shaken by the Land Agitation," written in 1910 and presenting the culture of the Anglo-Irish Big House as having given rise to the best of Irish politics and (most crucially for Yeats) art. The first two quatrains run:

> How should the world be luckier if this house,
> Where passion and precision have been one
> Time out of mind, became too ruinous
> To breed the lidless eye that loves the sun?
> And the sweet laughing eagle thoughts that grow
> Where wings have memory of wings, and all
> That comes of the best knit to the best? Although
> Mean roof-trees were the sturdier for its fall, (1–8)

Within Coole's hallowed confines, "passion and precision" transcend their merely alliterative proximity into the purer fusion of *sprezzatura*. This has been the case since "Time out of mind": a phrase that evokes the stately procession of generations while also implying that the (Catholic) masses have forgotten these noble (Protestant) forebears, egregiously putting "out of mind" the class whose role it has been "To breed the lidless eye that loves the sun." This line encapsulates the emergent aristocratic aesthetic of Yeats's middle period. With the infinitive "to breed" embodying the purely carnal aspect of generation, while also implying the nominal aristocratic trait of "breeding," the poem stands as early evidence of Yeats's nascent interest in eugenics, a foretaste of his eventual conviction—not stated explicitly until *On the Boiler*, a year before his death—that "unless there is a change in the public mind every rank above the lowest must degenerate, and, as inferior men push up into its gaps, degenerate more and more quickly" (*Later* 229). In fostering the idealistic mindset ("the lidless eye that loves the sun"), the aristocracy stands for Yeats as the primary bastion against the ever-encroaching materialism of the modern age—which is deeply ironic, of course, given how entirely aristocratic status depends upon the possession of land, estates, and other material assets that help to insulate their bearers against the necessity of working for a living, thus freeing their minds for "the sweet laughing eagle thoughts" that supposedly place them at society's aspirational vanguard.[7]

"Upon a House" exemplifies Yeats's tendency, especially after the turn of the century, to collapse economic questions into aesthetic ones. The note on the poem he offers in his diary illuminates his willingness to tolerate systemic societal inequality as long as it means preserving the "high laughter, loveliness, and ease" that allows the aristocracy to persist as a beacon of grace and refinement:

I wrote this poem on hearing the result of reduction of rent by the courts. One feels that when all must make their living they will live not for life's sake but the work's and all be the poorer. ... This house has enriched my soul out of measure because here life moves within restraint through gracious forms. Here there has been no compelled labour, no poverty-thwarted impulse. (qtd. in Jeffares 109)

Rather than see the lowering of Lady Gregory's tenants' rents as compassionately affording the laboring classes an opportunity to exert greater control over their livelihoods, Yeats worries about the consequences for art. Lacking inherited wealth—both material and, presumably, genetic—the "Mean roof-trees" must rely on the exigencies of "luck" to gain from the rent reduction any benefit beyond the basely economic. Ultimately, their enfranchisement forebodes the deterioration of Irish culture:

> How should their luck run high enough to reach
> The gifts that govern men, and after these
> To gradual Time's last gift, a written speech
> Wrought of high laughter, loveliness and ease? (9–12)

This final quatrain figures the aristocracy's superiority both spatially ("*high enough*") and temporally ("Time's *last* gift"), positioning the inhabitants of Coole and their class compatriots at both the hierarchical summit and the eschatological end point of moral and artistic development. The achievement of "written speech"—the natural yet poetic language Yeats strove for in this middle period—stands as both a gift of time and an artifact consciously crafted out of a lifestyle rife with leisure, free of the stultifying effects of "compelled labour."

Yeats thus casts the Protestant Big House as a kind of utopia, gesturing to its spatio-temporal boundaries and foundations, and elaborating how the place itself fosters the admirable character traits of its inhabitants. But this utopia, of course, depends for its maintenance on the exploitation of a tenant class whose sphere of existence serves as its necessary antithesis: not quite dystopian, but insidious to the extent that Yeats can so readily judge it to be lacking in the idealistic impulses that birth the finest in politics and art. The fearless idealistic freedom of the aristocracy is born, paradoxically perhaps, out of their insularity—a fact reflected not just in the curiously circular way Yeats phrases their virtues ("Where wings have memory of wings, and all / That comes of the best knit to the best") but also by the poem's formal delimitation. As a douzaine—a Shakespearian sonnet shorn of its couplet—"Upon a House Shaken by the Land Agitation" relinquishes the twist or about-face traditionally afforded by the final two-line tag, instead relying on the interrogative mode to provide the illusion of ambiguity. For despite consisting of three questions, the poem is rhetorically closed, a series of assertions feigning uncertainty. This does not mean, however, that we should read it as purely conservative in impetus, especially in formal terms. Helen Vendler highlights the politicized aspect of Yeats's refusal to fully adopt the Shakespearean sonnet, claiming that in "foregoing a formal 'match' between Coole and English Renaissance form, Yeats will be an Irish douzain-writer, not an English sonneteer" (*Discipline* 167). So, while reactionary in the context of Irish politics, the poem embodies a formal subversiveness in relation to English-language poetic tradition that speaks to Yeats's pride in the very specific virtues of the Protestant Ascendancy. Despite being written out of ideas of courtly *sprezzatura* derived from the Italian Renaissance, "Upon a House" stands not as a celebration of the aristocracy per se, but rather of the *Anglo-Irish* aristocracy, and the inhabitants of Coole in particular.

At the same time, Yeats implies the universal worth of the traits he exalts (after all, the poem asks "How should the *world* be luckier"?), an implication emphasized by the way the poem engages with the broader English tradition of the country house poem as inaugurated by Jonson's "To Penshurst," using an ostensible focus on the house itself to enact a celebration of the class whose virtues the edifice serves to foster and (precariously) protect. Yeats departs from the conventions of the country house poem in significant ways, however, both by practically voiding it of topographical content (in "To Penshurst," for example, the geographical situation and architectural features of the house are meticulously detailed) and by alloying its traditional panegyric emphasis with polemic, condemning the meanness of those who would have the aristocracy forfeit part of their inherited privilege. This touch of polemic helps the poem become utopian; for it introduces a tension between praise and criticism, ensuring that the poem's animating dynamic does not merely consist of a laudatory poet rhapsodizing to a passively receptive audience; instead, the poem implies a frustrated speaker propagandizing to an audience he imagines as resistant. Rather than hinging its effectiveness upon pleasing imagistic depictions, it achieves what resonance it manages primarily through a rhetorical embodiment of desire: desire to preserve the titular House as a microcosm of "passion and precision"—virtues that, if united in a ruling aristocracy recognized as such, will save the cultured world from the degradation to which it seems to be ever more inexorably giving way.

This sense of degradation is memorably captured in the famous refrain of "September 1913," which claims that "Romantic Ireland's dead and gone, / It's with O'Leary in the grave." Written three years after "Upon a House," the poem finds Yeats directing his disdain toward the urban mass whose material striving—a mockery of authentic aspiration—has drained Ireland of the idealism that once set it apart:

> What need you, being come to sense,
> But fumble in a greasy till
> And add the halfpence to the pence
> And prayer to shivering prayer, until
> You have dried the marrow from the bone;
> For men were born to pray and save:
> Romantic Ireland's dead and gone,
> It's with O'Leary in the grave. (1–8)

This first stanza's anaphoric linkage of "And add the halfpence to the pence / And prayer to shivering prayer" suggests that the Catholic middle classes have lost the urge to transcendence at the root of their faith, that the lure of the ideal—whether spiritual or, more crucially for the poem, national—no longer exerts its pull upon their souls; so thoroughly inured are they to a market ethic that even their prayers involve money. The second stanza begins with a hinge of contrast ("Yet they were of a different kind, / The names that stilled your childish play" (9–10)), and the remainder of the poem eulogizes the uncompromising idealism of the eighteenth- and nineteenth-century Irish (Protestant) nationalists Edward Fitzgerald, Robert Emmet, and Wolfe Tone, all of whom died in pursuit of the national cause. While the "you" to whom the poem is addressed have "come to sense," these revolutionaries exemplified "the delirium of the brave"—a distinction that highlights the radicalism of Yeats's anti-empirical rhetoric here, implying that it is better to die in pursuit of the unseen than to live in a world of mere "sense" (and cents). The final stanza casts this idealistic delirium as a form of desire verging on madness:

> Yet could we turn the years again,
> And call those exiles as they were
> In all their loneliness and pain,
> You'd cry, 'Some woman's yellow hair
> Has maddened every mother's son':
> They weighed so lightly what they gave.
> But let them be, they're dead and gone,
> They're with O'Leary in the grave. (25–32)

Because he attributes it to his disdained addressees, it remains ambiguous whether the speaker approves of this comparison between the heroes' nationalistic fervor and the carnal desire for an actual woman. On the one hand, Yeats could be using it to point up the inveterate gutter-mindedness of his satirical targets, who mistake the "delirium of the brave" for basic lust. On the other hand, however, at least until the 1920s, lust in Yeats's poetry is rarely without some hint of transcendence, and so the woman's "yellow hair" might signal her as a sort of Helen figure, an emblem of disastrous desire along the lines of the earlier Gonne/Helen in "No Second Troy" and a prefiguration of the apocalypse obliquely imaged in "Leda and the Swan." Regardless, the claim that "They weighed so lightly what they gave" resonates with both the political and amorous contexts; as the revolutionaries gave their lives, so "maddened" lovers give their sanity, each willingly relinquishing their attachment to this-worldly existence in desirous pursuit of a Blochian Not Yet. A readiness to shirk the actual for the possible lies at the conceptual heart of Yeats's image of "Romantic Ireland," and it is this readiness that he believes is increasingly lacking in the Irish middle classes—whose literal, democratic, and indeed utopian proclivities make them unwilling to abide in a state of unrequitement, determined to seek an end to desire rather than acknowledging its necessary endlessness, its status as the engine of the nation's cultural greatness.

Aristocratic Nation versus Democratic State

As much as the aesthetics of aspiration it exemplifies dovetails with Levitas's ontological conception of utopia as desire, Yeats would of course never have seen his idealization of the Anglo-Irish aristocracy and their Big Houses as "utopian" per se. As in the Gore-Booth elegy, the few occurrences of the word "utopia" throughout his writings show him always implicitly linking it to mass democracy and socialism, ideologies that he, like Nietzsche, disdained for their leveling impetus, their attempt to impose an equality that flouts the existence of the truly exceptional. Unlike Nietzsche, however, Yeats sees this exceptionality as embodied in groups as much as individuals. In the 1919 essay "If I Were Four and Twenty," for example, he condemns the "Utopian vapours" that delude so many into upholding the rights of individuals over those of families, and valuing "equal opportunity" over "social privilege" (*Later* 38–9). By the revised 1937 edition of his philosophical treatise *A Vision*, however, he has recast this dichotomy, critiquing the "Utopian dreams" that infect Greek society in the shift from the warrior-hero Achilles to the state-builder Aeneas (206). Common to both instances is his exaltation of the natural over the legislative realm: families and heroes embody the possibility of inherent (or at least inherited) superiority, while the discourses of statehood and individual rights rely on a legally imposed equality. According to this view, then, aristocracy hews more closely to the natural order than democracy, which comes to look artificial and naïvely utopian by comparison. Or to put it in terms that more closely reflect Yeats's concerns: aristocracy is artful, while democracy is philistine.

This dichotomy resonates with the poet's lifelong project of cultural nationalism and with the distinction he draws between nation and state. To Yeats, the nation emerges as a natural formation, a body of humanity unified into order by a common geographic and cultural inheritance, blossoming plantlike up from the land and its myths. Yeats would have readily assented to Benedict Anderson's conception, over half a century later, of the nation as an "imagined community"; in 1909 the poet wrote in his journal that "One cannot love a nation struggling to realize itself without an idea of the nation as a whole being present in one's mind. One could always appeal to it in the minds of others" (*Memoirs* 180). For Yeats, nation and aristocracy line up on one side of a divide with state and democracy on the other, the forces of idealism ranged against those of crass materialism—with "utopia" and its advocates standing firmly with the latter.

As Elizabeth Cullingford has elaborated at length, Yeats's flirtation with fascism arose partly out of the misconception that it entailed the rule of an idealistic elite with an almost paternal attitude to authority and that such an arrangement would foster the best possible environment for art.[8] Despite its apparent rootedness in wishful thinking, however, such a view remains for Yeats firmly *anti*-utopian, because regardless of his feelings as to its potential auspiciousness, the ascendancy of some form of authoritarianism was for him historically inevitable. His cyclical philosophy of history as set forth in *A Vision* foretells the imminent dawn of an age of violence and authoritarian rule; as the poet's alter ego Michael Robartes declaims: "After an age of necessity, truth, goodness, mechanism, science, democracy, abstraction, peace, comes an age of freedom, fiction, evil, kindred, art, aristocracy, particularity, war. Has our age burned to the socket?" (*Vision 1937* 52). The rise to prominence of Mussolini, then, seemed to affirm the mytho-historical speculations Yeats had begun consolidating as far back as 1917, when automatic writing sessions undertaken with his wife George produced the first scribblings that would become *A Vision*. This helps explain Yeats's mistaken willingness to see Italian fascism as the rule of a cultured elite that would banish philistinism and allow the national spirit to flourish, rather than the stifling and violent totalitarianism it was. But fascism appealed to Yeats for more than seeming to prove him right. Lifetimes of political instability in Ireland, culminating for Yeats in the Irish Civil War of 1922-3 and the Irish Free State's subsequent failure to produce the enlightened cultural haven he so ardently desired had produced in him a thirst for stability—a willingness to concede, with minimal lament, the imminence of tyranny. As he put it in a 1924 interview with the *Irish Times*: "Authoritative government is certainly coming, if for no other reason than that the modern State is so complex that it must find some kind of expert government, a government firm enough, tyrannical enough if you will, to spend years in carrying out its plans" (*Uncollected 2* 433). A decade later, when the emergence of the Irish fascist "blueshirts" made such authoritarianism an imminent possibility for Ireland, Yeats ominously declared: "We are about to exhaust our last Utopia the state" (*Letters* 813). Again—in this, the only occurrence of the word in Yeats's thousands of letters—"utopia" signals the artificial nature of the state, its status as a bureaucratic accrual that must be swept aside to make way for the nation's upsurge.

Poetry and Failure

Yeats's objection to both "utopia" and "the state" centers on the fact that inherent in each lies the promise of a lasting harmony, and so both concepts conflict with Yeats's antithetical vision of both history and (perhaps more crucially) the poet's struggle. If the ascendancy of fascism across Europe signals to him the imminent disintegration of the democratic state apparatus—thus apparently confirming his vision of the cyclical antagonism between democracy and aristocracy, the many and the few—it also dovetails with his view of the poet as engaged in an unending generative conflict with himself, a dynamic rendered most succinctly in Yeats's famous claim that "We make out of the quarrel with others, rhetoric, but of the quarrel with ourselves, poetry" (*Later* 8). Though often isolated as a statement against overt didacticism or argumentation in poetry—a proscription Yeats disregarded again and again—in context it works to assert the primacy of individual self-actualization over sociopolitical striving. Furthermore, it implicitly forges a distinction between rhetoric, which works to overcome conflict by out-convincing its opponents, and poetry, which depends upon the perpetuation of conflict for its genesis. In other words, rhetoric seeks the establishment of a status quo, while poetry abides in a state of continual overthrow. Or unsatisfied desire: for the long "Anima Hominis" section of *Per Amica Silentia Lunae*, the 1917 treatise in which the maxim on rhetoric and poetry appears, is largely a meditation on the poet's endless thirst to become his opposite, and the necessity that this thirst never truly be quenched. Naming this opposite the poet's "anti-self," "antithetical self," or "Daemon," Yeats repeatedly casts the generative dialectic between the two in terms of *desire*. Unlike the Hegelian or Marxist dialectic, however, Yeats's daemonic desire seeks no fulfillment; he writes of the "hollow image of fulfilled desire" that characterizes "happy art" (*Later* 7), claiming that "The poet finds and makes his mask in disappointment, the hero in defeat. The desire that is satisfied is not a great desire" (12). Poetry, in Yeats's view, is the fruit of unrelenting failure.⁹

Though phrased here in personal terms, the political dimension of this fetishization of unrequited desire is made explicit in many places elsewhere in Yeats's writings. Most basically, it stands as the most radical formulation of Yeats's anti-materialism, a tacit admission that his brand of idealism never actually seeks to attain its quested-after ideals. Just as he had characterized Lady Gregory and her aristocratic ilk as "Bred to a harder thing / Than Triumph"—thus twisting the decline of the Ascendancy class in the face of encroaching democracy into evidence of their status as the stewards of idealism—so Yeats sets out, during the first section of "Nineteen Hundred and Nineteen," an inversely proportionate relation between political harmony and poetic integrity. In the midst of Ireland's civil war, he reflects upon the "pretty toys" of the Celtic Revival years, the "law," "habits," and "Public opinion" that he and his compatriots deluded themselves into thinking "would outlive all future days," hubristically seeing themselves at the vanguard of a new peaceful dawn: "O what fine thought we had because we thought / That the worst rogues and rascals had died out" (9–16). The repetition of "thought" here issues in a kind of canceling double-positive, both tacitly condemning the thought's wrongness and implying that it had less to do with actual *thinking* and more with merely *wanting to believe*. Lacking the "Vision of Evil"—the capacity to "conceive of the world as a continual conflict" (*Vision* 1925 65)—the young Revivalists let their utopian hopes take the place of authentic perception. As a result, they find themselves unprepared for the sectarian violence of civil war, when "days are dragon-ridden" (25)—i.e., when the ruthlessness they thought had been consigned to the mythic dustbin of history re-rears its head to breathe destruction. In a milieu so brutal that the "drunken soldiery" of either side "Can leave the mother, murdered at her door, / To crawl in her own blood, and go scot-free," those who in their youthful fervor "planned to bring the world under a rule" find themselves "but weasels fighting in a hole" (26–32). Made joltingly aware that their world, wracked with sectarian strife, can obey no singular "rule," they find themselves reformed of their utopianism, confronted with the shifting amoral animality that constitutes the impulse to survive at all costs—the weasel within. The poetic temperament does not find itself disillusioned by this endless state of violent overturn, however; instead, it abides half-satisfied in the knowledge that the factional conflict in the outside world serves to mirror its inner artistic battle:

He who can read the signs nor sink unmanned
Into the half-deceit of some intoxicant

From shallow wits; who knows no work can stand,
Whether health, wealth or peace of mind were spent
On master-work of intellect or hand,
No honour leave its mighty monument,
Has but one comfort left: all triumph would
But break upon his ghostly solitude. (33–40)

The poet can "read the signs" that "shallow wits" who find themselves "unmanned / Into the half-deceit of some intoxicant" cannot, and such signs point to the bleak and simple fact that "no work can stand." This sweeping caveat applies of course to both political and poetic works, and so Yeats is asserting the extreme contingency not only of his youthful utopian self, but also of his current, presumably more clear-eyed, incarnation. According to the later Yeats's antithetical poetics, however, such conflictual contingency lies at the root of artistic identity. In taking comfort in the fact that "all triumph would / But break upon his ghostly solitude," Yeats implies that any political stability of the utopian sort he once hoped for would set the world at odds with his inner dissonance, with potentially deleterious effects upon the work that dissonance produces. The key phrase here is "ghostly solitude," which alludes to yet another epithet for the poet's daemonic foil, *the ghost*. A crucial passage in *Per Amica* runs:

> The Daemon comes not as like to like but seeking its own opposite, for man and Daemon feed the hunger in one another's hearts. Because the ghost is simple, the man heterogeneous and confused, they are but knit together when the man has found a mask whose lineaments permit the expression of all the man most lacks … The more insatiable in all desire, the more resolute to refuse deception or an easy victory, the more close will be the bond, the more violent and definite the antipathy. (*Later* 11)

Only when the poet deliberately and theatrically dons the mask of that which he most lacks can he achieve that coveted paradox of *antithetical unity*; only by questing to become the opposite of what he knows himself to be can he bind the daemon into intimate antipathy with him, achieving the conflictual coherence out of which the greatest poetry is birthed. Considered in the context of this antithetical poetics, the "triumph" referenced in "Nineteen Hundred and Nineteen" represents the "easy victory"—political or aesthetic—that the poet must avoid if he hopes to reap the half-fallow bounty of his "ghostly solitude," his haunted communion with personified lack. He repeats the formula in part III, this time making the poet's solitary pluralness explicit: "For triumph can but mar *our* solitude" (78; emphasis added).

"Unity of Being" as Utopian Harmony

Like most of Yeats's overtly political poems from *The Tower* and after, "Nineteen Hundred and Nineteen" finds him adopting the mask of the clear-eyed perceptor of violence's inevitability, delivering the news of perpetual disunity. And yet—just as his own antithetical poetics would mandate—something in Yeats remains ill-suited to this role. He never entirely quells the thirst for unity that informed his early cultural nationalism and led him to spend the early part of his career projecting an image of the Irish as "a people, a community bound together by imaginative possessions ... and by a past of great passions which can still waken the heart to imaginative action" (*Early* 158). Seeking as a poet to illuminate the imaginative bonds of Irishness, the young Yeats sought coherence on a personal level as well, striving to draw together his literary, philosophical, and nationalist interests according to the mantric directive to "Hammer your thoughts into unity" (*Later* 34). This command, though attributed retrospectively to himself at "twenty-three or twenty-four" in an essay written when he was in his fifties (*Later* 34), resurfaces in transfigured form throughout his writings of the 1920s and beyond, inherent in the much-exalted concept of "Unity of Being."

To understand what Yeats thinks he means by "Unity of Being"—a phrase he first encounters in an automatic writing session with George in 1918, and that reappears insistently throughout the remainder of his work—we must return to the dichotomy, foundational to his later thought, between democracy and aristocracy. In the final revised edition of *A Vision* published in 1937, two years before his death, Yeats places under the heading "The Two Conditions" the following couplet: "*Primary* means democratic. / *Antithetical* means aristocratic" (*Vision* 1937 104). Although he first elaborates the phrase "Unity of Being" specifically in relation to Dante—who he says thought of it as a kind of aesthetic self-organicism, "the subordination of all parts to the whole as in a perfectly proportioned human body" (*Explorations* 250)—it comes to take on a sociopolitical aspect as well, as in the early 1920s Yeats claims that as men in places of power attained Unity of Being "in great numbers" during the Renaissance, "their nations had it too, prince and ploughman sharing that thought and feeling" (*Autobiographies* 227). A nation achieves Unity of Being by preserving the political trappings of aristocracy while somehow having its leaders—antetypes of what we now know as 'the Renaissance man'—share their perfect inner proportions with their subjects, as if democratically. By the time of the first edition of *A Vision* in 1925, Yeats more directly idealizes this balance between aristocracy and democracy, writing that Unity of Being "implies a harmony of *antithetical* and *primary* life" (*Vision* 1925 51; emphasis in original). As the above examples imply, this harmony can manifest both politically and personally—or more to the point, poetically. In terms of politics, we can be reasonably clear from Yeats's examples of "nations" under Renaissance princes on what a balance of antithetical and primary elements might entail. In terms of the individual poet, however, the meaning of this balance is not immediately evident; throughout *A Vision* Yeats associates the primary with objectivity and the antithetical with subjectivity, claiming that "All men are characterised upon a first analysis by the proportion in which these characters or *Tinctures*, the objective or *primary*, the subjective or *antithetical*, are combined" (*Vision* 1925 13). Yeats thus sets out two strings of dichotomous terms according to which all personalities and all societies are proportionately structured: democracy-primary-objective and aristocracy-antithetical-subjective. And though he characterizes socialism, communism, and hence utopia as symptoms of the increasingly primary dispensation that defines the early twentieth century—as gusts of the "levelling wind" that "mock[s] at the great" in the final section of "Nineteen Hundred and Nineteen"—his own ideal of a harmonious "Unity of Being" is ultimately no less utopian in its attempt to define an ideal life state on both individual and societal levels. As I have discussed, what lies behind Yeats's condemnation of his era's apparent drive to democratic equality is not an opposition to the widespread improvement of humanity's material conditions per se, but a fear that such reforms would entail the virtual extinguishment of the conflictual conditions necessary for art.

Perhaps the most cogent claim to be extracted from *A Vision*—Yeats's grand mystical opus wherein historical eras and personality types alike correspond to the 28 phases of the moon—is that the artist (and especially the poet) is archetypal, embodying the dispensation of the age, or, as in Yeats's case, embodying the drive toward a more favorable dispensation.[10] In brief, Yeats's system sees history as progressing around a great wheel, through phases numbered from 1 to 28, with phase 1 (and its circumferential neighbor phase 28) representing complete objectivity or passivity, and phase 15 (its diametric opposite) representing complete subjectivity. Yeats labels the phases in the half of the wheel aligned around phase 1, from 1 to 7 and 23 to 28, *primary* phases. Those in the half around phase 15, from 9 to 21, he labels the *antithetical* phases. The world of 1927 stands somewhere between phases 23 and 25, near the apogee of primariness, moving gradually toward the near-total objectivity of phase 28, a stultifyingly literal and spiritually impoverished state that sees the death of idealism, when "men will no longer separate the idea of God from that of human genius, human productivity in all its forms" (*Vision* 1925 177). This evokes the revolutionary proletarianism of Russian communism, a state of art-as-labor: not the nobler labor Yeats Platonically distinguishes from gruntwork in "Adam's Curse," but rather a labor hierarchically indistinguishable from farming or the forging of steel girders, a mechanistically leveled state where work is work and art has forfeited its autonomy.

This also recalls his disdain for Eva Gore-Booth's "vague Utopia" and his portrait of her socialist sister Constance "conspiring among the ignorant"; written just two years after the first publication of *A Vision*, his 1927 elegy casts them as emblems of their over-democratized age, "image[s] of such politics," true denizens of the late objective phases. By contrast, Yeats himself walks out of step with such an age, inhabiting with Dante and Shelley the visionary phase 17, where "Unity of Being … is now more easy than at any other phase" (63). It is important to note here that although Yeats represents Unity of Being as a state of balance or harmony between the primary and antithetical dispensations, it is only achievable by individuals occupying the thoroughly antithetical phases 16, 17, and 18—and so, despite its pretensions to historical detachment, his system clearly privileges one hemisphere of the great wheel. The element of dispensational balance enters only through the reintroduction of his earlier concept of the Daemon (now spelled "Daimon"), which is cast as a kind of dialectical foil, at its most primary the more antithetical an individual is, and vice versa. Those occupying the primary phases—tending as they do toward democracy, objectivity, a general condition of uniformity—will tend to try to quell or let themselves be quelled by the Daimon, needing to live in either light or dark, unwilling to abide in perpetual conflict. By contrast, Yeats claims, "he who attains Unity of Being is some man, who, while struggling with his fate and his destiny until every energy of his being has been roused, is content that he should so struggle with no final conquest" (*Vision* 1925 26). From this point of view, the utopias pursued by Eva Gore-Booth and her socialist-leaning compatriots can be described as "vague" because they require their inhabitants to forego this generative struggle, allowing their own destinies to be subsumed into the common aim.

For Yeats, with the further advance of contemporary history through the primary phases, a time will arrive when "all personality will seem an impunity," until finally "with the last gyre must come a desire to be ruled or rather, seeing that desire is all but dead, an adoration of force spiritual or physical, and society as mechanical force be complete at last" (*Vision* 1925 175–6). This nightmarish vision of the end of desire and the "adoration of force" resonates with much twentieth-century dystopian thought that sees socialism as almost inevitably hinging into totalitarianism, recalling for instance Orwell's roomfuls of servile Party drones praising telescreen projections of Big Brother. But again, in *A Vision* as elsewhere, Yeats's thinking cannot straightforwardly be classified as anti-utopian, no matter how much he himself would have thought of it as such. For his famous account of Byzantium in the "Dove and Swan" chapter resounds with utopian longing:

> I think if I could be given a month of Antiquity and leave to spend it where I chose, I would spend it in Byzantium a little before Justinian opened St. Sophia and closed the Academy of Plato. I think I could find in some little wine shop some philosophical worker in mosaic who could answer all my questions … I think that in early Byzantium, and maybe never before or since in recorded history, religious, aesthetic and practical life were one, and that architect and artificers—though not, it may be, poets, for language had been the instrument of controversy and must have grown abstract—spoke to the multitude and the few alike. The painter and the mosaic worker, the worker in gold and silver, the illuminator of Sacred Books were almost impersonal, almost perhaps without the consciousness of individual design, absorbed in their subject matter and that the vision of a whole people. (*Vision* 1925 158–9)[11]

This passage is utopian in both a generic and an ontological sense: first, the dramatic situation of a visitor's question-and-answer encounter with a wise and eloquent Byzantine craftsman recalls the basic formula of the utopian narrative, from More to Bellamy and Morris; and second, the image of a society so organically unified that every artistic gesture expresses "the vision of a whole people" represents the apotheosis of Yeats's Romantic idealism.[12] Whereas the socialistic fulfillment of the primary gyre entails the erasure of subjectivity by the objective mass, Yeats's

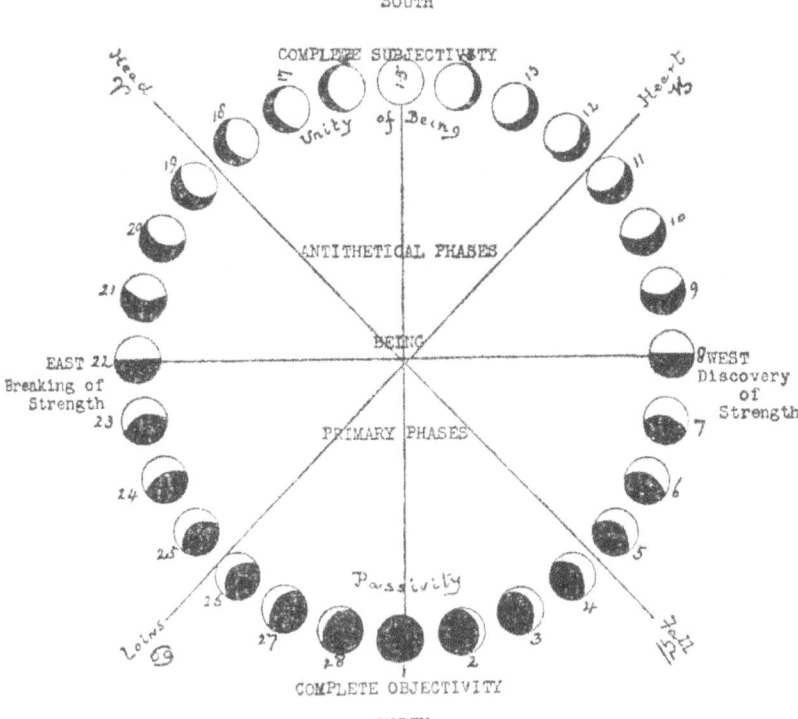

Figure 3 An illustration from the original 1925 version of *A Vision* depicting the phases of the moon in their relation to the primary and antithetical phases. Notice Yeats's own phase 17 near the apex, within the spectrum of Unity of Being (*A Vision* 1925 14).

Byzantium entails a harmony between the subjective and objective, antithetical and primary, that verges on fusion, gesturing beyond even Unity of Being to the "complete beauty" of phase 15, where "contemplation and desire, united into one, inhabit a world where every beloved image has a bodily form, and every bodily form is loved" (*Vision* 1925 58–9). Although phase 15, as the full moon of absolute subjectivity, has no human equivalent in *A Vision*'s system of personalities (with Yeats's own phase 17 being the nearest one can get), according to the book's historical scheme, civilizations may coincide with the fifteenth phase as with any other, and Justinian's Byzantium may well have achieved such fleeting perfection.

Byzantium as Good Place and No-Place

The tension between the permanence of the 28 phases in relation to personality types (or "embodiments" as Yeats calls them) and the utter transience of those same 28 phases in relation to the cyclical movements of history is illuminated in Yeats's poetic journey to his Byzantine utopia, "Sailing to Byzantium." Simply put, the poem delineates the difference between old age and ancientness, recasting the clichéd dichotomy between life's transience and art's permanence—given its quintessential expression in the figures on Keats's urn, "For ever panting, and for ever young"—as the poet's voyage between two countries: modern democratic Ireland ("no country for old men") and ancient imperial Byzantium ("the artifice of eternity"). The former place swelters with a fecundity memorably captured in the image of "mackerel-crowded seas," its youthful inhabitants reveling in the cycle of conception, birth, and decay, rapt in artless ecstasy: "Caught in that sensual music all neglect / Monuments of unageing intellect" (1–8). This spectacle elicits in the aging speaker a curious mixture of self-deprecation and aesthetic superiority; he is only "a paltry thing, / A tattered coat upon a stick" until "Soul clap its hands and sing, and louder sing / For every tatter in its mortal dress" (9–12). In other words, the very agedness that makes him a scarecrow-like object of aesthetic repulsion works to louden any song of transcendence his soul might sing. Despite this virtue of age and experience, however, singing is still a talent his soul must learn:

> Nor is there singing school but studying
> Monuments of its own magnificence;
> And therefore have I sailed the seas and come
> To the holy city of Byzantium. (13–16)

Notwithstanding some grammatical awkwardness in the service of meter here—as the subjectless "studying" works to cloud the first line—the "therefore" exerts a clarifying influence over the passage: the poet has come to Byzantium to study "Monuments of its [the soul's] own magnificence." The recurrence of the word "Monuments" (again at the beginning of a line and so capitalized), returns us to the first stanza's antithesis between "sensual music" and "Monuments of unageing intellect," a reminder that the poet's journey leads him away from the transience of carnal life toward an artifactual monumentality. His Byzantium exists less as a historical place than as a projection of the desire to be immortal; he wants to sail out of time.

The third stanza clarifies this trajectory. Beginning with an apostrophic "O," the speaker calls upon the "sages standing in God's holy fire / As in the gold mosaic of a wall" (17–18). Yeats deploys simile here to suggest that the state of saintly conflagration, of being engulfed in God's everlasting grace, is somehow akin to being an artwork upon a Byzantine wall. When the speaker asks these saints to "perne in a gyre" and "be the singing masters of [his] soul," he means that they should spiral down into history and teach his soul to sing itself up to their condition, yes, but a misspelled pun conceals a more urgent version of this request: that they should be "*singe*ing masters," should burn him into permanence:

> Consume my heart away; sick with desire
> And fastened to a dying animal
> It knows not what it is; and gather me
> Into the artifice of eternity. (21–4)

That the poet's heart "knows not what it is" speaks to the heart's dual signification, as chambered blood pump on the one hand ("fastened to a dying animal") and as metaphysical seat of love and aspiration on the other ("sick with desire"). Desire, of course, implies both lack and plasticity, relying upon the human ability to alter one's circumstances in pursuit of that missing fullness. Locked in a perpetual organic wholeness, art remains exempt from desire, and so "the artifice of eternity" into which the speaker wishes to be "gather[ed]"—brought together unto himself, into a state of wholeness, without lack—is anathema to his humanity. As hinted at by the inescapable connotation of falseness inherent in "artifice," at this point the speaker's utopian journey begins to seem delusory, perhaps even to himself.

A diversion back into *A Vision* will be helpful here. In describing the 28 phases, Yeats consistently focuses on the condition of desire within each phase; his own seventeenth phase, for example, is dominated by the specter of a self-inflicted loss that forces the imagination to endlessly "substitute some new image of desire; and in the degree of its power and of its attainment of unity, relate that which is lost, that which has snatched it away, to the new image of desire, that which threatens the new image to the being's unity" (*Vision* 1925 64). In other words, and using the poet himself as an example, one might say that Yeats must forever find substitutes for Maud Gonne as a lost object of desire (he does after all specify the initial loss as "some woman perhaps") and must recognize these substitutes as integral not only to her, but also to the part of himself that caused him to lose her—and indeed revels in the loss—in the first place. As I have pointed out, Yeats's antithetical poetics virtually mandates the constant pursuance of unrequitable desires; this, paradoxically, is what Unity of Being entails. Contrast, then, this endless generative incompletion with Yeats's description of the "complete beauty" of phase 15, a wholly subjective state impossible for any human to embody:

> Now contemplation and desire, united into one, inhabit a world where every beloved image has a bodily form, and every bodily form is loved. This love knows nothing of desire, for desire implies effort, and though there is still separation from the loved object, love accepts the separation as necessary to its own existence. (58–9)

Here desire's inextricability from the simple act of contemplation renders desire effortless, thereby absenting it from the definition of love, if not disappearing it altogether. Such a state would seem to be the remedy sought by desire-sick speaker of "Sailing to Byzantium," though the poem's conclusion implies the impossibility, at least in mortal terms, of such relief.

The final stanza shifts to the future tense "I shall," with the speaker imagining himself ensconced "out of nature," his "bodily form" distinct from "any natural thing" (25–6). The repetition of "nature" and its derived adjective within the stanza's first two lines evokes the related word "nation" and their common Latin root in the verb *nasci*, to be born; and indeed the speaker's journey entails his being both un-nationed—the "no country for old men" from which he departs in the first stanza is widely thought to allude to pastoral Celtic myths of Ireland's preternatural fertility—and unborn, shedding his carnality to become a golden bird, "such a form as Grecian goldsmiths make ... To keep a drowsy Emperor awake" (27, 29). The poet-bird's function here returns us to the poem's concern with the extent to which art can flout mortality. The Emperor is "drowsy" because he is mortal; like all rulers, he must eventually secede from life and throne alike. To secure even the most precarious of immortalities, he must leave monuments behind as testimony to his kingdom's grandeur—like the glittering mosaics Yeats had seen at Ravenna in 1907, which tonally inspired the poem's imagery. In thus emphasizing the temporality of the Emperor's rule, the speaker highlights not just Byzantium's historical contingency, but also his own; what began as an old man's journey out of time has become a subtle paean to the impossibility of such a journey, as the speaker envisions one last potential role for his golden-birded self:

> Or set upon a golden bough to sing
> To lords and ladies of Byzantium
> Of what is past, or passing, or to come. (30–2)

What is "passing," of course, is Byzantium itself. The poet might achieve a state of artifactual stasis, but such a transfiguration leaves him locked "out of nature," trapped inside a burnished body while the world declines and falls, rises and exults anew, before his always-open eyes. What might have been utopia becomes a gold-lit nightmare.

"Sailing to Byzantium" takes utopian longing as its launching point, and yet ends by underlining the impossibility of attaining the state of ageless, desireless stasis its speaker initially sought. The ideal Byzantium eulogized in *A Vision* may indeed have achieved the nearest-ever unity of "religious, aesthetic and practical life" (*Vision* 1925 158), but according to Yeats's cyclical philosophy such social unity cannot be reached through concerted human effort: peoples must simply abide in their destined point along the gyres of history; only those fortunate enough to live at the civilizational apogee of the antithetical phases will ever experience such unity—and even then, it soon passes:

> Each age unwinds the thread another age had wound, and it amuses one to remember that before Phidias, and his westward moving art, Persia fell, and that when full moon came round again, amid eastward moving thought, and brought Byzantine glory, Rome fell; and that at the outset of our westward moving Renaissance Byzantium fell; all things dying each other's life, living each other's death. (*Vision* 1925 152)

This final ouroborotic chiasmus is one of the signal motifs of Yeats's later work, encapsulating his conviction that both history and the individual lifespan proceed through antithetical struggle. In historical terms this struggle expresses itself through the cyclical rise and fall of civilizations; in individual terms, it is generative, both of art and (in the most propitious cases) of Unity of Being—that paradoxical state of harmony-in-antinomy accorded those who commit to an endless lustful war of attrition with the daimonic opposites within themselves.

Fredric Jameson ends his important essay "The Politics of Utopia" with an examination of "the fear of utopia, of the anxiety with which the utopian impulse confronts us" (51). As a prominent manifestation of this anxiety, he highlights "fear of aphanisis, or loss of desire" (53): in seeming to promise a lasting solution to the scarcity problem and the permanent satisfaction of all worldly needs (and thereby perhaps the elimination of all otherworldly ones), utopia confronts us with the specter of desire's obsolescence. That this specter menaced Yeats is shown throughout his later career in the way his narratives of poetic actualization— whether of individuals, classes, or nations—depend so thoroughly on antithetical striving. Furthermore, Yeats repeatedly links the idealistic aspects of such striving to the sexual urge—as in, for instance, his eugenicist emphasis on the need for aristocrats to literally outbreed their inferiors so that they may continue to infuse the culture at large with the more ephemeral refinements of "good breeding." His Unity of Being, too, has a sexual aspect, as in *A Vision* he writes that the "perpetual conflict or embrace" between man and Daimon "may create a passion like that of sexual love" (*Vision* 1925 25). For Yeats, to actively desire is to resist succumbing to the leveling pressures exerted by the primary, objective, democratic forces of the age.

At the same time, Yeats recognizes the universality of the urge to free oneself from desire. Depicting this urge acted upon in "Sailing to Byzantium," however— and virtually conflating it with the wish to escape time itself—he can only conclude by undermining it, implying that to be free from desire is to be a passive observer, a spectator rather than an agent of history, a static work of art rather than a shaping artist. In his later companion piece "Byzantium," Yeats further refines this antiutopian strain, portraying his one-time ideal as a place ultimately unfit for human habitation.[13] What begins as a continuation of the earlier poem's austere vision of art's immortality—contrasting the artifactual solidity of a "moonlit dome" or a bird of "changeless metal" with the "complexities of mire or blood" that define human embodiment (5, 22, 24)—becomes by the last stanza a hallucinatory rush of underworldly imagery, a roiling Yeatsian purgatory:

> Astraddle on the dolphin's mire and blood,
> Spirit after spirit! The smithies break the flood,
> The golden smithies of the Emperor!
> Marbles of the dancing floor
> Break bitter furies of complexity,
> Those images that yet
> Fresh images beget,
> That dolphin-torn, that gong-tormented sea. (33–40)

The theme here is still the breaking of *complexity* (a word whose variants appear in four of the poem's five stanzas), but unlike at the poem's beginning, it is broached in a fragmentary syntax that creates an impressionistic effect seemingly at odds with the paradisal simplicity toward which the dolphin-riding spirits surge. Byzantium's impetus is both iconoclastic and transcendent: not just to break images, but to shatter them into an artifactual apotheosis. This creative destruction—this "death-in-life and life-in-death" (16)—can only be told in poetry, however, through a glut of rhythmic language so abundant as to be almost torturous. The closing image of "That dolphin-torn, that gong-tormented sea"—a sea disturbed by crashes of wordless noise—evokes the inhospitability of a world becoming pure image, empty of any mortal hand to strike the gong. As the one residual form of life remaining amid this tumult of rarefaction, the dolphins represent not just the mammalian inverse of the denizens of the earlier poem's "mackerel-crowded seas" (making this final Byzantium perhaps "no country for young men"), but also—because they become the possessors of the "mire and blood" that belong to humans earlier in the poem—the gradual dissolution of humanity, a thalassic stage along our regression back to the nothingness of pure spirit, free of all complexity.

Taking up utopia's cognates, one might say that what begins in "Sailing to Byzantium" as a journey to *eutopia*—an old poet's voyage of hope toward the good place where immortal works of art reside—becomes in "Byzantium" a depiction of *outopia*, the true no-place where all such journeys must end. In the shift from the earlier poem to the later, then, one may sense the poet's conviction that *eutopia* cannot in fact be distinguished from *outopia*, that such places lose in humanity what they gain in perfection. This is not a new insight, of course; not only is it implicit in the combinatory nature of the word "utopia," but more explicitly, many twentieth-century thinkers call the distinction between utopia and dystopia into question, claiming that the permanence utopia implies can only be achieved by dehumanizing means. For Yeats, what begins in the first, 1925 edition of *A Vision* as a portrait of the historical Byzantium's exemplary Unity of Being has become by the 1933 poem "Byzantium" a hallucinatory exemplar of the fifteenth phase's utter inhumanity, of the corruption its perfection must suffer when looked at through imperfect eyes.

And yet the amorphous ideals behind all Yeats's versions of Byzantium—of a more complete integration of art into life, of a people more fully unified across classes and occupations, and more audaciously, of spiritual immortality—inflect his later work with a desire that can readily be called utopian. That he himself would never have characterized it as such is important only insofar as it serves to clarify that for him, utopians were materialists who sought the impossible achievement of a state of permanent perfection, while he was, as an idealist, seeking unities beneath and beyond the inevitable violences of material history. On the one hand, this may make him a quietist, an obscurantist, a fatalist, and an apologist for any status quo that may happen to prevail. On the other hand, it makes him (and he certainly would have seen it this way) a certain brand of realist, one who accepts the evidence of history-as-strife, and so seeks out ahistorical sources of harmony, ways of perceiving the interconnectedness of humankind without appealing to what he saw as the objectivizing platitudes of democratic rhetoric, and thus preserving subjectivity—and particularly the artist's subjectivity—as an overriding value. This last emphasis is what he claims most distinguishes him from utopians:

> We may come to think that nothing exists but a stream of souls, that all knowledge is biography, and with Plotinus that every soul is unique; that these souls, these eternal archetypes, combine into greater units as days and nights into months, months into years, and at last into the final unit that differs in nothing from that which they were at the beginning; everywhere that antinomy of the One and the Many that Plato thought in his *Parmenides* insoluble, though Blake thought it soluble 'at the bottom of the graves'. Such belief may arise from Communism by antithesis, declaring at last even to the common ear that all things have value according to the clarity of their expression of themselves, and not as functions of changing economic conditions or as a preparation for some Utopia. There is perhaps no final state except in so far as men may gradually grow better; escape may be for individuals alone who know how to exhaust their possible lives, to set, as it were, the hands of the clock racing. (*Explorations* 397)

This passage—containing his latest published use of the word "utopia"—finds him combining a vision of the deep spiritual unity of all humankind with a valorization of uniqueness. It remains unclear whether in claiming that "men may gradually grow better" Yeats means "men" as in *humanity*, or as in the most persistently ambitious and aspiring of individuals. This ambiguity is rich: for if his vision of unique souls ultimately combining into a balanced one-in-manyness represents the antithesis of communism—a system which for Yeats aimed at the virtual dissolution of individual uniqueness into an objectivized mass—then "men" here clearly resonates in both the inclusive and exceptionalist senses.

As evidenced by the above passage, and by the antithetical system of thought that dominated his later work, Yeats believed that our social and solitary selves exist at odds, and he reveled in the generative potential of the strife between the two. His universally pejorative use of the word "utopia" has its roots in his perception that utopia would entail the dissolution of the solitary into the social, the exceptional into the inclusive, and thus the extinguishment of the desirous struggle out of which art is produced.[14] His conception of utopia is a limited and yet prominent one, and so it serves to illuminate the grounds upon which the concept is defined and contested. A key alternate strain of thinking about utopia would locate the utopian impulse in precisely the desire for a more complete harmony between art and politics, and the individual and society, that Yeats exhibits in, for example, his original tribute to Byzantium in *A Vision*. If, as this strain of thinking would have it, utopia inheres in desire itself and not in its requitement, then Yeats is undoubtedly utopian. His explicit anti-utopianism arose not out of any enmity to visions of social improvement but out of his hatred of the doctrines of his time that equated the good place with both an achievable material prosperity for all and a concomitant leveling down of individuals into an objectivized mass. Though sharing with many tyrants a stringent idealism, he lacked their mania for permanence. Despite its frequently fatalistic tinge, Yeats's later work consistently presents us with the prospect, however distant, of transfiguring change. Not blueprints, but the glimmering lure of past and future worlds richer in harmony, beauty, and unity than the strife and dissonance his own lifetime afforded. Not affirmative futurity in the sense of striving toward a future end, but rather in the sense of accepting the desirous impulse to futurity as an end in itself and seeing poetry as the imperfect product of that impulse's exquisite futility. If his utopias are often naïve, ahistorical, or even (as in the case of "Byzantium") inhospitable—in other words, if they turn out to be no-places—this is to some extent inevitable, for art itself cannot be inhabited.

Notes

1 For an eloquent elaboration of this viewpoint, see John Gray's *Black Mass: Apocalyptic Religion and the Death of Utopia*, in which the author repeatedly defines utopia by its impossibility, claiming (for example) that "a project is utopian if there are no circumstances under which it can be realized" (20).
2 Though as we will see, Yeats's late interest in eugenics (outlined most thoroughly in *On the Boiler*, for which see *Later Essays*) allies him in at least one respect with the blueprint utopian tradition.
3 My emphasis on desire in this chapter owes a debt to the work of Ramazani, who points to the crucial function of desire in Yeats's aesthetic on several levels. As I discussed in the previous chapter, Ramazani highlights how "Yeats's nationalism ironizes itself in the knowledge that fulfillment would come at a great cost to a poetry built on melancholic desire" (*Hybrid* 30). In addition, Ramazani makes a similar point at greater length in relation to Yeats's love poems, claiming that they are "conscious that they depend on loss to produce their desire," and therefore "depict the psychic economy of traditional love poetry: erotic loss results in aesthetic gain, at least in an economy based on the loss, lack, absence, or death of woman" ("A Little Space" 68).
4 In her recuperative essay on Gore-Booth's work, Emma Donoghue writes that "without ever (as far as I can tell) casting herself as a political or sexual dissident, this woman quietly subverted her whole heritage" (17–18). As I will go on to show, it is this subversion of "heritage"—rather than the fact of her devotion to the women's labor movement—that most bothered Yeats about Eva.
5 Donoghue identifies Eva's "central image" as "that of one woman coming to rescue another from an urban prison, and leading her by the hand into a pastoral paradise" (18). This accords with Donoghue's emphasis on Gore-Booth as a sexual revisionist who "feminise[d] and lesbianise[d] the stories handed down to her" (17).
6 In the chapter of his *Romantic Image* entitled "The Dancer," Frank Kermode discusses how Yeats came to take the female body as a physical analogue of the organic beauty sought by the poet in imagery. Putting it bluntly, Kermode claims that for Yeats, "girls are like poems" (51). Or at least the ones he deemed pretty: for as Kermode notes, Yeats believed that intellectual labors worked to undermine the shapeliness and grace of the female body, breeding shrillness and—the trait most anathema to poetry— abstraction. Kermode's discussion illuminates how the basic fact of Constance and Eva Gore-Booth's political activities, rather than the specific nature of their chosen

causes, runs contrary to Yeats's view of women as aesthetic objects, embodiments of the Symbolist notion of the transcendent poetic image.

7 Seamus Deane explores this irony at length in his *Celtic Revivals*, particularly in the chapter "Literary Myths of the Revival," where he illustrates the degree to which, in order to associate the Protestant Ascendancy with Irishness, and Irishness in turn with anti-materialism, Yeats "distorted history in the service of myth" (32). More specifically, Deane claims that "Yeats's account of the Anglo-Irish tradition blurs an important distinction between the terms 'aristocracy' and 'Ascendancy,'" and that "had he known a little more about the eighteenth century, he would have recognized that the Protestant Ascendancy was, then and since, a predominantly bourgeois social formation" (30).

8 See her *Yeats, Ireland, and Fascism*, especially the chapter entitled "From Democracy to Authority," pp. 144–64.

9 In his 1917 poem "Ego Dominus Tuus" (which also serves as the prologue to *Per Amica Silentia Lunae*), Yeats characterizes Dante as having forged his artistic identity upon "A hunger for the apple on the bough / Most out of reach" (*Collected* 160). As we will see, Dante becomes a figure of supreme importance in Yeats's later work, as both originator and exemplar of the crucial concept of Unity of Being.

10 My emphasis here partly accords with (and partly diverges from) Helen Vendler's view of *A Vision* as essentially a poetics, "a stylistic arrangement of experience" (*Yeats's* Vision 2). According to Vendler, the differences Yeats posits between historical dispensations are merely codes for the differences between types of poetry, with the more florid conventionalities of his early verse hewing more closely to the waning "primary" dispensation, and the more chiseled vatic utterance of his later work corresponding to the incoming "antithetical" dispensation. "For Yeats," Vendler writes, "historical change is often a symbol for mental and artistic cataclysms" (107). While this reading contains a great deal of insight—for Yeats saw everything through a poet's lens—it does neglect the extent to which, as he repeatedly demonstrated in his comments on actual politics, Yeats really did believe that great historical changes were imminent. So although his historical chapters may amount to (as Vendler puts it) "nonsense at worst and wildly intuitive guesses at best" (109), we cannot write them off as literary-historical allegory simply for convenience's sake. The fact is Yeats sincerely held (to put it mildly) some strange beliefs.

11 In his *Faber Book of Utopias*, John Carey isolates this passage on Byzantium (along with the early poem "The Lake Isle of Innisfree") as Yeats's signal contributions to the history of utopian literature. See pp. 390–2.

12 Thomas Whitaker memorably characterizes the entire "Dove and Swan" chapter of *A Vision* as "a typically romantic achievement: a vision of history as art" (78).

13 There is a well-established tradition of seeing the Byzantiums of the two poems as two different places, both in their sources and in their execution. Curtis Bradford, in his seminal essay "Yeats's Byzantium Poems: A Study of Their Development," demonstrates through the evidence of Yeats's unpublished manuscript books that "Sailing to Byzantium" emerges out of Justinian's Byzantium as Yeats described it in "Dove and Swan," while "Byzantium" takes as its jumping-off point the Byzantium of over four hundred years later, at the end of the tenth century. Symbolically, Bradford interprets the two poems as respectively exploring the temporal and eternal aspects of Unity of Being. Harold Bloom cites the same disparate historical Byzantiums as sources for the poem, yet characterizes the symbolic distinction between them more succinctly than Bradford, noting that "the cities are both of the mind, but they are not

quite the same city, the second being at a still further remove from nature than the first" (344). As will be seen, this last claim readily accords with my own emphasis on "Byzantium" as depicting *outopian* no-placeness as compared to the *eutopian* good-placeness of the earlier poem.

14 Richard Ellmann traces this line of thinking back to Yeats's father J. B. Yeats, who wrote that "the work of art is the social act of a solitary man" (qtd. in Ellmann 17).

Chapter 3

"THE GOOD PLACE HAS NOT BEEN": THE PURSUIT OF UNITY IN EARLY AUDEN

As with Yeats before about 1910, Auden in his early career upholds unity as among the highest of values. But while Yeats's goal arose from nationalist motives, and so aimed specifically at *social* unity, Auden's pursuit of unity has psychological and even anthropological elements. Though Auden likewise wanted to see his own society unified, he also sought *personal* unity—to see the psychic wounds inflicted by the modern age healed—and the wider unity of *humanity*—to grasp and uphold the commonalities that define us as a moral species. In this chapter I work to illuminate both Auden's various motives for desiring these forms of unity and the myriad sources from which he drew his conceptions of these forms. As himself an alienated subject, as a young man with a thirst for social justice, and as a poet seeking the largest possible audience for his increasingly marginal art—Auden sought unity in all these guises over the course of his early career, drawing inspiration from contemporary psychological, political, and even mystical discourses in conceiving of ways to mend us back to whole. As should be clear from the context of my study, I contend that Auden's pursuit of unity is essentially a utopian pursuit, rooted in the desire for a better way of life, both individually and communally. Beginning with a discussion of Auden's diagnoses, in the poetry and prose of the late 1920s and early 1930s, of humanity's essential dividedness, I then move to explore his abortive attempts in essays of the mid-1930s to theorize for poetry a role in curing this condition, before concluding with an examination of his 1938 sonnet sequence *In Time of War*—a work that forcefully implies a conclusion toward which Auden had long been building, and which would increasingly dominate his thinking after his full return to the Christian faith in the 1940s: that our only true unity derives from our shared status as fallen beings, improving and sliding back in tragic increments, doomed forever to strive after unachieved utopias—and that the role of poetry is to urge this striving while also highlighting, as with Yeats, the unsatisfiable nature of the desire that fuels it.

The Obsolescence of Yeatsian Symbolism

In Auden's early writings, the human condition is cast as one of ever-increasing alienation, division, and severance. In the diary of 1929 that has come to be known as the Berlin Journal, he makes the sweeping claim that "Man is the product of the refined disintegration of nature by time" (*English* 298). Far from being simply a diaristic flourish scribbled in a fit of existential indulgence, this vision undergirds much of Auden's thought into the early 1930s. Elsewhere in the journal he elaborates three interconnected ways that our alienated condition manifests itself. First (and as the above quotation suggests), if we are in fact a product of nature's disintegration, this implies that we are somehow separate from the rest of nature, that what once existed as an integral whole including our proto-human ancestors is now irrevocably divided—and that this division is a condition of our humanity. Second, we are increasingly separate from each other: we have atomized ourselves virtually free of the communal feeling that defined earlier human societies, a fact that affords the individual unprecedented opportunities for self-actualization, but at the risk of teetering forever on the verge of pathology, having been forced to deny the communal urge to the point of feeling somehow un-whole. This brings us to the third manifestation of our disintegration, the wound of dualism. "It is the body's job to make," Auden writes, "the mind's to destroy" (*English* 298). Throughout the journal he casts the body as "communistic," a "Not-self" that yearns to be united with its fellow bodies (*English* 298–9). The mind, by contrast, is the essence of individuality and therefore identity, the "Me" that strives to differentiate itself from other human beings (298).

This tripartite dividedness—from nature, from each other, from within—holds both liberating and oppressive significance for the poet. In responding to Freud's vision in *Beyond the Pleasure Principle* of our drive to rejoin the state of union-in-stasis from whence we all emerge, Auden claims that "the real 'life-wish' is one of separation, from family, from one's literary predecessors" (*English* 299). In thus stressing the pursuit of individual distinctness, Auden (like Yeats, but for different reasons) implicitly exalts the writer's struggle to set themselves apart from their influences as a paradigmatic life gesture, a way of fulfilling the modern mind's drive to discrete selfhood. On the other hand, however, that very drive to discreteness works against the writer's desire to *share* their art, as it pushes them to define themselves too starkly apart from their fellows. Indeed, Auden goes so far as to claim that "only body can be communicated" (*English* 299). For a poet, of course, this raises the question of whether body can be conveyed in writing, and if not, whether poetry can actually be said to "communicate"—at least in the way the word occurs in the Berlin Journal, in a context that links it to "communal," "communistic," and "community."

Auden does not directly address either of these questions, but he does provide some clue as to how he might answer them in a passage that serves as a kind of interpretive skeleton key to his early poetics:

> Mind has been evolved from body, i.e. from the Not-self, whose thinking is community-thinking, and therefore symbolic. While Yeats is right that great

poetry in the past has been symbolic, I think we are reaching the point in the development of the mind where symbols are becoming obsolete in poetry, as the mind, or non-communistic self, does not think in this way. (*English* 298)

In attempting to outline the communicative dilemma of the modern poet, Auden refers specifically to Yeats's 1900 essay "The Symbolism of Poetry," and more generally to Yeats's early aesthetic as a whole, which, as I explore from the vantage of cultural nationalism in Chapter 1, is largely predicated upon the belief that poetic symbols have the capacity to unite us by appealing to the deep underlying commonalities within the human psyche. For Yeats—enthralled at the turn of the century with the Symbolists' numinous view of poetic language—all words are possibly symbolic, harboring almost mystical powers of evocation: "All sounds, all colours, all forms, either because of their preordained energies or because of long association, evoke indefinable and yet precise emotions, or as I prefer to think, call down among us certain disembodied powers, whose footsteps over our hearts we call emotions" (115–16). Yeats's persistent use of the first-person plural here and throughout the essay demonstrates his conviction that the emotional impact of poetic symbols is widespread if not universal; that poetry might actually serve to illuminate our dimmed sense of unity with one another and the world; and that (as he puts it later in the essay) "the laws of art ... are the hidden laws of the world" (120). By contrast, Auden asserts that the "community-thinking" of symbolism is becoming "obsolete in poetry" as a result of the "development of the mind" (or "non-communistic self") beyond the communal pull of the body. If for Yeats, symbolism linked poetry not just to the public but also to the cosmic realm, for Auden its obsolescence consigns poetry to the realm of tête-à-tête, with the poem addressing the reader not in their humanity, but in their individuality, inviting them to twist its coded meanings according to their psyche's private needs.

"The Watershed" and the Anguish of Disunity

Of course, such readerly freedom has always dwelt at the heart of lyric's appeal. But Auden's explicit rejection of poetry's equally long-standing communal attraction seems designed not to release readers into an interpretative *jouissance*, but rather to release the writer from the obligation to communicate, allowing him to cavort debtlessly in the fenced meadows of his own psycho-aesthetic preoccupations. After all, if (as Auden claims throughout the Berlin Journal) the eclipse of the communal body by the individuating mind is a historical fact, then originality becomes the artist's highest achievable end. Seen from this point of view, Auden's focus on the mind's development seems an attempt to provide a biologistic justification for Pound's imperative to "Make it new"—to claim with objective force that the modern poet *must* in fact do so, or else find himself swimming obscurely against the current of historical development. The model of poetry that emerges from the journal, then, is as follows: anti-symbolic, relentlessly original, and written in the conviction that any interpersonal communication beyond the bodily is virtually impossible. Auden's early poetry—particularly in *Poems* (1930), his first commercially published volume—exemplifies this model, with its clipped, hermetic style, the sense one gets of urgent subject matter honed down into an emotionless code. His most enduring poem from this period opens with a rigidity of voice that serves to highlight the barrenness of the landscape it describes:

> Who stands, the crux left of the watershed,
> On the wet road between the chafing grass
> Below him sees dismantled washing-floors,
> Snatches of tramline running to the wood,
> An industry already comatose,
> Yet sparsely living. (1–6)[1]

Written in 1927, "The Watershed" prefigures both formally and thematically the Berlin Journal's abiding concern with humanity's dividedness. As many commentators have pointed out, the poem's opening introduces multiple disorienting uncertainties. The first line deliberately leaves our expectations hung between question and statement, and the individual words within it abound in ambiguity. Should we read "crux" in literal Latin, as *cross*, or metaphorically, as *puzzle*? Is it *to the left* of the watershed, or *what's left* of it?

Geographically speaking, the poem describes a vantage in the northern English lead-mining district near Alston Moor, a region crucial to Auden's boyhood, and which he would later refer to as his "Great Good Place."[2] The poem's opening becomes markedly less mysterious when we trace its regional origins: the "crux" is likely Killhope Cross, a monument near the highest point of the Pennines; "washing-floors" are platformed areas at the surface of mines, equipped with troughed sinks for cleaning chunks of ore; and the "snatches of tramline" are vestiges of the abandoned transport routes so crucial to the mines' nineteenth-century boom period. While these facts clarify some of the imagery of these first lines, the key phrase "left of the watershed" resists such denotative unpacking. We know "watershed" can be taken as both a geographical division between waterways and a historical or existential turning point, and the relative accuracy of concrete detail elsewhere in the poem—along with the presence of significant waterways in the vicinity, such as Killhope Burn and Wellhope Burn—might cause us to favor the former. On the other hand, the determined hermeticism of tone along with the imprecision of "left"—not a cardinal direction, but a thoroughly subjective one—makes a psychologized reading attractive: perhaps the figure has returned to a site that changed him to scan the landscape for what might remain of its life-altering force.

I refer to the poem's central agent as "the figure" because he is denied full subjecthood, granted only the objective pronoun "him," left marooned as a spectral "Who." Had the poem been written in the first person (e.g., "Here I stand, at the crux left of the watershed ..."), it would readily fit into a Romantic tradition of lyric meditation on landscape whose *locus classicus* is Wordsworth's "Tintern Abbey." But by setting the speaker at an indistinct remove from the protagonist—beginning in third person and shifting in the last section to second—the poem occupies a liminal generic space between lyric and narrative. This lends the impression (reinforced by the Pennine lead mines' biographical significance to Auden) of a speaker recounting himself at a distance, observing himself observe. This self-objectifying poetic voice nicely exemplifies the formal implications of Auden's belief in the dividedness of mind from body: the figure yearning for communion with the landscape and the speaker who undermines that yearning are aspects of the same person.

Along these lines, Edward Callan sees the poem as exemplifying the common warning, reiterated throughout Auden's 1928 poems, "against the temptation to seek rest in natural harmony" (45). Callan develops this reading of the early poetry (as I do mine) through an analysis of the Berlin Journal, though he limits his focus to those passages in which Auden takes issue with Freud's characterization of the pleasure principle as "progress towards a state of rest" (*English* 299). Positing his own quick theory of fulfillment, Auden claims that "This is only one half of pleasure and the least important half. Creative pleasure is, like pain, an increase in tension" (299). I have already discussed the implications of this attitude above, in relation to Auden's claim that "the real life-wish is one of separation"—a claim that glorifies the artist's struggle for originality as a positive symptom of modern alienation. This exaltation of artistic striving is further evidenced by Auden's isolation of "creative pleasure" as a separate category beyond the purview of the Freudian schema. And indeed, this is the basis of Auden's refutation of Freud: that in casting pleasure's goal as a kind of regressive unity, Freud leaves room for the artist's strenuous pursuit of singularity to be dismissed as little more than an especially generative brand of neurosis. Callan's reading of the early poetry hinges on this tension; he vastly extends the implications of Auden's brief account of creative pleasure as an increase in tension, using it to support a reading of the poems as embodying a vitalist worldview according to which peace, stagnation, and death are virtually synonymous, and the temptation to rest is a potentially fatal obstacle to self-actualization. Situating "The Watershed" within this framework, Callan claims that it exemplifies Auden's early concern with "the disaster resulting from the attempt to regress to a simpler state," reading the poem as depicting a failed attempt "to return to Eden, to restore the 'wholeness' of nature before the Fall" (52). Before evaluating this reading, we should look at the rest of the poem:

> A ramshackle engine
> At Cashwell raises water; for ten years
> It lay in flooded workings until this,
> Its latter office, grudgingly performed,
> And further here and there, though many dead
> Lie under the poor soil, some acts are chosen
> Taken from recent winters; two there were
> Cleaned out from a damaged shaft by hand, clutching
> The winch the gale would tear them from; one died
> During a storm, the fells impassable,

> Not at his village, but in wooden shape
> Through long abandoned levels nosed his way
> And in his final valley went to ground.
>
> Go home, now, stranger, proud of your young stock,
> Stranger, turn back again, frustrate and vexed:
> This land, cut off, will not communicate,
> Be no accessory content to one
> Aimless for faces rather there than here.
> Beams from your car may cross a bedroom wall,
> They wake no sleeper; you may hear the wind
> Arriving driven from the ignorant sea
> To hurt itself on pane, on bark of elm
> Where sap unbaffled rises, being Spring;
> But seldom this. Near you, taller than grass,
> Ears poise before decision, scenting danger. (6–31)

Callan's reading of the poem as "Freudian allegory" focuses largely on the last verse paragraph, in which the "stranger" is informed in no uncertain terms that he will never achieve the Edenic connectedness to this landscape he evidently seeks: "This land, cut off, will not communicate." Auden's theory of creative tension is embodied, Callan claims, not only in the speaker's repudiation of the stranger's regressive desire—which the poem's final "danger" links to the Freudian death drive—but also in the patterning of assonance and internal rhyme that tightens Auden's blank verse into a tensile sonic web, straining beyond conversational ease.

I engage Callan's analysis at some length because it embodies two rare and crucial strengths among critics of the early work: first, it takes seriously Auden's interest in Freudian theory in this period, particularly his direct engagement with *Beyond the Pleasure Principle* and *The Ego and the Id* in the Berlin Journal just months after "The Watershed" was written; and second, it directly employs passages from the journal to illuminate both thematic and formal aspects of the poems written in the years around it—and does so quite convincingly within its limited purview.[3] I would, however, like to redress the limits of this analysis in regard to "The Watershed," particularly its neglect of the nascent sense of class consciousness to be detected in the poem, and the way this sense allows us to read the poem as more thoroughly bound up in the concerns of the Berlin Journal than Callan or any other critic has yet acknowledged, as a prefiguration of the more explicit social critiques Auden would set forth throughout the 1930s.

The poem's first verse paragraph deals half with the equipment and machinery the stranger can see from his promontory and half with people he cannot actually see but only foggily remembers through stories of their hardships and deaths. The presence of the "ramshackle engine," personified as performing its work "grudgingly," highlights the absence of the people it carries on without—though whether because the workday is over or because it has displaced them in this "comatose" industry we cannot know. The fact that "many dead / Lie under the poor soil" hints at both the danger and the low pay of mine work, but the figure is insulated from such arduousness: among the myriad broken lives that the scattered dead represent, "some acts are chosen / Taken from recent winters." The passive voice here (i.e., "are chosen") implies the distance not only between the figure and the laborers—whose stories he likely hears at several removes—but also between the figure and the speaker, divided aspects of the same post-Wordsworthian vista-gazer: while the former seeks warmth and solace in the minescape as his youth romanticized it, the latter knows that such seeking can only be in vain. The miners' anonymity ("two there were," "one died") undercuts the mythologizing impetus behind the figure's remembrance of them, as the vagueness of his memory stiffens them into "wooden shape." Finally, the description of the dying miner who "in his final valley went to ground" compounds the spatial distance between the perching figure and those he beholds, hinting that not only are they behind him in time and below him in space, but also beneath him on the socioeconomic ladder by virtue of being working class. Thus, the first verse paragraph of "The Watershed" not only bodies forth a divided *speaker-figure* through its use of the passive voice and its objectifying avoidance of the first person, but it also depicts a divided *society* by starkly distancing that figure from the world of labor he observes but cannot commune with.[4]

The figure's dual state of dividedness—within himself and from those he eulogizes—is underlined at the beginning of the second verse paragraph, as the speaker shifts to the second-person imperative mood, telling the figure to "Go home" and calling him "stranger" twice in the first two lines. The next line deepens this portrayal of the figure's alienation, adding a third aspect to his dividedness—his severance from nature: "This land, cut off, will not communicate." Nothing this vista presents to his sight can be meaningfully integrated into his experience; he can take "no accessory content" home from his touristic vigil. Nor, vice-versa, does his presence register upon either the human or elemental inhabitants of the scene; his incursion "wake[s] no sleeper," the sea remains "ignorant," and "sap unbaffled rises, being Spring" (this last detail underlining the comfortlessness here of that archetypal season of renewal, as well as the futility of the figure's attempt to revisit his youth). "The Watershed" thus depicts the three levels of disintegration he would begin to explore more systematically in the Berlin Journal less than two years later. So as not to model a merely extractive method of reading Auden's poetry, however—prosaically mining its interiors for conceptual content and tossing aside the verse-shaped husk—I must reiterate more explicitly a point I have earlier implied: namely that the *style* of Auden's early poetry conveys his conviction of humanity's essential dividedness just as forcefully as its subject matter does. If, as Callan claims in analyzing the sonic patterning of "The Watershed" in terms of creative tension, such patterning formally allegorizes the poet's desire to keep at bay the death drive's stultifying push toward a state of rest—then by analogy it also allegorizes his sense of a society out of harmony with itself, of living amid disunity.

As indicated by his comments in the Berlin Journal on the obsolescence of symbolism and the incommunicability of the mind, the young Auden saw the semantic aspects of poetic language as a kind of code, its meanings no longer drawn from a common reservoir, consigned instead to transmit hopefully resonant privacies. An exclusive focus on this private view of poetry defines readings of "The Watershed" like Callan's—which interprets the poem through a psychoanalytic lens of self-revelation, ignoring its concern with social incohesion—or that of Edward Mendelson, who claims of the poem's central figure that "His estranged condition, not the landscape of the mines, is true Auden country," while neglecting to make explicit that it is estrangement *from* "the landscape of the mines" and its inhabitants that defines the figure's "condition," instead treating it as a kind of metaphysical burden, vaguely dissociated from any material cause (*Early* 34). Such readings dominate critical treatment of Auden's early work, whose speakers are often cast as clear-eyed diagnosticians of modern alienation, rather than the more ambivalent and regretful elegists of lost unity—personal, natural, and especially social—that they can just as easily seem. In terms of "The Watershed," for example, one might as readily read the dense patterning of stresses and echoed vowels as working to offset the bleak subject matter and enigmatic syntax by appealing to a more communal sense of aural response: as the repeated sounds tighten the weave of the poem, they hope as well to bind the reader more tightly to the poetic voice. To take this analogy further, if on the level of subject matter the poem concerns itself with the death drive's dangerous pull toward what Freud calls in *Beyond the Pleasure Principle* "the inertia inherent in organic life" (309), then its sonic patterning might embody the counter-push exerted by the life instincts, an expression of "the efforts of Eros to combine organic substances into ever-larger unities" (315). Rather than see the taut aural fabric of Auden's early poems as simply betokening the young poet's struggle to extricate himself from his web of influences and achieve distinctness as a literary individual, one might also find—recalling the Berlin Journal's maxim that "Only body can be communicated"—a unifying gesture from poet to audience, a sonic appeal to the common ground of the body.

"The Watershed" exemplifies, both thematically and formally, the thrust of all of Auden's poetry written before 1930. Explicitly concerned with uncrossable borders, insuperable divisions, and irrecoverable turning points, it repeatedly hints through both its sonic patterning and its range of tones—clinical, laconic, portentous, yet tinged with pathos—at wishing the world might be otherwise. Although in the earliest work this wish remains at the level of implication, it becomes more explicit as the political upheavals of the 1930s increasingly capture Auden's attention. Whereas the Berlin Journal finds the young writer balancing the caustic aspects of his account of human alienation with an acknowledgment of the unparalleled opportunities for self-actualization allowed for by the breakdown of psychosocial cohesion, by the time of his 1932 essay "Writing" this hint of the celebratory has vanished: the loss of social unity is tragic for all of us, but especially for the artist, whose audience has shrunk to a mere niche among many.

I discussed in Chapter 1 how Yeats, recognizing much the same problem in Ireland in the last decades of the nineteenth century, sought to appeal through Celtic myth to underlying commonalities that might forge the Irish—and thus his audience—into a copious whole. In solving the problem of social disunity, then, poetry could also solve the problem of its own marginality. Rather than wallow bitterly in his sense of apartness from "the masses" who did not read his work, Yeats hoped to enjoy a special status—no less apart, but exalted rather than exiled—as an artist among the more harmonious formation of "the people," who would acknowledge him as having helped unite them into being. Although Auden lacks Yeats's crucial nationalistic impetus, the trajectory of his thinking over the course of the 1930s on poetry's relation to social unity remains remarkably similar to that of his Irish precursor. While Yeats appealed to the pastoral ideal of a lost Celtic Ireland to form the basis of his utopian vision for the emergent nation, Auden hearkened to an even less well-defined ideal of a lost social unity drawn from a mixture of sources both historical and theoretical: past European societies that purportedly embodied a "unity of interests" long since fractured, the Marxist vision of the classless society, the unselfconscious worship groups of the early Christian church, and the unifying force of Freudian Eros all intertwine in Auden's myriad sketches of how humanity might—and the paradox is intentional—*return anew* to a less fragmentary social mode. Like Yeats, Auden comes to entertain the notion that poetry might help usher in this new unified future, and this constitutes one aspect of the utopian element in his thinking. The other, earlier aspect resides in his repeated gestures backward to a lost past of social unity, and it is with these gestures that I will deal in the next section.

"Writing," Self-Consciousness, and the Bridge of Language

Written for a children's encyclopedia entitled *An Outline for Boys and Girls and Their Parents* rather than for any explicitly literary venue, Auden's 1932 essay "Writing" nonetheless stands as his key work of early prose, what Mendelson calls "a manifesto of his private ideology" that (key to my purpose here) shows that "dissociation from a longed-for unity" was the young poet's "sole subject at the time" (*Early* 15). It begins with a theory of the development of language, which Auden claims began because human beings, who once felt themselves a part of "a larger whole," found that their sense of wholeness had left them:

> At some time or other in human history, when and how we don't know, man became self-conscious; he began to feel, I am I, and you are not I; we are shut inside ourselves and apart from each other. ...
> The more this feeling grew, the more man felt the need to bridge over the gulf, to recover the sense of being as much part of life as the cells in his body are part of him. Before he had lost it, when he was still doing things together in a group, such as hunting, when feeling was strongest, as when, say, the quarry was first sighted, the group had made noises, grunts, howls, grimaces. Noise and this feeling he had now lost had gone together; then, if he made the noise, could he not recover the feeling? In some way like this language began. (303)

The origin story Auden presents here can readily be placed in dialogue with his earlier thoughts, in the Berlin Journal of three years previous, on the human condition of severance. Whereas there he identified a tension between the body's communal longing and the mind's drive to individuation, here he abandons the dualistic terms of this formulation in favor of a more holist language, casting humanity's emergent self-consciousness not as deriving from the mind as opposed to the body, but as a matter of "feeling," a mingling of the mental and corporeal. There are two distinct feelings in the above passage, with opposite trajectories: on the one hand, the feeling of emergent self-consciousness, of "I am I"; on the other, the feeling of which this self-consciousness deprives us and which must then be recovered, "of being as much part of life as the cells in his body are part of him." In contrast to the affirmative stance he adopted toward our separation in the Berlin Journal, "Writing" finds him comparing the impact upon the social whole of this entrance into self-consciousness to "a cancer growth in the body" (303). Furthermore, in place of the pessimism he espoused regarding language's ability to communicate amid such dividedness, he now casts language—in what seems a tacit response to the images of breaches, rifts, and gaps that proliferate in his earlier poetry—as "a bridge between speaker and listener," as a palliative if not a full-on remedy for the fissured psyches of the self-conscious (304).

The pseudo-anthropology Auden dabbles in here—and particularly his pinpointing of *self-consciousness* as the agent of humanity's division—is largely drawn from two of his most potent early influences: his crucial modernist predecessor D. H. Lawrence and the more obscure (but for Auden's thinking even more influential) philosopher-historian Gerald Heard. As Auden biographer Richard Davenport-Hines notes, Lawrence's 1923 book *Fantasia of the Unconscious* "enjoyed a powerful vogue" both among the literati at large and specifically with Auden and his group during the Berlin months of 1928–9 (94), and Mendelson confirms that "certainly he was quoting it a year or so later" (*Early* 57). Despite widespread acknowledgment of the book's influence on Auden, however, no critic has yet pointed out that the signal importance he accords to self-consciousness in "Writing" derives at least partly from Lawrence. Throughout *Fantasia*, Lawrence links self-consciousness to the triumph of idea over being, and to the modern tendency to mold ourselves into projections of our own self-images so that we forget to simply live. Lawrence's polemic largely focuses on how self-consciousness, in leading us to suppress our "sensual will" (62), reverberates this dysfunction through the modern family: from the parents, whose "sex in the head" drains their marriage of any "vital interchange" (121), to the child, whose familial and institutional education virtually ensure that the "spark of wholeness" will be swiftly quelled in them, reducing them to "another unit of self-conscious love-will" (143–4).

Though Lawrence's characterization of self-consciousness differs significantly from Auden's in seeing it as a product of modern culture, he does hint at its potential inherency to the human condition: "Every race which has become self-conscious and idea-bound in the past has perished. And then it has all started afresh, in a different way, with another race. And man has never learnt any better" (86). Still, Lawrence implies that humanity might indeed learn its way out of self-consciousness, while Auden allows for no such possibility, only that we might bridge through language the divisions it opens between us. Furthermore, Lawrence sees self-consciousness as anathema to individuality, and claims that "the polarizing of passionate blood in the individual towards life, and towards leader, this must be the dynamic of the last civilization" (183)—thus rooting his critique of self-consciousness in the belief that it has spawned the communal notions of love and brotherhood that weaken our sense of ourselves as individuals, and championing a fascistic emphasis on "the intense passionate yearning of the soul of a stronger, greater individual" as that which will "give men the next motive for life" (183). While an earlier Auden, from the Berlin Journal even up until a year before, may have been attracted to this ethic of leader-worship—indeed, looking back years later on his 1931 long poem *The Orators* Auden opined that it seemed to have been written by a young man "who might, in a year or two, become a Nazi"—the Auden of "Writing" evidences a marked yearning in the opposite direction, toward the communal. At this point the debt to Lawrence is lexical rather than ideological.[5]

A much more directly influential account of self-consciousness comes from Gerald Heard's book *Social Substance of Religion*, published in 1931. In setting out "The Problem" of his inquiry in the book's first chapter, Heard outlines a scenario whose contours resonate all too thoroughly with Auden's account in "Writing" of the compensatory origins of language:

> In all the thinking of mankind since the rise of reflective consciousness two assumptions are continually present: that the state in which he finds himself is not happy, but that he was made for happiness, and therefore he might again be so in the future. From these assumptions he also never fails to draw two conclusions: that he must have been happy in the past, and that therefore in order to be happy in the future he must know what his past state was, and thus learn how he may recreate that condition. (21)

Recall that in Auden's schema language arises out of the attempt to recapture the feeling of communality we lost with the development of self-consciousness. Similarly, in Heard's account, the "past state" of happiness whose loss we feel intuitively and which we strive to recreate is precisely "a state of unselfconsciousness and a completely diffused authority through a direct unreflective sense of the community" (38). Over the course of his psycho-historical survey, Heard charts the nature of human consciousness from its originary state of singleness to its present division into "a subjective and an objective mind," the result of which fragmentation is "the present individual, with his acute selfconsciousness and conflict" (63). Attributing this division to the competing pulls of family and community, the domestic and gregarious instincts, Heard posits the need for "refusion" (65): the unification of humankind through the reattainment of a past psychic state of "group identity" and the restoration of "the constant conviction that life has justified itself because we have recovered the immediate sense of our eternity in it" (58). As the key historical instance of this primordial sense of unity having been restored, Heard isolates the very early form of Christianity he calls Charitism, which through its feast ritual of Agape freed from individuality the consciousnesses of all involved, harnessing "a love which is so intense that it is more than self-forgetful, it is more even than self-destructive, it takes the self and expands it over a whole community, and (this is the step beyond) opens it out so that it can embrace and be embraced by the whole of life" (208–9). This concept of Agape—an all-encompassing communal love, devoid of the selfishness of erotic relations—would become extremely influential in Auden's thinking for the rest of the decade and into the 1940s, serving to image the social unity whose absence his work so often laments.

Within the essay "Writing," however, Heard's influence is registered more subtly; although Auden's emphasis on the fissuring effects of self-consciousness derives largely from Heard and more ephemerally from Lawrence, neither is explicitly acknowledged. Furthermore, while Heard prescribes a return to group consciousness—or what he elsewhere calls "co-consciousness"—as a remedy for modern isolation, Auden focuses on the palliative attempts of language. However much it ends up as one, Auden's essay "Writing" does not set itself out as an exploration of humanity's condition of mutual severance; as the title implies, it takes up the ostensibly more modest question of why people write. Even here, however, Heard's influence is strongly felt, for in enumerating the writer's motives Auden concludes that "Books are written for money, to convert the world, to pass the time; but these reasons are always trivial, beside the first two—company and creation" (309). In highlighting the motive of "company," Auden tacitly appeals to his earlier metaphor of language as a "bridge," claiming of writers that "They feel alone, cut off from each other in an indifferent world where they do not live for very long," and are driven by the question "How can they get in touch again?" (309). Similarly, Heard characterizes the Agape group of early Christianity as "a way, the only way, a *perilous bridge*, but the only one, that could lead the individual back, through a higher, more purely psychic level, to a state when he might be resolved in the reunion of his consciousness as a whole" (66; emphasis added). While Heard offers a psychological interpretation of history, choosing to frame the problem of social disunity in terms of the increasing dividedness of the human psyche, Auden focuses—in keeping with his complementary emphasis on "creation"—on the fate of a common language amid such fracture, seeing the division of the literary arts into innumerable niche markets as a symptom of a more thoroughgoing societal dysfunction. The closing paragraph of "Writing" cements this connection:

> Whenever society breaks up into classes, sects, townspeople and peasants, rich and poor, literature suffers. There is writing for the gentle and writing for the simple, for the highbrow and the lowbrow; the latter gets cruder and coarser, the former more and more refined. ... Since the underlying reason for writing is to bridge the gulf between one person and another, as the sense of loneliness increases ... What is going to happen? If it were only a question of writing it

wouldn't matter; but it is an index of our health. It's not only books, but our lives, that are going to pot. (312)

Instead of focusing on psychic fracture, Auden here singles out social stratification on the basis of beliefs, values, and most of all, wealth (though one might rather say "capital," since his reference to "classes" might just as readily refer to units defined by relative cultural status as by sheer money power). Still, Auden's critique here embodies a materialist slant largely absent from his sources in Heard and Lawrence, reflecting his well-documented interest in Marx and communism at the time. Of the beginning of the above passage Mendelson writes that "Auden's complaint is political only in the broadest sense, not specifically partisan" (*Early* 18)—a claim that embodies a perhaps overly narrow sense of what constitutes partisanship. For what Mendelson means is that Auden is not here espousing a card-carrying doctrinaire brand of communism—and indeed his characterization of the poet's position as one of "fraternal visionary communism" is apt—but what his caveat implies is that we should not take Auden's critique of social disunity and class disparity in "Writing" too seriously, that because "Auden had no political program for resolving town and country, highbrow and lowbrow," his concerns are so noncommittal as to be scarcely "political" at all (18).

On This Island and Auden's Utopian Poetics

In attempting to pinpoint how Auden's work can embody a distinctively political thrust without being strictly programmatic, the concept of *utopia* proves crucial, as it serves to signify the force of desire apart from any specific strategy to see it realized. In previous chapters I have cited Bloch's concept of utopia as "anticipatory consciousness," Jacoby's championing of an "iconoclastic" brand of utopianism as opposed to the meticulously planned "blueprint" utopianism that characterizes the prose narratives of the mainstream utopian tradition, and Levitas's definition of utopia as desire—all in the interest of theorizing more robustly the aspirational impulse that so often drives modern poetry and helps lend much of the work of Yeats and Auden in particular its enduring vitality and relevance: even when not explicitly political, their poems often thrum with a desirous energy, driven by the conviction that the world should be different. Rather than dismiss this pervasive energy as betraying a false consciousness—the artist's mistaken conviction that history will mend itself into harmony according to the visionary dictates of their art—I take seriously the impulse behind it, hoping to shed insight on the particularly potent mode of utopian striving that poetry embodies. This mode deals less with what is possible than with what is imaginable; or to reiterate this distinction through Levitas, "the essential element in utopia is not hope but desire—the desire for a better way of being" (191). The *OED* defines hope as "desire and expectation combined," so putting Levitas's distinction in terms of Auden, one might say that his lack of a political program diminishes only his *hope* for social unity, as he has little active reason to *expect* his *desire* to be achieved. But the crucial kernel of desire remains.

It is worth quoting Levitas further, as her work helps to illuminate the utopian impetus behind much of Auden's early writing. In continuing the passage cited earlier, she writes that utopia "involves the imagining of a state of being in which the problems which actually confront us are removed or resolved, often, but not necessarily, through the imagining of a state of the world in which the scarcity gap is closed or the 'collective problem' solved" (191). Auden's confrontation with his era's lack of social unity is what marks his writing as utopian, and his work throughout the 1930s constitutes a sustained reflection on the "collective problem." While the Berlin Journal and the early published prose broach this problem directly, the early poetry's fixation on images of division and failed crossings-over lends the whole of Auden's *Poems* (1930) a combined air of diagnosis and neurosis, as though its speakers suspect that what they cast as society's ills may just be projections of their own inner schisms. In the poems of his second volume, published in 1936 and titled *Look, Stranger!* in England and *On This Island* in the United States (the latter being the poet's own preferred title), Auden the diagnostician of severance shifts further along his utopian continuum to become Auden the chronicler of those desires for unity—sexual, social, and an inextricable mix of the two—to which our severed condition gives rise. Rather than clinically depict his figures' estrangement, leaving implicit their desire for connectedness, his speakers come to more overtly wish for escape, for both themselves and all of us.

The wishfulness that animates the poems of *On This Island* is evident from the first lines of its "Prologue," which immediately strike the volume's dominant tone:

> O Love, the interest itself in thoughtless Heaven,
> Make simpler daily the beating of man's heart; within,
> There in the ring where name and image meet,
>
> Inspire them with such a longing as will make his thought
> Alive like patterns a murmuration of starlings
> Rising in joy over wolds unwittingly weave. (1–6)

Thus the poem opens in atheistic prayer, with a personified Freudian Eros in place of God. Heaven is "thoughtless" both because it represents a realm beyond thought and because (at least according to the speaker's worldview) it is indifferent—a place not of omnibenevolence but of utter rarefaction, purged of categories. Indeed, the first line's appositional phrase defines Love as "the interest" in this place, implying the neo-Platonic doctrine that all small-L love merely shadows a grander yearning for transcendence. The speaker calls upon this personified Love to "Make simpler daily the beating of man's heart" and goes on to specify a location where this blissful simplifying should take place: "within, / There in the ring where name and image meet." John Fuller notes how this poem seems to have developed out of an abandoned line penned a month earlier—"O Love, sustainer of the unbreakable atomic ring"—and how "this ring is primarily the psychic field formed by the early Christians at their agape or love-feast" (146).⁶ This of course returns us to Heard's *Social Substance of Religion*, though while acknowledging this source Fuller chooses not to mine its explanatory value. For Heard, Agape served as a means by which each participant could recapture the state of unity that precedes the fracturing development of self-consciousness, generating a force of "immense love" that "can break down the barriers of his individualism, making him one with itself and with it" (212). The image in the third line of the finished poem, of "the ring where name and image meet," gestures to this Agapic unity, alluding not just to Heard but also to Auden's own earlier-stated ideas on the development of language out of self-consciousness: the speaker prays for a return to that "simpler" state before the dissociation of *name* and *image* compelled the development of *word*.

Recognizing the place of the "Prologue" amid the evolving discourse of lost social unity in Auden's writing helps to clarify the odd pronoun shift in the poem's fourth line, "Inspire *them* with such a longing as will make *his* thought" (emphasis added). In inquiring what the antecedent of "them" might be in this line, a perplexed Anthony Hecht offers that "the only possibility seems to be 'name and image,' but how can they feel 'longings'?" (42). Not taking account of the poem's roots in Heard and Auden's own speculative anthropology, Hecht misses a much simpler reading. The "them" refers to those gathered in the Agapic ring, whose inspiration by Love might generate such a force of "longing" as to lead "*his* thought"—the "man" of the first line individualized—into the patterned aliveness described by the subsequent lines. In other words, the blending of "them" into "his" serves to figure the experience of co-consciousness described by Heard and repeatedly yearned for throughout Auden's early work. Though the poem goes on to transmute this yearning from one for psychosocial connectedness to one for communion with a primordialized English landscape—asking Love to "make us as Newton was, who in his garden watching / The apple falling towards England, became aware / Between himself and her of an eternal tie" (10–12)—this shift only deepens the poem's status as a utopian artifact. For in addition to embodying, along with all the works I have been discussing, the utopian *desire* to see the collective problem solved, the symbolic rendering of England in the "Prologue" makes it a crucial instance of Auden's tacit engagement with the utopian *genre* throughout *On This Island*. As its title suggests, Auden uses island-ness throughout the collection to metaphorize both psychological and social isolation, and the wishes for unity to which such isolation gives rise. In his book *The English Utopia*, A. F. Morton cites the fact that England is an island to explain why the utopian genre has been so richly treated there: "For it is always easier to imagine anything in proportion as it resembles what we are or know, and it is as an island that we always think of Utopia" (9). Though Morton treats the concept of utopia with more generic strictness than I do here, his observation as to the prevalence of islands in utopian literature sheds valuable light on Auden's work of this period. In the "Prologue," England is variously designated as "these islands," "our little reef," and "This fortress perched on the edge of the Atlantic scarp, / The mole between all Europe and the exile-crowded sea" (8–9)—a range of characterizations that emphasize not only its isolation and vulnerability, but also (and more positively) its singularity and liminality. Indeed, throughout the poem England's island-ness registers its special status as a place where the poem's opening prayer to an all-uniting Love might be answered, where our aspirations of social unity might come to fruition, emerging "out of the Future and into actual History" (40).

"Paysage Moralisé," the Sestina Form, and the Cyclicity of Utopian Striving

Island imagery figures centrally, and to similar purposes, in four of *On This Island*'s other poems: "Look, stranger, at this island now" "The earth turns over, our side feels the cold," "August for the people and for their favourite islands," and most crucially for my discussion of utopia, the 1933 sestina beginning "Hearing of harvests rotting in the valleys" and later titled "Paysage Moralisé." Rather than directly express utopian longing, Auden here uses the strict patterning demanded by the sestina form to abstract from the utopian impulse, and to suggest a universal human propensity to aspire after paradise. The poem opens in a failing society:

> Hearing of harvests rotting in the valleys,
> Seeing at end of street the barren mountains,
> Round corners coming suddenly on water,
> Knowing them shipwrecked who were launched for islands,
> We honour founders of these starving cities,
> Whose honour is the image of our sorrow.
>
> Which cannot see its likeness in their sorrow
> That brought them desperate to the brink of valleys;
> Dreaming of evening walks through learned cities,
> They reined their violent horses on the mountains,
> Those fields like ships to castaways on islands,
> Visions of green to them that craved for water. (1–12)

The first stanza depicts settlements plagued by famine and natural calamity, having sent out scouting parties they know will never return. The initial order of the end words is suggestive: "valleys," "mountains," "water," "islands," and "cities" are punctuated by "sorrow," implying the ultimate futility of humanity's attempts to civilize a niche for ourselves amid the wildness with which nature presents us. The poem also suggests, however, that futile or not, the human flight from sorrow will continue in perpetuity. The "honour" of the cities' founders is "the image of our sorrow," and yet, as the first line of the second stanza adds, we cannot see this likeness of our sorrow in theirs. In other words, it was sorrow that drove the founders to seek out and build our civilization, which has only resulted in more sorrow, and the unwitting reemergence of that same founding drive—that same desire to launch out for new islands—in us. We flee from a sorrow that is already waiting to possess us at every new sanctum we reach. Having settled in the valleys, the founders almost immediately suffered in sorrow's grip:

> They built by rivers and at night the water
> Running past windows comforted their sorrow;
> Each in his little bed conceived of islands
> Where every day was dancing in the valleys,
> And all year the trees blossomed on the mountains,
> Where love was innocent, being far from cities. (13–18)

Auden here uses the sestina's reconfiguration of end words from stanza to stanza to suggest the tragic inexorable cyclicity of human striving, as the poem comes to depict our vacillation between the civilizing and pastoral impulses: the founders who had once dreamt of learned cities now decry the loss of innocence to which their own aspirations of urbanity have given rise. They lie in bed dreaming of an Arcadian paradise of abundance and unselfconscious love—a dream which, the poem suggests, can not only never be fulfilled, but will only bring sorrow in the wake of its unfulfillment, which in turn will dredge up the dream again, and then the sorrow, ad infinitum.

The poem's second half finds this pattern repeated, depicting how hunger ("a more immediate sorrow" (22)) sows the seed of another island-bound expedition, this time driven by religious proselytizing: "to moping villagers in valleys / Some waving pilgrims were describing islands" (23–4). From these islands, claim the pilgrims, gods come to deliver the settlers into a New Jerusalem: "Now is the time to leave your wretched valleys / And sail with them across the lime-green water" (27–8). As the sixth stanza suggests, however, some of the valley-dwellers have learned too much from history to plunge heedlessly into another cycle of sorrow begotten by unrequitable desire:

> So many, doubtful, perished in the mountains
> Climbing up crags to get a view of islands;
> So many, fearful, took with them their sorrow
> Which stayed with them when they reached unhappy cities;
> So many, careless, dived and drowned in water;
> So many, wretched, would not leave their valleys. (31–6)

The anaphoric repetition of "So many" conveys a sense of a society wracked by internal division. That even those who choose not to heed the pilgrims' false promises—the doubtful and the wretched—end up either dead or mired in sorrow bleakly epitomizes the poem's pessimistic worldview, inextricable by this point from the sestina form that embodies it. The final three-line envoi, however, takes a hopeful turn:

> It is the sorrow; shall it melt? Ah, water
> Would gush, flush, green these mountains and these valleys

And we rebuild our cities, not dream of islands. (37-9)

In one sense this ending marks the poem as explicitly anti-utopian, especially if one takes the proclivity to "dream of islands" as a quintessentially utopian one. In several other senses, however, it exemplifies Auden's ambivalent utopian*ism* in this period. The very suggestion that the sorrow might melt—while leaving the source of heat or happiness that might effect this melting unspecified—is a utopian gesture in the most colloquial and pejorative sense, as fruitless as the "dream[ing] of islands" it hopes to overcome. Furthermore, and more crucially, though the last line's wish that we might "rebuild our cities, not dream of islands" could superficially be read as the choice of a "realistic" option over a naïvely utopian one, the fact that both are equally predicated upon the revelatory melting of sorrow might rather lead us to read them as two different manifestations of the utopian impulse: to escape, or to stay put and work toward change, constructing our way out of the sorrow that pervades our societies.

"Paysage Moralisé" ultimately suggests, through its form and its subject matter alike, both the impotence of utopian striving and the universality of our propensity to strive nonetheless. Despite its veneer of pessimism, it clearly revels in the ceaselessness of humanity's desire to better our societies. These are the poles between which Auden's utopianism will shift throughout the latter half of the decade: beginning around 1935 he enters his most overtly political period—the period of topical poems like "Spain" and the sonnet sequence *In Time of War*—and although during these years his poetry less often expresses the utopian longing for societal unity that characterizes his earlier work, in his prose writings he wonders if poetry might help *effect* change rather than simply expressing the wish for it. Having shifted from the late 1920s to the mid-1930s from diagnosis to desire, the main tenor of Auden's work now becomes more audience-oriented, concerned less with the expression of desire than with desire's *education*. Like Yeats at the height of the Celtic Twilight, Auden comes to entertain a role for poetry in helping to overcome society's dividedness; at the same time, however—and also like Yeats, though in much different historical circumstances—he comes to realize that such dividedness can never be fully overcome, and that the communal space evoked by poetry is an aesthetic one, never to be actualized politically.

Poetry and Social Change

If the years from 1935 to 1938 find Auden at his most overtly political, they also find him at his most optimistic in thinking that the world can be changed. And indeed, politics for Auden in this period is not the judiciously nuanced matter implied by definitions such as that of the prominent leftist historian Bernard Crick—who describes it as "the activity by which differing interests within a given unit of rule are conciliated by giving them a share of power in proportion to their importance to the welfare and the survival of the whole community" (7)—but is rather an inherently revolutionary pursuit. Auden's politics has little to do with balancing the competing claims of interest groups; rather, he launches from the premise that the status quo is broken, and therefore its perpetuation is ultimately in no one's interest. In this charged context, to be political is to seek change. So, while Auden's diagnosis of society's ills remains much the same in its contours as it was at the beginning of the decade—rooted in his sense of the dividedness of self and society—he becomes much more proactive in imagining how the gaps within and between us might be sutured, and in envisioning for poetry a healing role.

Critics have often noted how the predominantly psychological reading of social dividedness offered by Auden's earliest work comes to be supplemented with a more materialist understanding of class disparity derived directly from Marx and (more generally) from the socialist fervor that gripped much of the European intelligentsia over the course of the 1930s. As Justin Replogle puts it, "In the 1930s, merely to be young, socially conscious, and outspoken was enough to mark one as a Marxist, or at least a 'leftist,' and Auden was all these things" (584). Though Replogle rightly highlights how the political climate of the era produced labels sounding much more decisive than the convictions behind them actually were, the fact is that Auden's socialist (if not strictly Marxist) leanings extended well beyond being "young, socially conscious, and outspoken." In his abiding concern with class disparity, especially—which, as I have pointed out, resonates through poems as early as "The Watershed" (1927) and is first directly expressed in prose in "Writing" (1932)—Auden evidences at least one fundamental point of concurrence with socialist thought. Of course, it might be argued that this concern arises not out of a sense of economic or social justice, but rather because class divisions disrupt the societal unity he longs for, both as a divided subject himself and (more crucially perhaps) as an artist who believes that only in a unified society can art be produced or received with the sympathetic breadth it deserves. In other words, given that so many of Auden's laments over social dividedness occur in the context of reflections on the place of art in contemporary societies, one might detect—as with the early Yeats—a good deal of self-interest behind his socialistic proclivities: the more unified his society, the larger his audience.

By the time of his 1935 essay "Psychology and Art To-day," however, his endorsement of socialism rings very sincerely, and comes with an acknowledgment of the near irreconcilability of socialist goals with those of his other pet paradigm in this period, the psychoanalytic. Spelling out the essential conflict between Marx and Freud—whom he claims both "start from the failures of civilisation, one from the poor, one from the ill"—he writes:

> The socialist accuses the psychologist of caving to the status quo, trying to adapt the neurotic to the system, thus depriving him of a potential revolutionary: the psychologist retorts that the socialist is trying to lift himself by his own boot tags, that he fails to understand himself, or the fact that lust for money is only one form of the lust for power; and so that after he has won his power by revolution he will recreate the same conditions. Both are right. As long as civilisation remains as it is, the number of patients the psychologist can cure are

very few, and as soon as socialism attains power, it must learn to direct its own interior energy and will need the psychologist. (341)

Most immediately striking here is the definiteness with which he affirms socialism's eventual attainment of power. As throughout his essays of this period, Auden casts socialism as the only just alternative to the status quo, and yet here he undermines its rootedness in vulgar economics, claiming that "the lust for money is only one form of the lust for power"—implying that socialists may just be riding inequality as an issue as the quickest way to steed themselves into the power after which they truly (though perhaps unconsciously) lust. By helping us to understand ourselves, then, psychology might keep the revolution honest, protecting the egalitarian goals of socialism from subsumption by the power-mongering of its figureheads. Of course, as Auden points out, it might just as likely convince us—wrongly—that the revolution is unnecessary, that the illness we attribute to society is in fact our own.

This, in the essay, is where poetry comes in: as an educative force that, without propagandizing in the service of specific aims, makes us more likely to choose consciously and therefore morally. Auden builds this notion of poetry's social role out of his earlier ideas about the birth of language out of humanity's severance through self-consciousness. While still believing that "the introduction of self-consciousness was a complete break in development, and all that we recognise as evil or sin is its consequence" (339), Auden now exalts the excessive self-consciousness of the artist as a kind of gift: "The artist like every other kind of 'highbrow' is self-conscious, i.e., he is all of the time what everyone is some of the time, a man who is active rather than passive to his experience" (334). Believing that "perfect satisfaction would be complete unconsciousness" (334), Auden casts the self-conscious artist as sublimely dissatisfied, both at odds with society and of great value to it, seething with what *could be* rather than abiding half-consciously in what *is*. The literary artist's potential significance derives from their choice of medium; not only is language the shared property of the collective, but (and here Auden credulously accepts Jung, who appears in the essay's bibliography) "every word through fainter and fainter associations is ultimately a sign for the universe" (337), and so the communicative possibilities of linguistic art are virtually limitless. In the earlier writings, Auden cast language as a symptom of our essential dividedness, averring that "only body can be communicated" (*English* 299). Now, however, he has come to see art not only as deeply communicative, but as potentially able to reunite us—at least with ourselves:

> The task of psychology, or art for that matter, is not to tell people how to behave, but by drawing their attention to what the impersonal unconscious is trying to tell them, and by increasing their knowledge of good and evil, to render them better able to choose, to become increasingly morally responsible for their destiny. (340–1)

Auden here allies psychology and art in their educative potential. In evoking the concept of the "impersonal unconscious," he implies that both can illuminate communal truths to help us increase our moral awareness, crediting them with the rather vague benefit of making us "better able to choose." Near the end of the essay he clarifies what sorts of choices this might entail, as he isolates "two kinds of art, escape-art, for man needs escape as he needs food and deep sleep, and parable-art, that art which shall teach man to unlearn hatred and learn love" (341–2).[7] As so often throughout his 1930s writings, "love" here functions as a panacea, in a rhetorical context that evokes Freud's all-uniting Eros, Heard's co-conscious Agape, and a Marxist sense of brotherhood and species-being. If art can teach us this sort of love, it can do no less than reunite us.[8]

While in "Psychology and Art To-day" Auden ascribes this unifying potential to art in general, another essay of the same year attributes this power specifically to poetry; in the Introduction to the anthology *The Poet's Tongue*, he calls poetry "the parabolic approach" and repeats almost word-for-word the description of the task he elsewhere assigned more broadly to psychology and art:

> Poetry is not concerned with telling people what to do, but with extending our knowledge of good and evil, perhaps making the necessity for action more urgent and its nature more clear, but only leading us to the point where it is possible for us to make a rational and moral choice. (329)

Though at pains to affirm throughout the essay that "poetry may illuminate but it will not dictate" (330)—a stance that has proven of much use to critics determined to prove that Auden was never "really" as political as he sometimes seems, and certainly no socialist—just as in "Psychology and Art To-day," the rest of the essay makes clear what his use of the stark dichotomy of "good and evil" only hints at: that Auden had rather firm ideas of what "rational and moral choice" might entail.[9] So although Mendelson's claim about Auden's stance here—i.e., that "he could not liberate his readers into the future that he chose for them, but he might be able to help them learn to choose a future of their own" (*Early* 257)—is compelling on the surface, his pithy summary somewhat obscures the fact that Auden's thematic preoccupations point to his desiring a specific quality of future for both himself and his readers: one no longer wracked with disunity. Elsewhere in his Introduction he returns to this theme, lamenting the Industrial Revolution's division of society into two classes, the working and the leisured, which in turn tended to split literature "into two streams, one providing the first with a compensation and escape, the second with a religion and a drug" (328). This development debases all:

> Artistic creations may be produced by individuals, and because their work is only appreciated by a few it does not necessarily follow that it is not good; but a universal art can only be the product of a community united in sympathy, a sense of worth, and aspiration; and it is improbable that the artist can do his best except in such a society. (329)

The latter half of this quotation could readily have been drawn from early Yeats.[10] Like Yeats, Auden exalts the unified society on the grounds that only there can art reach its full potential. Though his vision of communal unity does resonate with socialism—particularly in his evocation of a shared "sense of worth" and "aspiration," as opposed to the class hierarchies and rampant competitive individualism that mar capitalist societies—his emphasis derives first and foremost from his position as an artist. Still, Auden's frequent paeans to the unified society throughout his 1930s writings strongly evidence his belief in the essential good of such a prospect, just as his equally frequent criticisms of class-divided societies speak to their evil. Despite Auden's (and many of his critics') attempts to cast his educative poetics as neutrally promoting "rational and moral choice," it is clear that for him the exercise of true morality would result in a unity fundamentally at odds with the dividedness promoted by the status quo.

Christopher Caudwell and Poetry as a Communal Artform

Auden also shares with Yeats a certain strain of what I have called in Chapter 1 "pastoral utopianism"—a proclivity to look backward to a lost coherent past for an image of the future on which to fix his desire. I have already highlighted his appeal to this atavistic coherence in "Writing," where the development of language is cast as a symptom of its tragic dissolution, and in "Psychology and Art To-day," where he evokes an "impersonal unconscious" that links us to our ancient communion. Indeed, in this latter essay he gestures to the supposed pacifism and sociability of "Man's phylogenetic ancestors," using Freud to affirm that "a golden age, comparatively speaking (and anthropological research tends to confirm this), is an historical fact" (340). I have tried to convey how Auden subtly cast poetry as a potential spur to return anew to this golden age through its capacity to increase our knowledge of good and evil. But even more compelling evidence for his belief in poetry's connectedness to the lost communal world can be found in his brief review of Christopher Caudwell's 1937 book *Illusion and Reality: A Study of the Sources of Poetry*.

A neglected landmark of late modernist and Marxist criticism, Caudwell's work traverses similar pseudo-anthropological territory to many of Auden's early essays, but rather than emphasize language as a symptom of the communal tribe's tragic fragmentation into discrete self-conscious entities, he argues for the centrality of poetry to group identity: "Poetry is the nascent self-consciousness of man, not as an individual but as a sharer with others of a whole world of common evolution" (25). Caudwell theorizes poetry as both an evolutionary mechanism, developed out of songs sung in unison to ease the burden of communal work, and a medium of aspiration, attempting to sing into vision "a world of superior reality—a world of more important reality not yet realised, whose realisation demands the very poetry which phantastically anticipates it" (21). In contemporary terms, then, poetry embodies both an efflorescence of the dominant bourgeois ideology and the urge to drive beyond it. On the one hand, for example, it increasingly foregrounds the insularity of the lyric "I" in its self-reflective quest for actualization over the communal world of the dramatic—thus echoing the sham individualism of the bourgeois class, who refuse to recognize that what they take as their inborn freedom in fact derives from the forced unfreedom of the majority. On the other hand, however, this same poetry frequently embodies "the prophetic and world-creating power of dream"—not a solipsistic dream, but because poetry is inherently social, a broadly revolutionary one: "It is the dream, not of an individual, but of a man reflecting in his individual consciousness the role of a whole class, whose movement is given in the material conditions of society" (298). This is the ideal of a communist art set out by Caudwell in his visionary final chapter, "The Future of Poetry," in which he exhorts those bourgeois artists sympathetic to the proletariat (Auden is mentioned by name) to slough off their false ideas of artistic freedom and embrace the cause:

> There is no neutral world of art, free from categories or determining causes. Art is a social activity. Yours is the fallacious freedom of a dream, which imagines itself spontaneous when it is rigidly determined by forces outside consciousness. You must choose between class art which is unconscious of its causality and is therefore to that extent false and unfree, and proletarian art which is becoming conscious of its causality and will therefore emerge as the truly free art of communism. There is no classless art except communist art, and that is not yet born; and class art today, unless it is proletarian, can only be the art of a dying class. (318)

Being rooted in "the social solidarity of primitive communism," poetry is particularly well positioned to envision and assist in actualizing "a movement back to the collectivism and integrity of a society without coercion, where consciousness and freedom are equally shared by all" (323). Caudwell remains vague on what precisely might be the technical and thematic characteristics of art in such a society, but in his repeated insistence on the essential sociality of art, and that "the poet's public must become gradually coincident with society" (324), he echoes (albeit in much more strictly doctrinaire terminology) several crucial fixations of Auden's prose writings throughout the 1930s: that society suffers from its disunity; that only in a unified society can art reach its full integrity; and finally that art (and specifically poetry) can contribute to societal unification by resonating with our relict communal urge. Through its declamatory stance, its primal musicality, and its insistently desirous ethos, poetry echoes that part of us that senses that the world was once a better place and wishes it to be so again.

Like Auden, then, Caudwell ascribes to a pastoral utopianism, appealing to a lost coherence to justify his over-hopeful vision of the future.[11] Though the latter regarded the former's poetry as still clinging to bourgeois codes of self-actualization and personal striving, the critic clearly saw in the poet the potential to divest his art of such falsehoods, to "square art with life and life with art" and relinquish the illusion that any can be free when so many remain enslaved (318). Auden's review of *Illusion and Reality* appeared in the May 1937 issue of *New Verse*, and rather than respond to Caudwell's targeting of him, he delivered his briefest and most unconditionally laudatory critical assessment of the decade. Auden opens by casting the book as a major event: "We have waited a long time for a Marxist book on the aesthetics of poetry. *Axel's Castle* [by Edmund Wilson] was a beginning but it was about individual matters, not fundamentals. Now at last Mr. Caudwell has given us such a book" (*Prose I* 386). The two pages that follow consist of three-quarters quotation interspersed with brief summary, ending with the following: "I shall not attempt to criticise *Illusion and Reality* firstly because I am not competent to do so, and secondly because I agree with it. … This is the most important book on poetry since the books of Dr. Richards, and, in my opinion, provides a more satisfactory answer to the many problems which poetry raises" (387). Though his concrete political involvement always remained superficial—the 1932 letter in which he announced that "No I am a bourgeois. I will not join the C. P." is often cited as an index of his commitment—it is clear that he agreed with the essential elements of Marxist class analysis, and especially as it applied to poetry's history and its utopian potential.[12]

In Time of War and the Persistence of Utopia

It should be noted, however, that despite his obvious proclivities (and again like Yeats), Auden's few uses of the word "utopia" throughout the 1930s are universally depreciatory and reflective of a definition of the term much more rigid than the aspirationally oriented one of utopia as desire that I employ throughout this book. In the final canto of his 1936 *Letter to Lord Byron* he remarks that "The Great Utopia, free of all complexes, / The Withered State is, at the moment, such / A dream as that of being both the sexes" (*English* 199)—thus reflecting the common pejorative view of utopia as inherently unachievable (though his interjection of "at the moment" does hold out a sliver of possibility). Several years later, in the account of his "personal philosophy" he contributed to the essay collection *I Believe*, he opines that "no society can be absolutely good. Utopias, whether like Aldous Huxley's *Brave New World* or Dante's *Paradiso*, because they are static, only portray states of natural evil or good" (*English* 375). Auden here conflates utopias and dystopias as both inhering in the realm of the static, thus being equally incapable of actualization. What he rejects is not the desire for social reform at the root of the utopian impulse but rather the notion that any change can be effected once and for all—a delusion he links with fascism. Indeed, he affirms later in the same passage on utopia that "no society can be absolutely good; but some are better than others" (375), and further on that "I think that the Socialists are right and the Fascists are wrong in their view of society" (379), and he devotes much of the essay to setting out a counter-vision to fascism, a model of a more ideal society that owes much to the guild socialism of William Morris. Throughout this discourse he cautions against absolutism, urging us for example "to remember that while an idea can be absolutely bad, a person can never be" (380)—a warning that embodies a larger point: while a better or worse society is possible, perfection and its hellish inverse are beyond our human capacities.

This is the generative dialectic of much of Auden's work of the late 1930s: on the one hand his commitment in principle to a socialist vision of society and his utopian desire to see that vision furthered; on the other hand, his growing conviction—to put it in the religious terms he would soon explicitly adopt—of humanity's fallenness, our essential imperfection, and his suspicion of how reformers across the political spectrum tend to adopt absolutist views of human nature. This dialectic reaches its fullest expression in Auden's sonnet sequence *In Time of War* and its accompanying "Commentary," originally included as part of *Journey to a War*, the collaborative travelogue he wrote with Christopher Isherwood as the two toured China during the Sino-Japanese War of 1938. Though deriving some concrete detail from his frontline observations, Auden deals less with the particular historical war out of which the poems arose and more with humanity's trans-historical struggle against strife and violence—both psychological and physical, naturally occurring and human-caused. In fact, the sequence does much to call into question this latter distinction, repeatedly pointing out that just as humanity's fate is inextricably bound to the natural world in which we inhere, our violences are no less a part of nature—*human* nature—than thunderstorms or floods. Over the course of 27 sonnets and a 283-line "Commentary," spanning from creation and the Fall to the China of Auden's present, the sequence traces humanity's struggle to perfect itself in the face of its inveterate imperfection.

The first-person singular pronoun "I" does not appear in the sequence, a fact that helps *In Time of War* embody Auden's own prior ideal of the "parabolic method" while at the same time taking up Caudwell's challenge to divest his art of bourgeois tropes of individual actualization. Although not mentioning Caudwell, Stan Smith recognizes this, claiming that "By taking the personalized, self-regarding lover of the sonnet sequence, and dispersing him into the multitude of collective subjects who make a history, Auden deconstructs the political and literary traditions of bourgeois individualism" (110). The sequence tells the story, then, not of a lover's tormented quest for unity with his beloved, but of humanity's persistent desire to unify itself—psychologically, societally, and with nature—despite the apparent futility of this desire. Sonnet II chronicles the initial fracture, tracing the fate of a humanity who once "knew exactly what to do outside" (4) as they enter the post-lapsarian era:

> They left: immediately the memory faded
> Of all they'd learnt; they could not understand
> The dogs now who, before, had always aided;
> The stream was dumb with whom they'd always planned.
>
> They wept and quarrelled: freedom was so wild.
> In front, maturity, as he ascended,
> Retired like a horizon from the child;
>
> The dangers and the punishments grew greater;
> And the way back by angels was defended
> Against the poet and the legislator. (5–14)

Figure 4 Auden (right) and Christopher Isherwood at Victoria Station, London, en route to China in January 1938.

This poem recapitulates, a full decade later, the levels of dividedness the younger Auden set out in his Berlin Journal: the dogs and streams will no longer communicate; the newly ungardened humans quarrel with one another; and the ever-receding horizon of maturity leaves each at odds with themselves. There are, however, some key points of divergence. First, the initial moment of severance is cast, for the first time in Auden's writing, within the Judeo-Christian narrative of the Fall, rather than within a psychological or sociopolitical paradigm. Second, this moment is here cast as a *choice* ("They left"), rather than an imposition—a move that deviates both from scripture and from his own earlier account of the spontaneous emergence of self-consciousness. This emphasis on the torment of choice ("freedom was so wild") continues throughout the sequence, attesting to the gradually emerging Christian-existentialist strain in Auden's thinking (upon which Kierkegaard would become the major influence throughout the 1940s). While Auden has not entirely abandoned his vision of the poet's utopian role—in a half parody of and half homage to Shelley he links "the poet and the legislator" as those who seek to help return us to the lost Garden—their "way back" is barred "by angels," a fact that both hews to Genesis and additionally suggests that our proclivity for redemptive quests may in fact be destructive, something from which we need to be saved by benign force.

This central contradiction is taken up again and again throughout the sequence: that humanity's guiding desire has always remained a utopian one—again, in Levitas's words, "the desire for a better way of life"—but that no improvement has ever been achieved widely or permanently enough to see that desire quelled by lasting happiness. As Sonnet XIII puts it: "History opposes its grief to our buoyant song: / The Good Place has not been; our star has warmed to birth / A race of promise that has never proved its worth" (9–11). Even here, however, Auden sparks at the utopian torch; he could just as easily have written "The Good Place *will never be*," and his gesture to the infinitesimally small twist of chance by which our planet harbors life rings as an affirmation that all hope, however miniscule the possibility of its achievement, ought to be kept alive. We are, after all, "A race of promise." Auden again strikes this essential note of hopefulness (albeit in a darker timbre) in Sonnet XX; after meditating through the first two quatrains on war's rootedness in the mutual fear of its antagonists ("They carry terror with them like a purse, / And flinch from the horizon like a gun" (1–2)), he shifts in the sestet to the first-person plural:

We live here. We lie in the Present's unopened
Sorrow; its limits are what we are.
The prisoner ought never to pardon his cell.

Can future ages ever escape so far,
Yet feel derived from everything that happened,
Even from us, that even this was well? (9–14)

Bluntly asserting material presence ("We live here"), the speaker goes on to imply both that we are limited by what the present affords us and, more optimistically, that the present's only limits are our own. Its sorrow remains "unopened" only as long as we acquiesce in its closure—which we should not do: "The prisoner ought never to pardon his cell." In the final three lines the speaker grasps after a sense that present suffering is necessary to ensure humanity's "escape," and wonders hopefully whether "future ages" will look back and find "that even this was well." A tension persists here between Auden's emergent Christian worldview, which sees humanity as fallen and valorizes suffering in the name of future redemption, and his long-held secular reformism, which maintains that humanity can be the ultimate agent of that redemption. Common to both, however—and resonating through the dialectical interplay of the two—is utopian desire, the *shared* aspiration (emphasized by the prevalence of the pronoun "We") for a better, more peaceful, more unified way of life.

The sequence ends in a way that lets this desire resound, while also acknowledging that it may never be satisfied. Sonnet XXVII stands as a crucial transition point between the early utopian Auden, guided by the hope that we might return anew to our past coherence, and the Christian-existentialist Auden of the 1940s, driven by the belief that our essential imperfection will never be overcome:

> Wandering lost upon the mountains of our choice,
> Again and again we sigh for an ancient South,
> For the warm nude ages of instinctive poise,
> For the taste of joy in the innocent mouth.
>
> Asleep in our huts, how we dream of a part
> In the glorious balls of the future; each intricate maze
> Has a plan, and the disciplined movements of the heart
> Can follow for ever and ever its harmless ways.
>
> We envy streams and houses that are sure:
> But we are articled to error; we
> Were never nude and calm like a great door,
>
> And never will be perfect like the fountains;
> We live in freedom by necessity,
> A mountain people dwelling among mountains. (1–14)

If this poem stands as an example of the parabolic method, its intention is less to clarify the distinction between good and evil so that we might choose more morally, and more to assert that we cannot *not* choose—and that this necessity of choice, as much as our fallenness, defines us as humans. Indeed, because "we are articled to error," there is no guarantee that we will ever be correct in our moral assessments, so that even when we try to choose rightly, history often proves us in the wrong. We quest after "an ancient South"—the "warm nude ages" once rife with "the taste of joy"—because we falsely believe this lost past to have been a place beyond morality, where choices are either always good or entirely unnecessary. But such a state of choicelessness (as Auden would point out many times during the 1940s, to be discussed in the next chapter) can only mean tyranny. Although in the "Commentary" to *In Time of War* he attributes the claim that "*Man can have Unity if Man can give up freedom*" to the fascists who "make their brazen offer" across Europe—thus holding out the utopian hope that unity and freedom might one day be fully achieved together—the sonnets themselves often imply that by the late 1930s Auden was at least beginning to regard the two as mutually exclusive, and to suspect that our tragically fruitless *desire* for unity might in fact be the only thing that ever unites us.

Notes

1. All citations of poems in this chapter are of the versions printed in *The English Auden*.
2. For further geographical detail, see John Fuller, *W. H. Auden: A Commentary*, p. 9. The quotation "Great Good Place" comes from a letter to Geoffrey Grigson, quoted in Richard Davenport-Hines, *Auden*, p. 236.
3. Many readers who have encountered the Berlin Journal only as excerpted in Edward Mendelson's edited volume *The English Auden* are likely unaware of the full extent to which Auden used his diary to respond directly to Freud. In my own examination of the journal manuscript in the New York Public Library's Berg Collection, I found for example that the comment about "the real 'life-wish'" actually appears under the heading *Beyond the Pleasure Principle*. *The Ego and the Id* also serves as a heading in the journal. These headings are not reproduced in *The English Auden*'s selections. See *The English Auden*, pp. 297–301.
4. Both Fuller and Mendelson mention in passing the class divide that separates the poem's speaker figure from those he regards, but they do not shape their readings in any significant way around this observation. See Fuller pp. 9–10, Mendelson, *Early*, p. 34.
5. The comment about his younger self "who might well, in a year or two, become a Nazi" comes from the preface to the third edition of *The Orators*, published in 1967, and is quoted in Stan Smith, *W. H. Auden*, p. 55.
6. In support of Fuller's interpretation of the image of the ring, note Heard's description of the early Christian Agape:

    It began with a real meal. Food, as the nucleus of the group, is therefore retained. After the feast there was singing. Rhythm is added, as we have seen it was added to the food interest in the building up of religion. The Primitive Church in its dynamic rite is recapitulating the history of religion's evolution. The small group of about a dozen leant over the cushion of the pulvinus, or sigma, and so formed an inward-looking group—perhaps a ring. (213)

7. Auden's distinction between escape art and parable art resonates with one of the key distinctions of utopian theory, which in Levitas takes the form of a kind of continuum, along which might be plotted the compensatory, critical, and finally transformative functions of utopia. See *The Concept of Utopia*, esp. Ch. 8 "Future Perfect: Retheorizing Utopia."
8. On the subject of "love" as a panacea for the early Auden, Lucy McDiarmid comments that "one word for the spiritual richness that the poems cannot reach is 'love': this was the great unmentioned in the early essay 'Writing,' which traced the 'urge to write' to the 'sense of personal loneliness'" (39). In his seminal essay "Freud to Paul: The Stages of Auden's Ideology," Randall Jarrell provides a memorable summary of Auden's politicized attitude to love in this period: "Love is a place we stop at when we should go on, a power or insight we bury selfishly or uselessly, instead of using in the social situation. It *should* be sublimated in social service. Eros is—at least potentially—a

secular humanitarian Agape" (447). See also my own essay "Love and Other Gods: Personification and Volition in Auden."

9 For a particularly torturous (and unfortunately influential) attempt to downplay the political content of both essays, see Samuel Hynes, *The Auden Generation*, pp. 166–9. Hynes's book is valuable in many ways, but his insistence on transposing the later Christian Auden backward onto the early secular one seems, more than anything, an attempt to de-emphasize and trivialize Auden's actual socialist sympathies because the critic himself finds them distasteful. Granted, the poet himself encouraged this revisionism, but this academic form of what really amounts to red-baiting has marred much otherwise very fine scholarship.

10 See, for example, Yeats's essay "Ireland and the Arts" (1901): "I would have Ireland recreate the ancient arts … as they were understood when they moved a whole people and not a few people who have grown up in a leisured class and made this understanding their business" (*Early Essays* 152). Or "The Galway Plains" (1903), where he simply asks: "Does not the greatest poetry always require a people to listen to it?" (158).

11 In his *Marxism and Literary Criticism*, Terry Eagleton posits a fundamental contradictoriness in Caudwell's view of art, disparaging him for being "unable to discover any more dialectical theory of art's relation to reality than an efficient channelling of social energies on one hand, and a utopian dreaming on the other" (55). One might respond that the two are in fact dialectically related, according to the standard Marxist reading of history. For if capitalism produces in the proletariat the agents of its own overthrow, then the presence of a utopian impetus in art might emerge out of the artist's marginalization (and indeed proletarianization) by the bourgeois order. This applies especially well to poetry, among the most marginal of the arts. In other words, poetry embodies *both* the ideology of the dominant order *and*, because its forced marginality allies it with the proletariat against that order, the utopian drive beyond it. The problem remains of whether one can reasonably assert such commonality between poet (no matter how marginal) and proletariat, but nonetheless Caudwell's conception remains more thoroughly dialectical than Eagleton gives it credit for.

12 Letter ("I am a bourgeois") quoted in Davenport-Hines, p. 157, Mendelson, *Early*, p. 19, and Adrian Caesar, *Dividing Lines*, p. 53. For convincing (if somewhat prickly) refutations of Auden's status as an authentic leftist, see Caesar's chapter "Auden and the Audenesque," pp. 41–66, and Eagleton's essay "First-Class Fellow-Travelling: The Poetry of W. H. Auden."

Chapter 4

"THE UNGARNISHED OFFENDED GAP": UTOPIA AND NEGATIVE POETICS IN LATER AUDEN

After the 1930s, Auden's work becomes markedly less political; with his return to the Anglican communion in the early 1940s, the thirst for unity that characterized the first decade of his work becomes reoriented more and more toward personal union with the divine. Though he is no less concerned with making the world a better place, his conception of "world" becomes more circumscribed, less broadly social and more strictly salvational. The only notion of human unity that survives in his work of this period is rooted in his conviction of our mutual fallenness, and of our shared erroneous tendency to behave as though our existences are self-authorizing when in fact they depend entirely on divine caprice—what he called in a 1940 poem the "grace of the Absurd." In this Christianized paradigm, the secular ideal of utopia is largely supplanted by dreamlike visions of a heavenly afterlife or a prelapsarian Eden. But curiously (and as with the later Yeats), it is in this period of having repudiated his earlier utopian longing for widespread human reconciliation—and his hope that poetry might help effect such a unity—that the word "utopia" begins to appear in Auden's work. As expected, many of his uses occur in a pejorative context, with Auden joining the strong current of anti-utopian thinkers in the twentieth century who disdain the concept as inevitably fostering totalitarianism. But as we will see, he also uses the word in relation to poetry's thrust toward formal and thematic integrity, to theorize his intuition that poetry can analogize the state of wholeness that—whether in his early secular politicized stage or his later salvationary Christianized one—is never absent from his aspirations. This chapter examines Auden's ambivalent treatment of the concept of utopia from the time of his move to the United States in 1939 until the mid-1950s—a period during which the concept plays a crucial role in his formulation of what I am calling a *negative poetics*: a sense that rather than directly aid in the reconciliation of humanity (as his earlier writings maintained), poetry analogizes such a state of unity, thereby serving to illuminate how achingly distant from it we always remain.

Poems as Utopias

In an essay composed in the early 1950s entitled "The Virgin and the Dynamo," Auden comments on the relationship between poetic forms and social formations:

> Every poem ... is an attempt to present an analogy to that paradisal state in which Freedom and Law, System and Order are united in harmony. Every good poem is very nearly a Utopia. Again, an analogy, not an imitation; the harmony is possible and verbal only. (*Dyer's* 71)[1]

Auden's insistence upon the purely analogical relationship between poem and utopia presents an implicit response to the Romantic stance epitomized by Shelley's *Defence of Poetry*, which exalts poetry as actually exerting a patterning or even directly causal influence over social formations. Though this exaltation is most notoriously embodied in his characterization of poets as "the unacknowledged legislators of the World" (508)—a phrase that Auden ridiculed as "describ[ing] the secret police, not poets" (*Dyer's* 27)— Shelley asserts poetry's foundational role more directly elsewhere in the *Defence*, in claiming for example that "a poem is the very image of life expressed in its eternal truth," and that poets are "the institutors of laws, the founders of civil society, and the inventors of the arts of life" (482). For Shelley, the relationship between poetry and utopia transcends both the analogical one Auden allows for and the imitative one he refutes; in the Shelleyan schema, poetry so utterly embodies the drive toward utopia that the two words edge toward synonymity.

Auden regarded this vision of poetry promulgated by Shelley and his early twentieth-century inheritors (especially Yeats) as not only delusional but dangerous, albeit for ever-changing reasons over the course of his career. Throughout the 1930s he works to refute it on the basis that it seems to justify the production of propaganda, thus threatening poetry's integrity as itself. As I discussed in Chapter 3, his 1935 introduction to the anthology *The Poet's Tongue* finds Auden characterizing poetry's proper approach as "parabolic," and claiming that "poetry is not concerned with telling people what to do, but with extending our knowledge of good and evil ... only leading us to the point where it is possible for us to make a rational and moral choice." In other words, poetry helps prepare us for the moment of choice without ever telling us what to choose. Three years later, in the introduction to another anthology entitled *Poems of Freedom*, Auden downscales even this relatively modest vision of poetry's social role, claiming rather vaguely that "the primary function of poetry, as of all the arts, is to make us more aware of ourselves and the world around us," and adding, "I do not know if such increased awareness makes us more moral or more efficient: I hope not" (*English* 371). While thus rescinding his previous claim for poetry's positive contribution to our moral progress, he does go on to accord it at least a preventative role: "I think it makes us more human, and I am quite certain it makes us more difficult to deceive, which is why, perhaps, all totalitarian theories of the State, from Plato's downwards, have deeply mistrusted the arts" (*English* 371–2). From "extending our knowledge of good and evil" to "mak[ing] us more difficult to deceive" may not seem a drastic transition, but in shifting from the language of active improvement to that of *reactive* protection, Auden displays a growing unwillingness to attribute to poetry any measurable effects upon the social and moral realms.

This unwillingness arises not only from poetry's limitations, however, but also from the instability of society and morality themselves. In his contribution to the 1939 anthology *I Believe: The Personal Philosophies of Certain Eminent Men and Women of Our Time*, Auden claims that:

> No society can be absolutely good. Utopias, ... because they are static, only portray states of natural evil or good. ... People committing acts in obedience to law or habit are not being moral. As voluntary action always turns, with repetition, into habit, morality is only possible in a world which is constantly changing and presenting a fresh series of choices. No society is absolutely good; but some are better than others. (*English* 375)

In this passage, the earliest occurrence of the word "utopia" in Auden's body of work, he implies that the realized utopia, at least the sort in which absolute goodness stands as an achieved fact, must by necessity be amoral—having voided goodness of its moral standing by transfiguring it into obedience. By the same token, if poetry were to make us "more moral," it would contribute to this habituation of goodness, because morality is actualized only at the moment of choice, and is not otherwise measurable. Taken together with Auden's earlier allusion to Plato's *Republic*—often discussed as among the earliest utopian texts—this warning against the statical aspirations of utopian thought serves to highlight one of the deceptions to which poetry might make us less susceptible: the notion that a perfect society is achievable or even desirable. Absolutist utopians like Plato would do away with poetry not only because it fails to measurably contribute to our social or moral advancement, but also because it works to affirm that such advancement can at best be intermittent and may always be vitiated or regressed by bad future choices.

Yeats and the Happening of Poetry

This alertness to contingency lies behind what has become Auden's most-quoted line (and indeed one of the most quoted lines in modern poetry), from the 1939 elegy "In Memory of W. B. Yeats": "poetry makes nothing happen." Against the colloquial tendency to engage with the line as a maxim shorn of its surrounding context (both within the poem and within Auden's career) and to treat it as his culminating statement on poetry's real-world efficacy, I would venture that it simply marks another phase in his struggle to shun the megalomaniacal tendencies of Shelleyan poetics while still preserving a crucial role for poetry in the pursuit of the Good Place. It is of course no accident that Auden should choose to offer such a stark repudiation of poetry's causal force in an elegy for Yeats, Shelley's most prominent modern inheritor—and this speaks in favor of reading the line literally, with all its aphoristic firmness. On the other hand, if read as "poetry makes *nothing* happen"—as in, it opens up a space in which inaction and non-occurrence take precedence—then the line offers another way of conceptualizing the space of possibility that lends our active choices consequence. The remainder of the stanza supports such a reading:

> For poetry makes nothing happen: it survives
> In the valley of its saying where executives
> Would never want to tamper; it flows south
> From ranches of isolation and the busy griefs,
> Raw towns that we believe and die in; it survives,
> A way of happening, a mouth. (*Collected* 246, lines 36–41)

Poetry's topographical distance from "executives"—linked to both the mortal act of execution and, in their deeper etymology, to *following through*—marks the poetic realm as a haven of inconsequence. Cradled down away from the urgent world of isolation, grief, belief, and death, poetry persists as a kind of anti-occurrence, "A way of happening, a mouth." Stan Smith points to the way this "strange, dehumanizing metonymy," embodied but not tied to any subjectivity, highlights the paradox of poetry's "double historicity," its status as both historical product and free-floating discursive utterance that reenters history upon being read, with "the moment of the reader quite distinct from that of the originating author" (4). Reading the Yeats elegy alongside the much later essay I cited at the outset of this chapter—"The Virgin and the Dynamo," with its claim that "every good poem is very nearly a Utopia"—Smith points to how poetry "reconciles the historical anxiety of its genesis with the utopian bliss of its reading." In Smith's view, then, poems are near-utopias in the way they insulate us from the historical circumstances that occasion their composition, offering us the assurance that—and here he cites one of the later Auden's key statements of belief—"the historical world is a redeemable world" (71).[2] In existing not as a causal force, but rather as an endlessly repeatable event-in-itself whose readerly impact may vary each time it reenters history, a poem embodies a temporal space between the static and the kinetic, a no-place of possibility that is paradisal in its simultaneous insulation from and engagement with the vicissitudes of history.

Beyond just its second section, the overall structure of "In Memory of W. B. Yeats" supports such a dialectical reading. When Auden first published the poem in *The New Republic* of March 8, 1939, it consisted only of its first and third sections; the second had not yet been written. Critics have often taken this original version as setting out two starkly contrasting views of poetry's real-world impact—in Mendelson's terms, the first section "acknowledges that the most a poet can achieve in the world is to be acknowledged by his admirers," while the closing section "celebrates poetic language as a force more powerful than time or death" (*Later* 3)—and this standard reading does ring true to a certain extent. In terms of the first section, such interpretations hinge on the lack of objective impact the poet's death has on the world around him; contrary to elegiac convention, for example, his loss does not resonate through the natural world—a fact ironically embodied in the refrain "O all the instruments agree / The day of this death was a dark cold day" (30–1). Furthermore, that Yeats's death means nothing to his actual written works ("The death of the poet was kept from his poems" (11)) implies that as a poet, his identity resides in his poems rather than his person, so that "he became his admirers" in the sense that, just as poems are revitalized with each new reading, so lives the figure of "Yeats" in each of his readers' guises. But if, as the section's climax proclaims, "The words of a dead man / Are modified in the guts of the living" (22–3), then this is just as much an assertion of poetry's power as the poet's powerlessness. Implicit throughout this entire first section is the point made more boldly in the later-added second: poetry, as distinct from the poet himself, *survives*. It may be "modified in the guts of the living," but this says nothing about its real-world importance or impotence because we are not told what it does once it gets to those guts—which for all we know may be very great things indeed.

The first section thus presents less a stark contrast to the final one than a sober prelude, taking objective stock of Yeats's death while acknowledging his poems as an enduring presence in the world, rumbling with potential. So while the exaltation of the final section no doubt represents a marked shift—effected in large part by Auden's adoption of the same trochaic tetrameter catalectic line Yeats employed for his own self-elegy in "Under Ben Bulben"—it should strike us less as a refutation of the first section's sobriety than as its logical next step, elevating its somber refrain into a fuller-throated lamentation. Beginning with an elemental apostrophe ("Earth, receive an honoured guest; / William Yeats is laid to rest"), the section eventually shifts to address the poet himself, ending with a series of hopeful exhortations:

> Follow, poet, follow right
> To the bottom of the night,
> With your unconstraining voice
> Still persuade us to rejoice;
>
> With the farming of a verse
> Make a vineyard of the curse,
> Sing of human unsuccess
> In a rapture of distress;
>
> In the deserts of the heart
> Let the healing fountain start,
> In the prison of his days
> Teach the free man how to praise. (54–65)

The shift in apostrophic addressee from "Earth" to "poet" is accompanied by a concomitant shift from the personal to the archetypal: whereas the section started in singling Yeats out by name, he is now subsumed into his role. At the same time, however—and especially within the final three-part structure of the poem—this entails a degree of humanization: whereas the first section emphasized the *poems* "modified in the guts of the living," and the second section declared that "*poetry* makes nothing happen," in this section the weight falls on the figure of *the poet* and his "unconstraining voice." This trajectory, from poems to poetry to poet, means that Auden's tribute closes in a much more conventional elegiac mode than it began, moving from the specific to the general and finally to the archetypal, and thus vaguely spiritualizing Yeats in the process.[3] Furthermore, these two trajectories are accompanied by a third, from *words* to *mouth* to *voice*. While on one level the poem abstracts ever further from the death of Yeats the man—moving from "The day of his death" in section one, to the trials of his life in "mad Ireland" in section two, before finally leading his shadow self "To the bottom of the night" in section three—on another level it brings us ever closer to him, first showing us his inert words, then his disembodied mouth, and then at last allowing us to hear his voice (indeed almost literally, as by the end of the poem Auden has not only adopted a classic Yeatsian meter, but is also practically ventriloquizing Yeats's early stance on poetry's ability to uplift and transfigure, to "Make a vineyard of the curse").

Of course, this ending cannot be taken to summarize Auden's actual views on poetry's effectiveness any more than "poetry makes nothing happen" can. But while the subsequent insertion of this latter maxim and the second section that contains it no doubt serve to undermine somewhat the hopeful imperatives of section three—marking them as perhaps a temporary and insincere capitulation to Yeatsian notions of poetry as panacea, for tributary purposes only—the fact is that here, in the landmark first poem Auden wrote after moving to the United States, he chose to let such affirmations resound. The previous year he had mildly characterized poetry as "mak[ing] us more aware of ourselves and the world around us," but "In Memory of W. B. Yeats" finds him both revoking even that modest agential force and attributing to poetry a much more active, healing role. In its three-section movement from the objective present, to the subjectivized historical past, to the only glimmeringly hypothetical future, the poem at once affirms poetry's causal powerlessness and displays its capacity to lend shape and coherence to hopeful possibilities—and thus to redefine causality for us. This capacity is reflected structurally as well, as the poem begins in free verse, becomes a pseudo-sonnet in section two, and finally ends in resolute elegiac quatrains that formally testify to the poet's ability to defy (and beautify) our mortal dissolution, thus making a happening of nothingness despite its explicit protestations to the contrary.

The difficulty of determining exactly what Auden believes poetry can do in this period of his move to the United States is only compounded by an essay he published in *Partisan Review* soon after writing the original two-section version of the elegy, "The Public v. the Late Mr. William Butler Yeats." The essay sets out a pair of dissenting statements, the first from The Public Prosecutor and the second from The Counsel for the Defence, to debate Yeats's status as "a great poet" (*Prose II* 3). The Prosecutor claims that such greatness hinges not only on the memorability of a poet's language, but also on his having "a profound understanding of the age in which he lived," and "a working knowledge of and sympathetic attitude towards the most progressive thought of his time" (3). According to these criteria, claims the Prosecutor, Yeats is disqualified from greatness due to his "feudal mentality" in political matters, and his lifelong devotion to "irrational superstition," from his early belief in "fairies" to his later turn to "the mumbo-jumbo of magic and the nonsense of India" (4–5). The Prosecutor even challenges Yeats on the level of linguistic mastery, pointedly asking "How many of his lines can you remember?" and holding up his editorship of *The Oxford Book of Modern Verse*—which he calls "the most deplorable volume ever issued under the imprint of that highly respected firm which has done so much for the cause of poetry in this country, the Clarendon Press"—as evidence of the poet's general bad taste (3).

The Defence directs the first portion of his counterstatement at the Prosecutor's critique of Yeats's political and spiritual beliefs, which rests on the assumption that poetry is little more than "the filling up of a social quiz; to pass with honours the poet must not score less than 75%"—an assumption the Defence dismisses as "utter nonsense" (5). But it is in his response to the other aspect of the Prosecutor's critique—that relating to Yeats's language and its memorability—that the essay dialogues most directly with the elegy and its concern with poetry's real-world impact. The Defence cautions that he is "not trying to suggest that art exists independently of society" and affirms that "the relation between the two is just as intimate and important as the prosecution asserts" (6)—but the two sides differ greatly in the way they conceive the *nature* of this relation. "Poetic talent," claims the Defence, "is the power to make personal excitement socially available" (6). Great poets are thus those who (a) react more strongly to the world than the average person; and (b) are able to vividly communicate this reactive strength—and "the nature of the reaction, whether it be positive or negative, morally admirable or morally disgraceful, matters very little; what is essential is that the reaction should genuinely exist" (6). The Defence goes on to justify Yeats's nationalism by calling it "a necessary stage toward socialism," and points to his co-establishment of the Abbey Theatre as a "useful form of social action" (7). He even defends the early fairies and later "doctrine of Anima Mundi" as "attempt[s] to find through folk tradition a binding force for society," noting of Yeats's poems overall that "from first to last they express a sustained protest against the social atomisation caused by industrialism, and both in their ideas and their language a constant struggle to overcome it" (7).[4] Auden's Defence thus sets out poetry as capable of lending meaningful expression to social alternatives, if not itself effecting these alternatives. The essay's closing paragraphs further nuance this distinction:

> For art is a product of history, not a cause. Unlike some other products, technical inventions for example, it does not re-enter history as an effective agent, so that the question whether art should or should not be propaganda is unreal. The case for the prosecution rests on the fallacious belief that art ever makes anything happen, whereas the honest truth, gentlemen, is that, if not a poem had been written, not a picture painted, not a bar of music composed, the history of man would be materially unchanged.

But there is one field in which the poet is a man of action, the field of language, and it is precisely in this that the greatness of the deceased is most obviously shown. However false or undemocratic his ideas, his diction shows a continuous evolution toward what one might call the true democratic style. The social virtues of a real democracy are brotherhood and intelligence, and the parallel linguistic virtues are strength and clarity, virtues which appear ever more clearly through successive volumes by the deceased.

The diction of *The Winding Stair* is the diction of a just man, and it is for this reason that just men will always recognise the author as a master. (7)

The first of these paragraphs stands as Auden's most extreme statement of the doctrine that poetry makes nothing happen, with the sheer exaggerated falseness of the claim that in the absence of art "the history of man would be materially unchanged" serving to remind us of the essay's dialogic structure, and to implicitly caution us against assuming (as many critics have done) that just because the Defence is granted the final word, he must transparently represent Auden's actual position.[5] A less overtly doctrinal view of the relationship between poetry and the social realm comes in his characterization of Yeats's "true democratic style." While on the one hand the phrase is simply a figurative way of praising the virtues of "strength and clarity" in Yeats's mature diction, on the other it embodies Auden's belief—displayed again over a decade later in his claim that "every good poem is very nearly a Utopia"—that political values can be analogically embodied in poetic elements. Again, an unmistakable whiff of falseness taints the claim that despite Yeats's beliefs being "undemocratic" (a word synonymous for the Auden of this period with "unjust"), his diction nonetheless marks him as a just man—and this discrepancy once again points to the essay's formal ambivalence, hinting that Auden's actual position lies in a synthesis of those of the Prosecution and Defence.[6] In order to retrieve this position, then, we must be skeptical of poetry's ability to exert any influence upon the social realm, while also remaining open-minded about its ability to analogically embody more ideal—for example, true democracy, utopia—sociopolitical arrangements.

Poems as Verbal Societies

But, as Auden repeatedly cautions throughout his career, this embodiment can be verbal only. To shift forward once again to the early 1950s, and "The Virgin and the Dynamo": in the final paragraph he underlines the potentially evil effect of poetry's inner harmony, which might lead us to believe that "since all is well in the work of art, all is well in history. But all is not well there" (*Dyer's* 71). Poetry does not urge us to dwell in the possible to the neglect of the actual; as what Auden calls a "verbal society," a poem presents a model of a "natural organism," a "pseudo-person" in which "meaning and being are identical" (67–8). As such, it embodies by analogy the possibility that "the unfreedom and disorder of the past can be reconciled in the future" (70); it embodies—but *by analogy only*—"the possibility of regaining paradise" (71). This string of co-analogies and qualifications serves both to clarify and to muddy what Auden means by "every good poem is very nearly a Utopia," and as Lucy McDiarmid points out, this is likely intentional: "The proximity is teasing," she writes, "it establishes, or rather reaffirms, the border between ... literary textuality and extraliterary value" (19). Elsewhere, Auden did worry that his linkage of poetry and paradise might be taken to too literally espouse an excessively organizational definition of utopia:

> A society which was really like a good poem, embodying the aesthetic virtues of beauty, order, economy and subordination of detail to the whole, would be a nightmare of horror for, given the historical reality of actual men, such a society could only come into being through selective breeding, extermination of the physically and mentally unfit, absolute obedience to its Director, and a large slave class kept out of sight in cellars. (85)

Clearly Auden wishes to militate against the notion that poetry's analogical relationship to utopia is purely or even primarily formal; this would issue, as the passage illustrates, in an archetypally dystopian model of society. At the same time, however, the poetry/utopia analogy still does reflect meaningfully upon how we might reorder and improve our societies. As I have argued, in claiming that poetry both "makes us more difficult to deceive" and "makes nothing happen," Auden points to how poetry foregrounds the contingency of the social order while opening up a space of as-yet unfilled possibility into which alternate contingent arrangements can be safely dreamed. And yet, poetry's role is not primarily escapist or compensatory: as he claims in another essay of the early 1950s entitled simply "Writing": "Poetry is not magic. In so far as poetry, or any other of the arts, can be said to have an ulterior purpose, it is, by telling the truth, to disenchant and disintoxicate" (27). In other words, to un-sing and un-poison: to coax us free of our immersive complacency, reminding us—through its "reconciling [of] contradictory feelings in an order of mutual propriety" (71)—how far from paradise we still are.

I have phased back and forth between the late 1930s and the early 1950s in order to highlight several crucial shifts in Auden's attitude toward both utopia and, concomitantly, poetry's potential real-world effectiveness in the decade and a half after his move to the United States. First, between the initial occurrence of the word "utopia" in his *I Believe* essay of 1939 and his final sustained engagement with the concept in the early 1950s—both in the essays I have been citing and his poetic sequence "Horae Canonicae," to be discussed at the end of this chapter—Auden's treatment of "utopia" moves from one of total disdain for its impossibility and its totalitarian implications to a more moderate position, which (while still suspicious of these faults) sees the concept of utopia as a useful one through which to analogize both a poem's formal organization as a "verbal society" and the way this organization reflects upon our existing societies, illuminating the distance between the actual and what is ideally possible.[7] This relates very closely to the second shift I wish to emphasize: in the decade and a half after

1939, Auden's statements on poetry's relevance to the sociopolitical realm work to problematize any straightforward interpretation of "poetry makes nothing happen," urging us to read this assertion as not only a dismissal or repudiation of poetry's causal efficacy (in which case it would be more appropriately phrased "poetry doesn't make anything happen") but also as an affirmation of poetry's ability to open up a no-place of possibility—to make "nothing" a thing that happens. Throughout the rest of this chapter, I will argue that throughout the 1940s Auden sets forth (often tacitly, but sometimes quite explicitly) a *negative poetics*, whereby poetry's utopian function consists precisely in its analogization, whether formally or thematically, of the more ideal states of existence from which we forever remain so far.

"Atlantis" as No-Place of Hope and Salvation

This distance is explicitly thematized in Auden's 1941 poem "Atlantis," which begins by highlighting the futility of any attempt to actually reach utopia:

> Being set on the idea
>   Of getting to Atlantis,
> You have discovered of course
>   Only the Ship of Fools is
> Making the voyage this year (*Selected* 125, lines 1–5)[8]

Of the seven 12-line stanzas that comprise the poem, the speaker devotes each of the first six to detailing one of the imperfect places the addressed "You" may land along their quest. In each case, the speaker instructs the quester to fully imbibe the place's imperfection: in Ionia, for example, whose "witty scholars ... have proved there cannot be / Such a place as Atlantis," the quester must:

>   Learn their logic, but notice
> How its subtlety betrays
>   Their simple enormous grief;
> Thus they shall teach you the ways
>   To doubt that you may believe. (20–4)

The void left when one subscribes solely to logic—the scholars' "simple enormous grief"—might be described as spiritual, in keeping with Auden's ongoing process of return to the Anglican communion at the time; but it might also (and more in keeping with the explicitly utopian character of the poem) be conceptualized as the absence of the possible. Observing the Ionians' absolute abidance by the actual illuminates for the quester what is missing behind their erudition, their utter dearth of the purposive futurity Atlantis symbolizes. The doubt learned from them thus leads the quester—and by second-person implication, the reader—ever more firmly onward.

Each stop along the quester's way fulfills a similar negative function. When we reach Thrace, "that stony savage shore," the speaker tells us to:

> Strip off your clothes and dance, for
> Unless you are capable
> Of forgetting completely
> About Atlantis, you will
> Never finish your journey. (32–6)

The speaker similarly instructs us, while in "gay / Carthage or Corinth" to "take part / In their endless gaiety," for:

>   unless
> You become acquainted now
> With each refuge that tries to
> Counterfeit Atlantis, how
> Will you recognize the true? (44–8)

Like the God of the *via negativa* to which Auden variously alluded throughout the subsequent decades, Atlantis thus emerges as an entity without positive qualities, a no-place taking its outline from our growing knowledge of what it is not.[9] In fact, the entire poem hinges on the tension between the quester's inferred desire to arrive at Atlantis, to capture an image of it for themselves, and the speaker's determination that Atlantis should remain tantalizingly imageless. "Atlantis" thus embodies the dichotomy identified by Jacoby between "blueprint" utopianism—which demands utopia's visualization—and an alternative "iconoclastic" utopianism, which emerges out of the Old Testament prohibition on graven images, and according to which "the refusal to describe God transmutes into the refusal to describe utopia, which can only be depicted in negative terms" (35).[10]

One might see "Atlantis" as effecting the inverse movement, as the poem shifts gradually away from its Greco-mythological context to become a recognizably Christian quest, and the refusal to describe Atlantis transmutes into the refusal to name God. The penultimate stanza begins with the speaker issuing the imperative to "Stagger onward rejoicing" (61), a phrase that hints at the poem's Christianization, as the command "Rejoice" resonates loudly in the very next poem Auden wrote, the epithalamion "In Sickness and in Health"—an examination of marriage's "round O of faithfulness" from an explicitly Christian perspective. Here he uses the word to prepare the quester for failure, and to encourage glorying in it: if nearing the end of our journey we should "collapse / With all Atlantis shining / below" (64–6), we should not despair but rather:

>   still be proud
> Even to have been allowed
> Just to peep at Atlantis
> In a poetic vision:

> Give thanks and lie down in peace,
>   Having seen your salvation. (67–72)

The introduction of the concept of "salvation" shifts the poem's *telos* from one of harmonious social existence in this life—for Atlantis is an earthly kingdom counterfeited by those less-perfect societies the quester visits along the way—to one of individual deliverance from sin and admission to the next life. God's presence can be inferred by the fact of our having "been allowed" to glimpse Atlantis, implying that the success or failure of our quest will have depended solely upon His grace. This sense of paradise deferred is compounded by the fact that salvation can only be "seen" rather than strictly arrived at, a further indication that the prospect of this-worldly bliss upon which the poem initially hinges has by this late stage been largely subsumed into the promise of afterlife. Whether we conceive of this as the poem's shedding of its utopianism or as its shifting from one utopian mode to another will depend on exactly how we define *utopia*, and how strictly secularism figures in our definition. This much is certain, however; in transforming from a secular pagan to an explicitly religious poem, "Atlantis" both illuminates the connection between iconoclastic utopianism and negative theology gestured to by Jacoby and highlights the two different modes of futurity these two ways of thinking embody: while the former sees the gap between our actual societies and any possible more harmonious future society as at least theoretically closeable through human intervention in this world, the latter sees this gap as a function of the unnameable divine.

The poem's last stanza effects not just this philosophical or theological shift, but a narrative one as well, as it makes clear that the poem up until this point has abided in the realm of the hypothetical, and that the quester's journey has not yet actually begun:

> All the little household gods
>   Have started crying, but say
> Good-bye now, and put to sea.
>   Farewell, my dear, farewell: may
> Hermes, master of the roads,
> And the four dwarf Kabiri,
>   Protect and serve you always;
>   And may the Ancient of Days
> Provide for all you must do
>   His invisible guidance,
> Lifting up, dear, upon you
>   The light of His countenance. (73–84)

This coda serves as a kind of prayer, calling upon the relevant entities to protect a quester suddenly addressed as "my dear"—a move that simultaneously distances the "you" from the reader and brings them into a more intimate relation with the speaker—as they set out on what we now see as an allegorical life's journey toward salvation. The "household gods" further suggest some domestic relation between speaker and quester, while also nodding to the pagan context in which the poem began. Indeed, the appeal to "Hermes" and the "four dwarf Kabiri"—who John Fuller tells us "are thought to be Phrygian deities who protected sailors and promoted fertility," though they are not traditionally dwarves (391)—affirms this sense of the speaker inhabiting a polytheistic world, with a presiding god for every eventuality. But just as the previous stanza ended with the resonantly Christian concept of "salvation," this one invokes "the Ancient of Days"—a name for God that appears three times in the book of Daniel (and serves as the title for one of William Blake's most well-known etchings)—before ending on the unmistakably hymnal "The light of His countenance." This closing image resonates with the previous stanza's "Atlantis shining"—even spatially, as Atlantis is "Below" while God is "Lifting up" His light. I have already discussed the convergence and slippage between utopian and theological discourse to which this resonance points, but it is worth focusing more closely on how the vague imaging of luminescence in both instances serves to displace any more concretely visual description of the phenomena in question. Neither Atlantis nor God is attributed any positive qualities beyond light; nothing about them is presented for our contemplation, and so they are left as functions of desire—one for social utopia, the other for personal salvation. The poem's shift from one desire to the other can thus be interpreted in several (by no means exclusive) ways. On the one hand, "Atlantis" can be read as almost Christian propaganda, reflecting the increasingly devout Auden's claim, in an essay of just a few months earlier, that "without an adequate and conscious metaphysics in the background, art's imitation of life inevitably becomes, either a photostatic copy of the accidental details of life without pattern or significance, or a personal allegory of the artist's individual dementia" (*Prose II* 87). According to this reading, the poem stands as a metaphysical refutation of the utopian impulse as a chimera, an assertion that the only paradise to be found inheres in one's individual communion with God—and that the gap of desire that leads us to seek out more perfect societies is simply a measure of His present absence in our lives. This interpretation is borne out not only by the shift from a utopian to a theological emphasis, but narratively, in the shift from an addressed "you" that includes the poem's readership to a "my dear" that seems designed to exclude us, to cast us back out upon our own salvationary roads.

This repudiation of social unity in favor of our isolated status as fallen individuals before God is supported by statements Auden made the next year, in the second of a series of Kierkegaardian "Lecture Notes" published in *Commonweal* under the pseudonym "Didymus," on the poet's relation to his audience. Here he claims that the poet's purpose is not "to arouse or communicate emotions" but rather "to find out what his feelings really are, and, of course, most of these will be neither pleasant nor good" (*Prose II* 167). He then goes on to cast this exercise in self-discovery as potentially containing the seed of a wider—though precarious—solidarity, claiming of the poet that:

He sings alone before God, but he may be overheard by other men and what they hear may cause them, one by one, to undergo a similar process of discovery. If the result is to make them feel in unity with each other, it is not because they are all filled with the same emotion, but because they share the same knowledge of weakness, and dare not therefore judge each other. (167)

This represents a drastic shift from the claim he made just three years earlier, that poetry "makes us more difficult to deceive"—much less his more ambitious assertion in the mid-1930s that it is concerned with "extending our knowledge of good and evil." In both these statements, poetry's effects are unambiguously registered in the first-person plural ("makes *us*," "extending *our* knowledge"), whereas here in 1942, Auden casts any sense of unity that poetry might foster as almost incidental, the result of a chain reaction of solitary self-discoveries, leading a series of individuals to realize that they "share the same knowledge of weakness." Reading "Atlantis" alongside this view of poetry as at most working to illuminate our mutual fallenness only further suggests a reading of the poem as a repudiation of socially oriented utopian goals in favor of personal salvation.

Concurrent with this interpretation, however—with its emphasis on the contrast between secular utopia and divine salvation as goals of a quest—one might just as readily emphasize their shared liberatory ends. I have already highlighted the negativity in which both Atlantis and God are cloaked, and how neither is granted positive qualities for the reader's contemplation. In light of this fact, one can see "Atlantis" as enacting an implicit critique of the "bourgeois-classical aesthetics" of "contemplative appeasement" cast by Bloch (in volume two of his monumental *The Principle of Hope*) as the dominant mode in Western thinking about art since Kant (808). According to Bloch, the realm of contemplation conjured by such an aesthetics serves to stultify the utopian impulse: "Art is always a sedative here," he writes, "not an appeal, not even a comforting song; for this too presupposes the restlessness of the will" (808). In its place Bloch longs for the ascendancy of the aesthetics of hope he sees embodied in the "wishful landscapes" that characterize what he calls "perspective art": works that, instead of impressing upon us the sense of "fully-constructedness" characteristic of the Kantian aesthetics of contemplation, rather project "an unfinished world" that draws the will beyond its glimmering horizons (808–9). Bloch does not limit his use of the word "perspective" to the visual arts, and in fact points to literature (and elsewhere in his study, poetry in particular) as able to embody the aesthetics of hope he valorizes. In typically enigmatic fashion, he claims: "The word points differently from the start when it aims very far. It is taut, has a premonition which has nowhere yet become solid and enterable" (807). Exalting language's capacity to present possibility as such without reifying it as false actuality, to embody *futurity* rather than any concrete *future*, Bloch illuminates how Jacoby's concept of iconoclastic utopianism serves as a contrast not just to the blueprinting of utopian texts in the tradition descending from More, but as a critique of the aesthetics of completion such texts embody— an aesthetics that, in striving to convey a holistic experience, betrays our crucial intuition of the world's unfinishedness.

I would argue that "Atlantis," in both its secular utopian and its Christian aspects, works to preserve this intuition, and thus displays the perspectival and even premonitory capacities of language that Bloch stresses as so vital to an unfolding aesthetics of hope. More broadly, I would also point out how the concept of an aesthetics of hope can help to further flesh out the paradoxical sense of "making nothing happen" that I am working with in this chapter, for in presencing possibility while also preserving it *as* possibility, such an aesthetics makes nothing happen in a double sense: first, it exhibits what has not yet been actualized, and second, it illuminates the gap between the actual and the possible, lighting the no-space of potential that all change requires. That Auden still ardently desires change at this point in his career is widely evident, even if the change he desires concerns less the social organism than the individual soul. Indeed, one might claim—as I did of the later Yeats in Chapter 2—that Auden shifts from seeking after the good place (in the 1930s) to the more exclusive good life (in the 1940s)—though the difference between Yeats's and Auden's visions of the good life is of course immense. For the Auden of 1942, firmly in the thrall of a Kierkegaardian existentialism, social ills are reducible to the sum of individuals who refuse to accept their own fallenness and thus behave as self-authorizing agents, dooming themselves to futility. Further on in his "Lecture Notes" as Didymus, he clearly delineates the role of art in such a fallen society: "Art cannot make a man want to become good," he writes, "but it can prevent him from imagining that he already is; it cannot give him faith in God, but it can show him his despair" (*Prose II* 167). In positing both art's limitations and its capabilities, this formulation nicely captures the essence of Auden's negative poetics in the 1940s; while admitting that art cannot *create* the will to goodness, he avers that it can open us to the emptiness that something better might fill.

The Sea and the Mirror and the Limits of Art

Auden's most concerted fleshing-out of art's revealing negativity comes in what is often cast as his greatest work of the 1940s, the long poem *The Sea and the Mirror*. Composed between 1942 and 1944, in the midst of the Second World War, and subtitled "A Commentary on Shakespeare's *The Tempest*," the poem re-inhabits the play's characters to build a labyrinthine meditation on the relation of art (the titular *Mirror*) to the world we inhabit (the *Sea*). In a letter to Theodore Spencer, Auden characterized the poem as "my Ars Poetica, in the same way I believe *The Tempest* was Shakespeare's," and added: "I am attempting, which is in a way absurd, to show, in a work of art, the limitations of art" (qtd. in Mendelson, *Later* 205; Kirsch 58). Taking as its starting point Prospero's freeing of Ariel and his relinquishing of his magical powers at the end of Shakespeare's play, the poem sets out to refute *The Tempest*'s treatment of "art" and "magic" as synonymous.[11] Unlike what we normally mean by "magic," art has no ability to actually conjure new realities, only to distort the existing ones into shapes consolatory in their privileging of form, their commitment to what Caliban calls in his long speech at the end of the poem "*a felicitous pattern*" (33; emphasis in original). Indeed, art's ability to console represents perhaps a greater danger than its being mistaken for magic, at least from the Christian perspective Auden inhabited at the time of writing *The Sea and the Mirror*: for in imaging alternate worlds more felicitously patterned than our own, it implicitly exalts the human ability to fashion such worlds for our actual lives, promoting the illusion that our existences can be self-authorizing, without need of God's grace.

In his 1942 "Lecture Notes," Auden opined: "As a writer, who is also a would-be Christian, I cannot help feeling that a satisfactory theory of Art from the standpoint of the Christian faith has yet to be worked out" (*Prose II* 163). *The Sea and the Mirror* would seem to constitute his attempt to embody such a theory in his work, as he told Ursula Niebuhr in a letter after the poem's completion that it was "really about the Christian conception of art" (qtd. in Mendelson, *Later* 205). So far, however, I have only alluded to how *The Sea and the Mirror* highlights art's potential falseness from a Christian perspective, and so the questions remain: What positive role might art fulfill within the Christian worldview? And how does the poem theorize this role? Auden provides a partial answer to the first of these questions in his 1943 essay "Purely Subjective," a long meditation on the necessity of religious faith:

> The religious function of art is the destruction of auto-idolatry, i.e. of the notion that the faith required to make a subjective decision is faith in myself. Since Art can only deal with what is manifested, it cannot say that the faith I require is a faith in God; it can only say: "Those who trust in themselves lose the power to react correctly to actual situations and are destroyed by what appear to them to be objects outside their own control." That is why art deals in the exceptional and the unexpected, in heroes and reversals of fortune. (*Prose II* 190)

This veers precariously close to a view of art as fulfilling a proselytizing function. According to this view, tragedies are cautionary tales, the falls of their protagonists object-lessons in the perils of the faithless life. More moderately, however—and more in keeping with this book's framework—art in this view can be seen as a warning against any attempt to actualize our utopian impulses in purely secular terms. As I discussed earlier, "Atlantis" performs just such a warning role, insisting that utopia is attainable only as a God-granted vision. With its long semi-dramatic form allowing for a greater semblance of plot, *The Sea and the Mirror* sets out a similar insistence more circuitously, refracting the folly of "auto-idolatry" through several different characters, each of whom separately come to understand that the products of our own creativity cannot truly ameliorate our existences, that they mostly serve as escape or consolation, realizing their metaphysical purpose only if they illuminate our distance from the divine.

The poem embarks from its very beginning on an exploration of art's limits, with the opening Preface (*The Stage Manager to the Critics*) serving less to support or promote what the audience has just witnessed—for the poem is meant to take place immediately following a performance of *The Tempest*—than to undermine its potential effectiveness. Wary of art's ability to reside in hubristic fantasy (he imagines hero and heroine "Waltzing across the tightrope / As if there were no death / And no hope of falling down") and to mesmerize its audiences into calculatedly irrational responses ("How the dear little children laugh / When the drums roll and the lovely / Lady is sawn in half"), the Stage Manager turns his attention almost immediately to actual lived experience, inferring that it proves significantly less predictable than plot-driven artifice: "O what authority / Gives existence its surprise?" (3).[12] In thus pitting the ability of divine "authority" to generate real "surprise" against the relative expectedness of the effects generated by the artist's creative magic, the Stage Manager lets God beat Prospero at his own game, subordinating art to life in casting the former as at best able to caution against the self-pride that can ruin the latter:

> Art opens the fishiest eye
> To the Flesh and the Devil who heat
> The Chamber of Temptation
> Where heroes roar and die. (3)

The odd epithet "fishiest" evokes a glazedness (Elizabeth Bishop would later memorably liken the glaze of a fish's eyes to "old scratched isinglass"), implying that even those most mesmerized by art cannot help somehow absorbing its lesson on the dangerous "Temptation" of auto-idolatry: when "heroes roar"—i.e., when they attempt to embody a sublimity beyond their human limits—they meet only an unsaved death. The stanza goes on to further refine this claim:

> We are wet with sympathy now;
> Thanks for the evening; but how
> Shall we satisfy when we meet,
> Between Shall-I and I-Will,
> The lion's mouth whose hunger
> No metaphors can fill? (3–4)

The "We" here is both the audience who weeps and the performers who bask in their tears. Both can successfully fill their roles (or "satisfy") only within the action-driven theatrical economy, a world where heroes boldly authorize their own choices and suffer or reap the consequences. But confronted with the prospect that our decisions are not entirely ours to make, but also partly God's to make for us through the precarious agency of faith, both performers and audience must fall stilly silent before the unportrayable. In other words, when confronted with the volitional paradox of active passivity inherent in the concept of grace—a dilemma beautifully captured in Augustine's cry to God to "Grant what you command, and command what you will" (202)—the theatrical economy stalls. Stealing the "roar" from the "lion's mouth" does not abate its "hunger."

The Preface closes by equating silence with the divine, praising Shakespeare for recognizing that "this world of fact we love / Is unsubstantial stuff" and affirming that:

> All the rest is silence
> On the other side of the wall;
> And the silence ripeness,
> And the ripeness all. (4)

Auden here cobbles together lines from *Hamlet* and *King Lear*, transfiguring their various meditations on mortality and the acceptance of death into an assertion of the primacy of the divine realm of silence that art cannot portray. Where "ripeness" in *Lear* connotes a readiness to die, here it gestures toward the inassimilable richness on "the other side of the wall": not the so-called fourth wall between audience and performance, but that between creatures and creator, of which the former is merely a porous travesty. Like the preface as a whole, these lines contain much of the poem's thematic thrust, with its central assertions recurring throughout the poem: in Chapter 1, for example, Prospero concedes that "I never suspected the way of truth / Was a way of silence" (11), while near the close of his Chapter 3 speech to the audience, Caliban eulogizes "that Wholly Other Life from which we are separated by an essential emphatic gulf of which our contrived fissures of mirror and proscenium arch—we understand them at last—are but feebly figurative signs" (52). Arthur Kirsch has deftly characterized this thematic thread of the poem as claiming that "art is doubly illusory, because it holds the mirror up to nature rather than the truth that passes human understanding" (58). But in keeping with my own emphasis on Auden's evolving negative poetics and its utopian implications, I would amend Kirsch's formulation to acknowledge that although *The Sea and the Mirror* does cast art as illusory, it also stresses how this very illusoriness is itself illuminating, shedding light on the distance between us and the "Wholly Other Life" we strive toward.

Caliban acknowledges this illuminating function in the snippet from his speech quoted above ("we understand them at last"), and indeed his speech itself not only *theorizes* but *enacts* this illumination, a process that I shall explore in greater detail shortly. But although Caliban's famously Jamesian sermon that comprises the whole of Chapter 3 no doubt serves as *The Sea and the Mirror*'s rhetorical climax and thematic culminating point, its take on art's capacity to light the gap between utopian desire and its fulfillment is well prepared for by the earlier sections. In Chapter 1, for instance, Prospero makes Ariel a metaphor for the force of artistic inspiration, opining of him that "from your calm eyes, / With their lucid proof of apprehension and disorder, / All we are not stares back at what we are" (6). Here Ariel—whom Auden dubs in a later essay on *The Tempest* the "spirit of imagination" (*Dyer's* 132)—symbolizes the orderly purity of art as against the "disorder" of lived experience: the word "apprehension" here draws on its etymological connotations of *laying hold of* in order to contrast the graspable placeness of "what we are" with the rarefied no-place of "All we are not." Similarly, in Chapter 2—devoted to *The*

4. Utopia and Negative Poetics in Later Auden 143

Supporting Cast (Sotto Voce)—Alonso, King of Naples, advises his son and heir Ferdinand to:

Learn from your dreams what you lack,

For as your fears are, so you must hope.
The Way of Justice is a tightrope
Where no prince is safe for one instant
Unless he trust his embarrassment,
As in his left ear the siren sings
Meltingly of water and a night
Where all flesh had peace, and on his right
The efreet offers a brilliant void
Where his mind could be perfectly clear
And all his limitations destroyed:
Many young princes soon disappear
To join all the unjust kings. (20)

Here Alonso urges Ferdinand not to seek escape from the trials of princehood into either a sensual oceana or an intellectual ivory tower, but rather to gain from his "dreams" of these places a keener sense of his own hopes and fears, so that he may more deftly walk the "tightrope" of this-worldly "Justice." The stanza break after "lack" not only emphasizes the word's denotative meaning through whitespace, but also signals that the competing visions of utopia that follow both arise from a source of incompletion in ourselves. The idea of dream realms tempting from the left and the right of this world was also used by Auden in a chart he prepared for his students at Swarthmore College in the spring of 1943, while in the midst of writing *The Sea and the Mirror*. The chart is divided into three primary columns: the middle one labeled "This World," the left representing the "Search for Salvation by finding refuge in Nature," and the right the "Search for Salvation by finding release from nature." Down the full page, Auden fleshed out these antithetical headings in rows of categories ranging from "Metaphysical Condition" to "Sin" to "Political Slogan" to typify the denizens of each realm (the seekers of refuge in nature, for example, are given to the sin of sensuality, while their counterparts who seek release from nature are most susceptible to pride). Auden would later label these two categories of people "Arcadian" and "Utopian," and his characterization of the two realms in Alonso's speech certainly prefigures this distinction: to Ferdinand's left "all flesh *had* peace," while to his right "his mind *could be* perfectly clear"—a difference in tenses that accords with Auden's later conception of the Arcadian as yearning backward for Eden while the Utopian forges ahead to the New Jerusalem. Put simply, Alonso is advising Ferdinand to avoid both Arcadian and Utopian longing, while learning from the temptations with which each presents him (his "dreams" of past solace or future reconciliation) how better to abide in the temporal present.

In a sense, Alonso's counsel stands as a secularized microcosm of the argument finally set forth by Caliban in his Chapter 3 speech. While Alonso focuses on

Ferdinand's learning from his *dreams* what he lacks as a representative of the "Way of Justice," Caliban emphasizes how we can all learn from *art* how distant we are from the divine "Wholly Other Life." Similarly, the distinction between the arcadian realm where "all flesh had peace" and the utopian realm where the "mind could be perfectly clear" is recast in Caliban's speech as the distinction between himself

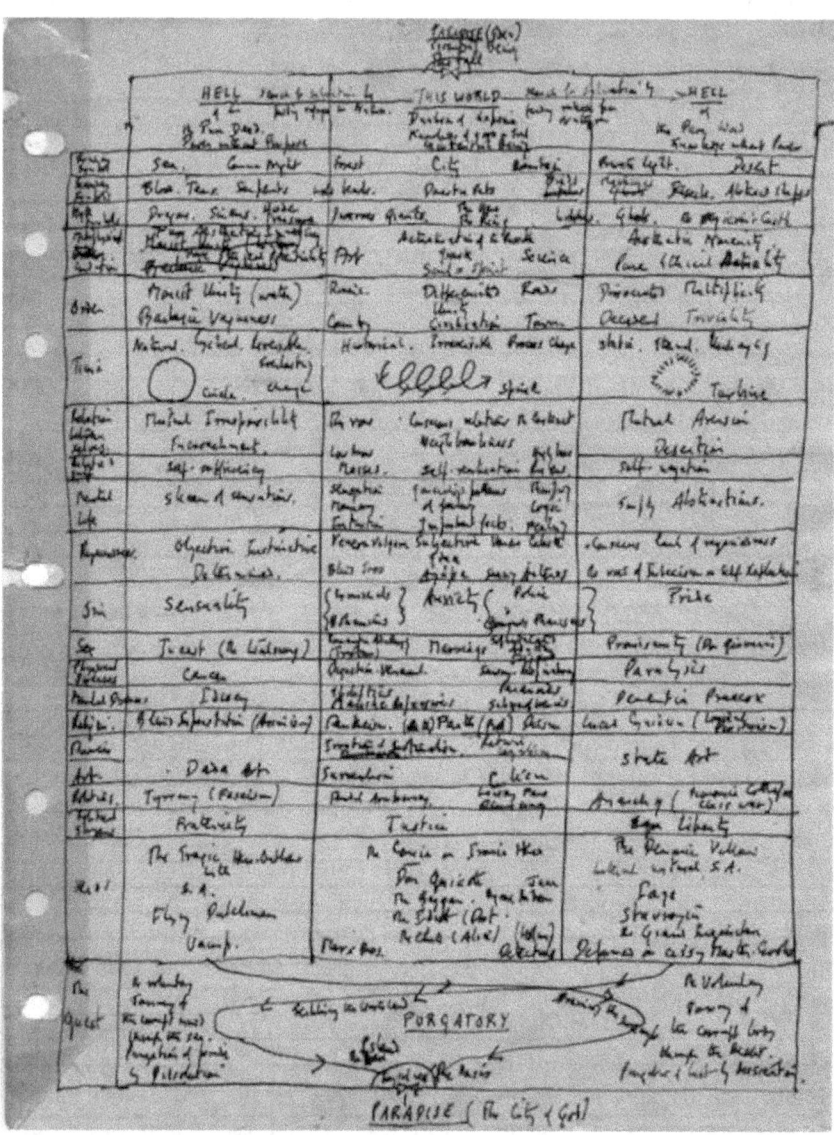

Figure 5 The handwritten chart on Romanticism that Auden produced for his students at Swarthmore College in the spring of 1943. Reproduced with permission from The Estate of W. H. Auden.

and Ariel. Most broadly, Caliban represents the body, the brute sensual nature in which refuge might be sought, while Ariel represents the spirit, the temptation of escape into rarefied disembodiment. Auden uses this symbolic contrast not just to illustrate the tension between the two characters, or to recapitulate Alonso's point that a tightrope-like balance between the two must be achieved, but most potently, to highlight how one or the other—an escape into sensuous nature or the utter transcendence of it—is usually sought from art, which can only provide a fragile illusion of either. This recognition of art's inadequacy lies at the basis of the Christian conception of art that Auden sets forth in *The Sea and the Mirror*, and especially in this climactic chapter.

Caliban's Utopian Gap

Chapter 3 (*Caliban to the Audience*) takes the form of the eponymous character's circuitous pontification on the relationship between art and life from several adopted viewpoints: first he ventriloquizes the audience to itself, then he addresses as a mentor any potential artists in the audience before finally speaking more directly as himself, experiencing his own revelatory awakening as to the religious function of art even as he reveals it to audience and reader. Overall, Caliban's speech stands as the most complete exposition of Auden's negative poetics as I have been elaborating it in this chapter, deftly embodying both the straightforward claim that art "makes nothing happen" and the more elusive one that it makes *nothing* happen—that is, it makes an event of nothingness. This ambivalence is most fully embodied in Caliban's account of the audience's response to art. In his opening ventriloquization of the audience, he has them detail some of the utopian discrepancies between the Muse's world and the real world that attract them to art—it is a place, for example, where "*it is the socially and physically unemphatic David who lays low the gorilla-chested Goliath with one well-aimed custard pie*"— but also has them insist that (unlike Yeats's speaker in "Sailing to Byzantium," for instance) they would never want to live in such a place: "*Into that world of freedom without anxiety, sincerity without loss of vigour, feeling that loosens rather than ties the tongue, we are not, we re-iterate, so blinded by presumption to our proper status and interest as to expect or even wish at any time to enter, far less to dwell there*" (31; italics in original). As their reason for this rejection they (as Caliban) offer the need for conflict and contradiction to give individual existence meaning; chastising art for always presenting "*the perfectly tidiable case of disorder*" (31), they claim that "*without our privacies of situation, ... our specific choices of which hill it would be romantic to fly away over or what sea it would be exciting to run away to, ... without, in short, our devoted pungent expression of the partial and contrasted, the Whole would have no importance and its Day or Night no interest*" (32-3). This objection implies that the world of art—where all conflicts are dramatically interesting and aesthetically integrated—is a lot like the utopias imagined by fanatical social reformers, and susceptible to the same accusations of inhumanity-through-uniformity that such utopias have often been.

As this section of the speech continues, the audience/Caliban goes further to maintain that everything about the experience of art—the audience being there, the artist being who he is and not someone else—is dependent on the disorderly exigencies of real life, and so to abolish those exigencies (as artists and utopians in common can sometimes seem to want to do) would be to destroy what art feeds upon, to be left with a mirror with nothing to meaningfully reflect. Either that, or the intrusion of the ideals of art into the real world—the inverse of Caliban's presence in *The Tempest*, intruding brute bodily reality into the world of magic—would lead to a kind of aestheticized anarchy:

> *For if the intrusion of the real has disconcerted and incommoded the poetic, that is a mere bagatelle compared to the damage which the poetic would inflict if it ever succeeded in intruding upon the real. We want no Ariel here, breaking down our picket fences in the name of fraternity, seducing our wives in the name of romance, and robbing us of our sacred pecuniary deposits in the name of justice.* (35)

Caliban thus ventriloquizes the audience as holding the view that art should not make anything happen, at least in the sense of changing the material conditions of the real world. In rejecting the incursion of artistic ideals of fraternity, romance, and justice into their real lives, they/he imply that art's relationship to utopia should remain entirely analogical—that any reformist elements of art should serve escapist rather than educative or (worse) revolutionary purposes.

The first section of Caliban's speech, then, seems to confirm through the audience Auden's repudiation, in the Yeats elegy and beyond, of his earlier life-altering hopes for poetry. But the subsequent sections offer several caveats to the escapist view of art promulgated by the audience/Caliban. In the second section, for example, Caliban points out to any potential artists that what they perceive as their Ariel-inspired "lyric praises of the more candid luxurious world to come" (41) are in fact transfigurations of Caliban himself, "a gibbering fist-clenched creature" who stands as "the only subject that you have, who is not a dream amenable to magic but the all too solid flesh you must acknowledge as your own" (39). In contrast to Auden's own defense of art from this Freudian reductionism nearly a decade earlier in "Psychology and Art To-day," Caliban here casts the artistic drive as above all a narcissistic one, revealing Ariel the muse to be, at root, simply a sublimated incarnation of Caliban the id. Such a view of art heavily problematizes the escapism sought by the audience in the first section, at least from the religious stance out of which *The Sea and the Mirror* develops: for if art is spawned from the artist's attempt to ennoble and rarify her or his own raw bodily nature, then to escape into such a construct entails escaping into a deception. Rather than working to shatter our auto-idolatrous illusions by forcing us to confront our flawed natures—as the Auden of this period thought art at its best should do—such an aesthetics allows both artist and audience to indulge in fantasies of self-authorization, believing the crucial gap to be that between their actual lives and those their desires imagine, rather than that between their fallenness and the divine.

It is these fantasies—and the extent to which art can seem to sanction them—that Caliban attacks in the speech's final section. He splits the audience into two types, corresponding to the tempting left- and right-hand worlds of Alonso's warning to Ferdinand: those Edenists who seek to be absorbed into "the whole rich incoherence of nature" (45), and those New Jerusalemites who long for "that blessed realm, so far above the twelve impertinent winds and the four unreliable seasons, that Heaven of the Really General Case" (47). Both mistakenly seek the Oneness of an "ultimately liberal condition" (45)—the former through regression to kind of infantile pan-egoism, the latter through rarefaction to an intellectual shedding of the ego. And both searches lead to despair: "Such are the alternative routes," Caliban proclaims, "the facile glad-handed highway or the virtuous averted track, by which the human effort to make its own fortune arrives all eager at its abruptly dreadful end" (49).[13] Having returned to the poem's major theme—that the human attempt to make meaning of our own lives without God's help is doomed to futility—Caliban goes on to evaluate art's role in illuminating our distance from the divine, and to isolate the dilemma of the religiously minded artist:

> Having learnt his language, I begin to feel something of the serio-comic embarrassment of the dedicated dramatist, who, in representing to you your condition of estrangement from the truth, is doomed to fail the more he succeeds, for the more truthfully he paints the condition, the less clearly can he indicate the truth from which it is estranged, the brighter his revelation of the truth in its order, its justice, its joy, the fainter shows the picture of your actual condition in all its drabness and sham, and, worse still, the more sharply he defines the estrangement itself—and, ultimately, what other aim and justification has he, what else exactly *is* the artistic gift which he is forbidden to hide, if not to make you unforgettably conscious of the ungarnished offended gap between what you so questionably are and what you are commanded without any question to become, of the unqualified No that opposes your every step in any direction?—the more he must strengthen your delusion that an awareness of the gap is in itself a bridge, your interest in your imprisonment a release, so that, far from your being led by him to contrition and surrender, the regarding of your defects in his mirror, your dialogue, using his words, with yourself and about yourself, becomes the one activity which never, like devouring or collecting or spending, lets you down. (50)

Presented in its dramatic context as a revelation that dawns on Caliban rather than an insight he possessed before he took the stage, the sudden urgency of "what you are commanded without any question to become" marks the most explicitly religious moment in the poem until this point. As in "Atlantis," however, no direct reference is made to the He who does the commanding, once again leaving God cloaked in negativity so as to emphasize "the ungarnished offended gap" of which "the artistic gift" serves to make us "unforgettably conscious."[14] But we must be cautious, Caliban warns, not to fall into the trap of believing that consciousness of the gap can be enough, as though awareness alone can save us from the necessity of "contrition and surrender." This places the religious artist in a dilemma, whereby their art is ideally conversionary but actually often exacerbates our tendencies to self-authorization, lending us a mirror in which to see our follies vainly reflected without providing the necessary prod toward spiritual reform. Through Caliban, Auden once again veers close here to the view of art as Christian propaganda exemplified by "Atlantis," though this view is only ever theorized negatively. In the final paragraph of his speech Caliban evokes "that Wholly Other Life from which we are separated by an essential emphatic gulf," and once again stresses the gap revealed by the mirror of art as key to spiritually suturing the divide: "it is precisely in its negative image of Judgement that we can positively envisage Mercy; it is just here, among the ruins and the bones, that we may rejoice in the perfected Work which is not ours" (52). The phrase "Wholly Other Life" bridges the concepts of God (who remains unnamed throughout *The Sea and the Mirror*) and utopia, highlighting that both take on greatest significance in our distance from them—a distance both the poem itself and art as theorized by it find their purpose in illuminating.

Arcadians and Utopians

So far in this chapter I have been drawing together two strands of Auden's thought from the late 1930s to the 1950s, with the first strand embodied in a revisionist reading of the claim that "poetry makes nothing happen"—in the sense that it opens and illuminates a no-place of possibility into which alternatives can be imagined—and the second inherent in the claim that "every good poem" (or "every work of art" as the earlier iteration runs) "is very nearly a utopia"—in the sense of providing a patterned analogue to a more perfect society. As I discussed in the previous two sections, *The Sea and the Mirror* stands as the point in Auden's work at which these two strands most explicitly and thoroughly intertwine into a fully fledged negative poetics, as the poem casts art's felicitous mirror as serving to reflect our distance from what its last words call "the restored relation." Because of *The Sea and the Mirror*'s religious impetus, however, this is a relation not to one another in a more perfect society, but rather to the divine unnameable. As in much of Auden's work throughout the 1940s, religious imperatives largely subsume utopian ones, though the hope for a state of unity more encompassing than a strictly personal salvationary one consistently glimmers through. Implicit behind Auden's 1940s stance on the function of art as "the destruction of auto-idolatry" lies the idea that a society in which all had come to realize, accept, and seek forgiveness for their essential fallenness would be a society of mutually loving neighbors—the fulfillment of utopia in a postlapsarian Eden.

I have already pointed to *The Sea and the Mirror*'s prefiguration of Auden's later distinction between Arcadians and Utopians, Eden and the New Jerusalem. But these dichotomies are never made explicit in his work until later in the decade, most concertedly in the 1948 essay "Dingley Dell and the Fleet." Asserting a "characterological gulf" between "the Arcadian whose favourite daydream is of Eden, and the Utopian whose favourite daydream is of the New Jerusalem" (*Dyer's* 409), Auden goes on to flesh out these distinctions at length, focusing on the pastness of Eden as opposed to the futurity of the New Jerusalem. The "backward-looking Arcadian" accepts the irrevocability of his banishment from Eden, and so knows that his vision of the Good Place must remain "a wish-dream that cannot become real" (410). By contrast, "the forward-looking Utopian" does not accept the impossibility of establishing the Good Place on earth, but in fact "believes that his New Jerusalem is a dream that ought to be realized so that the actions by which it could be realized are a necessary element in his dream" (410). According to Auden, such "actions" will almost inevitably be violent ones—revolution, purgation, even genocide—and so the Utopian temperament is marked by an "indulgence in aggressive fantasies" utterly foreign to the Arcadian (410). In one sense Auden concurs here with a persistent strain of anti-utopianism in the twentieth century, exemplified in Hannah Arendt, Karl Popper and more recent thinkers like John Gray, which sees impossibility as inherent in the definition of utopia and posits the virtual inevitability of totalitarianism whenever utopian ideals are actually implemented.[15] In another sense, however, "Dingley Dell and the Fleet" finds Auden at last clearly delineating the distinction between religious and utopian hope implicit in much of his work for over a decade. The Arcadian—whose essential Christianity is hinted at by the name given to his Good Place, Eden—roots their hope in an acceptance of fallenness, and so their yearning serves primarily to image their redemption in the afterlife. By contrast, the Utopian's fervor for the New Jerusalem may be religious in character, but it is blasphemous in its auto-idolatry, its prideful conviction that heaven can be brought to earth.

Auden's one explicit treatment of this distinction in his poetry comes in "Vespers," written in 1954 as the fifth of seven sections of the sequence "Horae Canonicae" (*Collected* 635). Structured according to the canonical hours of prayer, the sequence takes as its foundational event the crucifixion of Christ, extending the metaphoric resonance of that specific historical murder to include any societally sanctioned act of violence. Throughout the sequence, Auden's speaker meditates on those upon whose invisibility, disenfranchisement, or death any peaceful civic existence depends. In keeping with this theme, "Vespers"—the formal name for evensong—recounts a twilight meeting between the speaker, who identifies himself as an Arcadian, and his "anti-type," a Utopian—each with his own exclusionary vision of the perfect society. Structured in short blocks of prose, the poem proceeds through a series of comparisons that largely reiterate the distinctions made in "Dingley Dell and the Fleet," with the Arcadian speaker embodying harmless aesthetic values while the Utopian remains stridently political: "Glancing at a lampshade in a store window, I observe it is too hideous for anyone to buy: He observes it is too expensive for a peasant to buy" (636). Though most of the poem finds the speaker obviously favoring his own playful vision of Eden (where "the only source of political news is gossip") over the Utopian's severe and rigorous New Jerusalem (where "a person who dislikes work will be very sorry he was born"), in its final third he reflects more equivocally on the meaning of their encounter:

> Was it (as it must look to any god of cross-roads) simply a fortuitous intersection of life-paths, loyal to different fibs?
>
> Or also a rendezvous between accomplices who, in spite of themselves, cannot resist meeting
>
> to remind the other (do both, at bottom, desire truth?) of that half of their secret which he would most like to forget,
>
> forcing us both, for a fraction of a second, to remember our victim (but for him I could forget the blood, but for me he could forget the innocence),
>
> on whose immolation (call him Abel, Remus, whom you will, it is one Sin Offering) arcadias, utopias, our dear old bag of a democracy, are alike founded:
>
> For without a cement of blood (it must be human, it must be innocent) no secular wall will safely stand. (637)

The suggestion that Arcadian and Utopian might simply be "loyal to different fibs" once again argues against taking the speaker to straightforwardly represent Auden's viewpoint. That their meeting might be "fortuitous," and indeed that they might even be "accomplices," suggests a dialectical relation between the two, as if each is fully actualized only by the presence of the other. In speculating that each reminds the other "of that half of their secret which he would most like to forget"—in the Arcadian's case, "the blood" without which his vision of Eden could never be safely dreamt; in the Utopian's, "the innocence" that must be sacrificed to bring his New Jerusalem to fruition—the poem suggests that neither mode of conceiving of the Good Place can be coherent in itself, that both lack a fully rooted understanding of the present conditions from which their visions emanate. In emphasizing how each illuminates for the other the absent presence of their mutual "victim"—without whose "cement of blood ... no secular wall will safely stand"—"Vespers" tropes the very concept of negative poetics I have been exploring in this chapter: Arcadian and Utopian each make nothing happen for the other, presencing the invisible suffering figure whose very existence both makes their visions of the Good Place necessary and proves how distant they remain from achievement.

To return to the idea with which I began this chapter—and which was formulated in the very same year "Vespers" was written—one might read the poem as exemplifying Auden's claim that "every good poem is very nearly a utopia" in more than just a formal sense. One might also see it as highlighting the distance inherent in that concept of *nearness*; in suggesting that even the walls within which poetry is safely written are themselves cemented with blood, "Vespers" makes clear that a good poem can never be as insulated from the conditions of its composition as its formal coherence might suggest. Furthermore, from Auden's claim that specifically *good* poems share this nearness to utopia, one might infer the critical assertion that an awareness of poetry's inadequacy—and the inadequacy of the better worlds it analogizes—is an essential criterion of any poem's goodness. In the years after "Horae Canonicae," Auden's poetic voice becomes increasingly defined by a modesty of tone, an indication that he had given up thinking of poetry as performing anything more ambitious than eulogizing our bodily and domestic existence and admitting the utter impotence of any one individual in the face of the world's many problems. The word "utopia" disappears from his writing, along with any hint that poetry can fill any more than a consolatory role. No longer concerned with negatively illuminating what our worlds—societal or personal—might be missing with an aim to filling those gaps, his work tends to content itself with gently chiding and forgiving us for our inevitable imperfections.

This insistence that poetry acknowledge its fundamental inadequacy in the face of suffering and other material tribulations also registers in Auden's responses to Yeats in the period after the Second World War. As I discussed earlier in this chapter, while the 1939 essay "The Public v. the Late Mr. William Butler Yeats" certainly castigates the ludicrous and even reprehensible aspects of Yeats's worldview—from his belief in "mumbo-jumbo" to his "feudal" political outlook (*Prose II* 4–5)—it ends by affirming him, on the evidence of his diction and his "true democratic style," as "a just man" (7). Throughout that essay, the Counsel for the Defence repeatedly acknowledges the extent to which Yeats's work is fueled by social and political aspirations, recognizing that his mythological and mystical predilections arose from a desire "to find through folk tradition a binding force for society" and claiming of his poems as a whole that "from first to last they express a sustained protest against the social atomisation caused by industrialism, and both in their ideas and their language a constant struggle to overcome it" (7). In other words, Auden engages with Yeats as a poet who—like Auden himself earlier in the decade—conceives of poetry as potentially exerting a unifying influence in the collective realm. By the 1948 essay "Yeats as an Example," however—the other major essay on Yeats of Auden's career—Auden has disavowed this utopian conception of poetry, instead marveling at the fact that "though there is scarcely a lyric written to-day in which the influence of his style and rhythm is not detectable, one whole side of Yeats, the side summed up in the *Vision*, has left virtually no trace" and posing the question as to "why Celtic mythology in his earlier phases, and occult symbolism in his later, should have attracted Yeats when they fail to attract us" (*Prose II* 385). Ignoring the fact that he had answered this question nine years earlier (i.e., that such recourses to folk tradition and mysticism are attempts to forge an underlying unity amidst social atomization, particularly in the context of a colonized and fragmented Ireland), Auden goes on to reach the more modest and markedly less politically inflected conclusion that Yeats used myth to meaningfully structure his experience, recognizing himself as "living in a society in which men are no longer supported by tradition" and accepting himself as "forced to do deliberately ... what in previous ages had been done for him by family, custom, church, and state, namely the choice of the principles and presuppositions in terms of which he can make sense of his experience" (387). It is the clear-eyed manner in which Yeats faced up to this responsibility—and the beauty and lucidity of what he produced through that confrontation—that makes him, as the essay's title has it, an "example." Notwithstanding the truth value of this analysis (and it is certainly true that Yeats's capacity to structure his experience through mythic and mystical frameworks is both extraordinary in itself and productive of extraordinary work), the fact that it is conspicuously voided of Auden's earlier nuanced acknowledgments of Yeats's social, political, and indeed utopian motives reflects how vigorously, by this point in his career, he had worked to expel such motives from his own poetics.[16] On the one hand, he respects Yeats's non-Christianity enough to praise him for what might amount to auto-idolatry in Auden's own terms—i.e., for constructing an essentially self-authorizing mythic framework rather than seeking out God's grace—while on the other hand, his critique of specifically *artistic* auto-idolatry persists in the fact that he no longer even acknowledges Yeats's (or his own prior) vision of poetry as a unifying, morally edifying, and ultimately meliorating force.

Notes

1 Although I quote from the final version of the essay in *The Dyer's Hand*, first published in 1962, most of the material from "The Virgin and the Dynamo" was contained in successive versions of the essay "Nature, History, and Poetry," first in 1949 (unpublished) and then in the September 1950 issue of the journal *Thought*. The utopia analogy does not appear, however, until a talk Auden gave at a Smith College symposium entitled "Art and Morals" on April 23 and 24, 1954, in which he claims that "every successful work of art is very nearly a utopia" (*Prose* III 666).
2 In the 1950 version of "Nature, History and Poetry," for instance, Auden includes the following as the third of three "absolute presuppositions" that every poet holds (consciously or not) "as the dogmas of his art": "(3) The historical world is a redeemable world. The unfreedom and disorder of the past can be reconciled in the future" (*Prose III* 232). He reiterates this belief again in "Art and Morals," for which see *Prose III*, p. 666.
3 Ramazani highlights this renovatory aspect of Auden's elegy, pointing out for example how in "With your unconstraining voice / Still persuade us to rejoice," he echoes "The Gyres" ("Out of Cavern comes a voice / And all it knows is that one word 'Rejoice'"), and remarking how "Auden appropriates the harshest poem in the Yeats canon and assimilates it to the humanistic counsel of his elegy … Apostrophizing Yeats as master, forgiving him his politics, recycling his elegiac method, and recirculating his words, Auden lets 'the healing fountain start' in the heart of his elegy" (*Mourning* 188).
4 For a thorough exploration of Yeats's attempt to find in folk tradition a binding force for society, see Chapter 1.
5 See for example Lucy McDiarmid's reading of the essay's relation to the poem, which claims that the Defence Counsel "announces an uncrossable border between poetry and the rest of life," and then goes on to claim that Auden "paraphrase[d] his own prose" in adding the second section of the elegy, thus repudiating his previous vision of "a poet who persuades and teaches and causes agricultural miracles" (27). Of course, this ignores the fact that Auden chose to allow this latter vision to resonate at the end of the elegy. Curiously, though she and other critics are perfectly willing to read the

essay according to this last-is-truest methodology, none to my knowledge is willing to read the elegy this way—which would of course entail positing the third section's soaring Yeatsian affirmations of poetry's ability to heal as Auden's true position.

6   Auden returns to this laudatory emphasis on Yeats's diction a year later in his brief review of the latter's posthumously published *Last Poems*, in which—after once again asserting the mistakenness of some of Yeats's ideas (e.g., his "determinist and 'musical' view of history")—he ends on the following resonant note of praise: "In lyric writing what matters more than anything else, more than subject-matter or wisdom, is diction, and of diction, 'simple, sensuous and passionate', Yeats is a consummate master" (*Prose II* 63).

7   It should be noted that Auden also liked to deploy the concept of utopia humorously, as in the opening of his 1941 address to the *Yale Daily News* Banquet: "There can hardly be a person less fitted by nature than myself to the honour of addressing a university dinner sponsored by a newspaper. Until the year 1933 I never opened a daily paper, and, I must confess, that, for me, Utopia would be a place and time where I no longer felt it my duty to read one" (*Prose II* 119).

8   I refer to the version from the *Selected Poems* rather than the *Collected*, because this represents the earliest printed version of "Atlantis" rather than Auden's final revision.

9   Though Auden never discusses the concept of the *via negativa* at length, he refers to it in letters and essays throughout his later writings. See for example his letter of May 30, 1957 to Ursula Niebuhr, in which he discusses Simone Weil's book *La pesanteur et la grace* as "An exposition of the via negativa carried almost to heretical lengths, i.e. for her it is not the cross that is the stumbling block, but the Incarnation, or rather any of the references in the Gospel to Christ enjoying himself" (qtd. in Newlands, p. 114). See also his 1964 essay "The Protestant Mystics," in *Forewords and Afterwords*, esp. pp. 73–4.

10 The rest of Jacoby's passage runs: "Yet like the resistance to naming God, the reluctance to depict utopia does not diminish but exalts it. It bespeaks the gap between now and then. It refuses to reduce the unknown future to the well-known present, the hope to its cause" (35–6). Jacoby's use of "gap" here dovetails with my own use of the word throughout this chapter.

11 Prospero's magic is referred to as "art" several times in *The Tempest*, for example when Miranda pleads: "If by your Art, my dearest father, you have / Put the wild waters in this roar, allay them" (I.ii.1).

12 Because so much of *The Sea and the Mirror* is in prose, rather than citing line numbers, I cite page numbers from Arthur Kirsch's 2005 edition of the work.

13 Alan Jacobs sees a critique of Romanticism inherent in this distinction between two paths: "As Caliban details his warnings to those who give themselves over to him or to Ariel, two of Auden's convictions become increasingly clear: first, that the victims of both fates share the delusion that it is possible to exercise full control over their destinies; and second, that the desire for such self-determination is the characteristic disease of Romanticism" (21). Jacobs relates the Edenic impulse to Wordsworth and the obverse impulse to rarefaction to Shelley, and though I find this analogization very interesting, I cannot see any hint that Auden is taking aim specifically at Romanticism in Caliban's speech, rather than generally at the hubris of considering oneself a self-determining being rather than a creature indebted to a creator.

14 McDiarmid claims that "*The Sea and the Mirror* is incapable of referring to a deity directly," and that "the point of this is not simply to show off a Jamesian circumlocutory style, but to dramatize the poem's inability to refer to any extrapoetic

reality" (99). That McDiarmid chooses the words "incapable of referring" rather than "unwilling to refer" evidences the determination with which she pursues her conviction that "the poem's only raison d'être is to undermine the spiritual significance of all art" (117). As should be clear from my own reading, I disagree, believing that *The Sea and the Mirror* portrays art's spiritual significance as residing in its illumination of our perpetual distance from spiritual plenitude.

15 Gray, for example, claims that "Utopianism does not *cause* totalitarianism—for a totalitarian regime to come into being many other factors are necessary—but totalitarianism follows whenever the dream of a life without conflict is consistently pursued through the use of state power" (53).

16 Auden does address the political impetus of Yeats's poetry in a 1955 *New Yorker* review of Yeats's *Letters*, in which he praises him as "probably the only poet in this century who has written great poetry on political subjects" (*Prose III* 519). Even here, however, his chief emphasis is on Yeats's "luck" in having an authentically personal connection to the chief actors and events of the Easter Rising and the Irish Civil War (a fact that accounts for the quality of his work on these subjects) and not on poetry's capacity to exert a shaping influence on the political sphere. Indeed, he notes that "the political pronouncements of artists should be heard with great caution" (521).

Chapter 5

DRAPED IN BLACK: EKPHRASIS AND THE END(S) OF UTOPIA

Anti-Utopianism and the Liberal Consensus

In ending with what might be construed as a dismissive gesture toward the apparent quietism of Auden's late work, the previous chapter struck perhaps too firm a note of finality. For while its occasional formal looseness, its overriding tone of modesty and self-deprecation, and its chatty didacticism have often led readers to downgrade Auden's late poetry—one of the early work's greatest admirers, Philip Larkin, famously disparaged the poems of *Homage to Clio* (1965) by opining that "their poetic pressure is not high"—much remains to be learned from both the poems themselves and their historical situatedness amidst the decades following the Second World War, especially in the context of this study's focus on the poetics of utopia (127). As Jacoby amply documents in *Picture Imperfect*, the postwar era saw the emergence and consolidation of "a liberal anti-utopian consensus ... that has not only endured but has gained strength with each passing decade" (50). According to Jacoby, the key progenitors of this liberal anti-utopianism—figures such as Karl Popper, J. L. Talmon, Isaiah Berlin, and Hannah Arendt (the last of whom became a friend of Auden's after his admiring review of her book *The Human Condition* in 1959)—tended to be expatriates to the United States who had left or fled the countries of their births, whose thinking came to be significantly shaped by the evils of the Holocaust, and who developed out of these experiences of exile and trauma theories of totalitarianism that classed together communism and fascism as twin manifestations of an insidious zeal for social control that they branded with the label of "utopian." As Jacoby puts it, "Their liberal criticism became the conventional wisdom of our time; it damned utopianism as the scourge of history" (52). While not sharing the Jewish descent of these thinkers and therefore lacking their close sense of ancestral trauma in the face of the Holocaust, Auden embodies in his post–Second-World-War work an analogous conception of utopia as inherently likely to entail murder in pursuit of a permanent order. As we saw in Chapter 4, when he directly confronts the idea of utopia in this work, Auden envisions it as the product of an overweening auto-idolatry, ascribing to its advocates a zealotry that will stop at nothing to advance its impossible vision of a paradisal stasis. While the previous chapter framed these conceptions mainly in terms of his return to the Anglican communion in the early 1940s, this chapter extends that analysis to take account of the wider historical circumstances informing their evolution, particularly the marked anti-utopian turn taken by many prominent Western intellectuals—and, it would be fair to say, the societies that harbored them—in the wake of the Second World War and the horrors of the Holocaust.

In historicizing the anti-utopianism of Auden's late work, it will prove instructive to first return to Yeats, whose own late anti-utopian stance is also rooted in an abhorrence of what he takes to be utopians' fetishization of permanence. While the two poets share this abhorrence, however, it arises in each from different sources and ultimately contributes differently to the positions each adopts regarding both the poet's obligation to his audience and poetry's relation to history. In Chapter 2, I elaborated Yeats's anti-utopian utopianism, a position rooted on the one hand in his disdain for what he saw as the inveterate materialism of the utopian ideologies of his day (particularly Marxism) and on the other in his abiding commitment to setting forth in his work images of worlds more wholly reconciled than our own—even if (as with "the artifice of eternity" into which the speaker longs to be subsumed in "Sailing to Byzantium") these "worlds" often thwart concrete habitation. While disdaining utopian blueprints, then, Yeats's work nonetheless continually embodies the utopian impulse posited by Bloch, an urge toward the Not Yet driven at its root by what the latter characterizes as "a longing that is the pervading and above all only honest quality of all human beings" (*Utopian Function* 4). One can readily see Auden as likewise impelled by this longing; as I have elaborated at length, both poets' work abounds in poses of what I have called affirmative futurity, not only accenting some crucial lack in the status quo, but also frequently advancing—in the exploratory, experimental, speculative, eventual way that poetry "advances" anything—some ameliorating alternative. And yet, like Yeats, Auden comes to disdain blueprint utopianism, going further than the elder poet to specifically criticize the utopian plotting of artists. In his 1962 essay "The Poet and the City," Auden alleges an inversely proportionate relationship, particularly among poets, between artistic success and radical dissatisfaction with the status quo:

> If he is a successful poet—though few poets make enough money to be called successful in the way that a novelist or playwright can—he is a member of the Manchester school and believes in absolute *laisser-faire*; if he is unsuccessful and embittered, he is liable to combine aggressive fantasies about the annihilation of the present order with impractical daydreams of Utopia. Society has always to beware of the utopias being planned by artists *manqués* over cafeteria tables late at night. (*Dyer's* 84)

From a poet who, three decades earlier, had entertained ambitious claims for poetry's utopian capacities—averring variously that it makes us harder to fool and increases our knowledge of good and evil, while also flirting with the notion that it might help to conjure a more communalist social order—this denigration of "impractical daydreams" registers as a marked about-face. In attributing such "aggressive fantasies" to money hunger, Auden joins Yeats in associating utopia with blunt materialism, while also avowing (as a successful poet himself) a *laisser-faire* economic stance. That the one-time poetic champion of the 1930s left, who wrote of the eventual triumph of socialism in Britain as a virtual inevitability, should by the early 1960s be declaring his allegiance to the Manchester School attests to a spectrum of factors, from the personal to the historical, that set Auden's anti-utopianism distinctly apart from Yeats's, despite their superficial similarities.

On a personal level, Auden's anti-utopianism is rooted in his post-conversion notion of auto-idolatry; like Yeats, he is suspicious of materialism, but for religious reasons rather than ones linked to secular idealism. Believing that art cannot concretely ameliorate our lives but rather only illuminate (as *The Sea and the Mirror*'s Caliban puts it) "the ungarnished offended gap between what you so questionably are and what you are commanded without any question to become," Auden increasingly infuses his later work with images of human fallenness, paeans to our consequent imperfections, and wry admissions of poetry's practical impotence in the face of these follies. Beyond these personal religious motives, however, Auden's later disparagement of the concept of utopia seems deeply informed by his place in history. The pervasive anti-utopian cast of Western societies in the wake of the Second World War was accompanied in the United States by what has come to be known as the Liberal Consensus, a consolidation of national confidence informed by two chief convictions: first, that the overwhelming postwar success of American capitalism in increasing the general prosperity of the populace had rendered moot the possibility of serious domestic conflict; and second, that the greatest threat to this buoyant prosperity lay in foreign communism. According to Gregory Hodgson—whose critique of the liberal consensus in his 1976 book *America in Our Time* is still regarded as foundational—so pervasive was this atmosphere of liberal self-assurance that "in the United States (though nowhere else in the world) socialism was utterly discredited" (77), with the eventual result that the American political scene took on a perilously homogenous cast: "Thanks to the liberal triumph," Hodgson claims, "the powerful emotions and interests that always work for conservative policies were not balanced by equally powerful forces and interests of the Left. Instead, they were opposed by a liberalism that was in effect hardly to be distinguished from a more sophisticated and less resolute conservatism" (98). The influence of the era's combination of widespread prosperity, domestic harmony, and political homogeneity—especially as relative to the fractious pre-Second-World-War era— permeated the American literati; no less a spokesman than Lionel Trilling declared in the preface to his (tellingly titled) essay collection *The Liberal Imagination* (1950) that "In the United States at this time liberalism is not only the dominant but even the sole intellectual tradition. For it is the plain fact that nowadays there are no conservative or reactionary ideas in general circulation" (xv). This is not to say that Auden would have agreed outright with Trilling's assessment; even after gaining American citizenship in 1946, he remained a cosmopolitan European, keenly attuned to "intellectual tradition[s]" outside the United States. As Peter Firchow points out, however, Auden conceived of the United States as fostering "an open and indeterminate view of the future" according to which "political action became relatively unimportant if not altogether irrelevant" (191). Claiming of Auden that "by 1939 [he] had come to the conclusion that literature and politics do not mix well," Firchow goes on to suggest that "it must have been part of the appeal of the United States that literature in general and poetry in particular no longer needed to concern themselves unduly with such matters" (191). Larkin makes an analogous point amidst his famous disparagements, eulogizing Auden's earlier incarnation as "a tremendously exciting English social poet" and claiming of his emigration on the eve of the Second World War: "At one stroke he lost his key subject and emotion—Europe and the fear of war—and abandoned his audience together with their common dialect and concerns. For a different sort of poet this might have been less important. For Auden it seems to have been irreparable" (125). While it would be wrong to claim that the American Auden avoided political subjects as such, Larkin's lament for Auden the "social poet" rings as justified; whereas the poems before 1940 teem with *engagé* content urgently rooted in the historical moment of their composition, those afterward—and I think here of such significant political poems as "The Fall of Rome," "Memorial for the City," and "Horae Canonicae"—take (as their very titles suggest) a transhistorical approach to the subject of justice. To "the wide-angled rhetoric" that Larkin praises in the early work, these poems add a lacquer of erudition and abstraction, making them politi*cal* without attempting to intervene in *politics* in the sense of any ongoing struggles over power and provision (123).

Here we can return to Yeats, whose career trajectory likewise entails a shift from concrete political engagement to more abstract meditations on what might be characterized (given their focus on the mystical cyclicity of temporal power) as the place of the political in history. While Auden's post–Second-World-War work emerges out of the ideologically settled intellectual climate of the burgeoning Liberal Consensus, however, Yeats died in 1939, and so his late work is produced in the anxious lead-up to the war whose arrival so irrevocably altered the course of Auden's career. In other words, Yeats's poetry of the mid- to late 1930s emerges out of an era of fierce sectarianism whose consequences he did not live to see, whereas Auden's postwar oeuvre is predicated upon those very consequences. That this difference in historical positioning profoundly affected how each poet conceived of the function of poetry in relation to history—that is, how poetry might embody a utopian stance toward the possible and thereby alter history's course—can be readily observed in comparing the poems from each poet's later period that most explicitly meditate upon the artist's role amidst the specter of global conflict. Both "Lapis Lazuli" and "The Shield of Achilles" directly confront the violence of a world in crisis; both employ the ekphrastic mode to address art's responsibility toward that violence; and both dramatize the conflict, in times of such upheaval, between what an audience might expect of art and what the artist is willing to dispense. In juxtaposition, however, it becomes clear that the two poems adopt nearly opposite stances toward the transfigurative capacities of art; while both seem to agree that the creative act should not be undertaken, in made-to-order fashion, as a direct fulfillment of consumer demand, the artist figures they depict diverge widely in the terms of how, why, and to what aesthetic ends they refuse the pressures of a troubled marketplace. As we will see over the course of this chapter, a focus on these divergences serves to potently illuminate Yeats's and Auden's distinct utopian poetics, thus serving to distill—against the backdrop of the twentieth century's most decisively *anti*-utopian event—the points of tension that render them essentially irreconcilable as artists, despite sharing a basic conviction in the importance of their art and mutually grappling throughout their careers with the ever-shifting nature of that importance.

"Lapis Lazuli" and Utopian Gaiety

Written in July of 1936, "Lapis Lazuli" stands as Yeats's most explicit poetic reckoning with the question of art as propaganda outside the context of Irish nationalism. While his early career had found him embracing the role of propagandist, cloaking himself in the mist of the Celtic Twilight in the name of cultural nationalist advancement, his explicit stance on the matter after the First World War remains best encapsulated by his notorious distinction, elaborated in *Per Amica Silentia Lunae* (1917), between poetry and rhetoric: "We make out of the quarrel with others, rhetoric, but of the quarrel with ourselves, poetry" (*Later* 8). As many have noted, Yeats's own poetry makes surface nonsense of this high-sounding claim, quarrelling with others both explicitly and implicitly to generate some of its most vital animating tensions. "Lapis Lazuli" is one such poem born of quarrel, its first stanza cast in a snide, defensive tone:

> I have heard that hysterical women say
> They are sick of the palette and the fiddle-bow,
> Of poets that are always gay,
> For everybody knows or else should know
> That if nothing drastic is done
> Aeroplane and Zeppelin will come out,
> Pitch like King Billy bomb-balls in
> Until the town lie beaten flat. (1–8)

Edna Longley connects this opening to an essay of a quarter-century earlier, "J. M. Synge and the Ireland of His Time" (in which Yeats personifies Irish politics as a "hysterical woman" obsessed with a "fixed idea"), noting of this stanza that "Yeats's old enemy (inner enemy too), the political mind, has resurfaced in new guises: 'if nothing drastic is done' mocks the urgent voice of all politics" (63). Given that the speaker's imagined antagonists in this stanza are not just feminized objects of misogyny, but also, more implicitly, infantilized and Catholicized objects of patrician disdain, one might question the newness of their "guises" here. For in casting their fears in such blatantly sequential alphabetic form ("Aeroplane and Zeppelin"), Yeats makes of those fears objects of bathos, the bogeymen of timorous children. And while "King Billy bomb-balls," with its allusion to the nationalist ballad "The Battle of the Boyne," could seem to be an earnest evocation of military threat by way of one of Ireland's most momentous historical conflicts, its full context suggests otherwise. For the ballad wistfully recounts the founding victory of the Protestant Ascendancy, depicting the defeat of the Catholic James II by the Protestant William of Orange ("King William threw his bomb-balls in / And set them all on fire") and thus eulogizing the emergence of the very class to which Yeats belonged and which he expended considerable energy throughout the latter half of his career in exalting. The voices of these "hysterical women" are thus conflated with those of the ignorant and opportunistic Catholic masses, the "Mean roof-trees" who serve as antagonists of such middle-period poems as "Upon a House Shaken by the Land Agitation," "September 1913," and "Paudeen." Yeats rhetorically isolates the mindset that would denigrate "poets that are always gay" in favor of "drastic" action as emanating from an inferiorized gender, class, religious, and (therefore, it is implied) temperamental position. Indeed, the word "drastic," rooted in the Greek verb *dráō*, "to do," implicitly opposes hoi polloi's clamorous thirst for extreme action to the dignified Nietzschean gaiety of the poet, who parodies their histrionic fear of societal breakdown in the shift from the perfect rhymes of the stanza's first quatrain (say/gay, bow/know) to the disintegrative slant rhymes of its second (done/in, out/flat), thus both internalizing formally the ostensible consequences of "nothing drastic [being] done" and advertising his own authority as the keeper of formal order.

Having so thoroughly caricatured his opponents, the speaker shifts in the second stanza to extolling those able to abide stoically in the knowledge that "All perform their tragic play" (9). Evidencing the fatalism at the core of *A Vision*'s historical system, the speaker draws a valuating line between the hysterics of the first stanza and those who are "worthy their prominent part in the play"—actors who, when confronted on stage while playing Hamlet or Lear or Ophelia with the tragic destinies of these heroes, "Do not break up their lines to weep" (14–15). While serving as thespian extensions of the first stanza's parodying of drastic action, these actors also exemplify a more ideal audience for art. For as the poem goes on to emphasize, the actors' proper performance of their tragic parts depends upon their having absorbed the play's edifying lessons before attempting to embody them:

> They know that Hamlet and Lear are gay;
> Gaiety transfiguring all that dread.
> All men have aimed at, found and lost;
> Black out; Heaven blazing into the head:
> Tragedy wrought to its uttermost.
> Though Hamlet rambles and Lear rages,
> And all the drop scenes drop at once
> Upon a hundred thousand stages,
> It cannot grow by an inch or an ounce. (16–24)

The shift in immediacy from the simple present ("They know") to the present continuous ("Gaiety transfiguring") thrusts us into the poem as witnesses to the dramatic act of transfiguration, with the "Gaiety" for which poets are denigrated by the hysterics of the first stanza emerging as the very mechanism by which the "dread" of those selfsame hysterics can be artistically ennobled. The necessary challenge for any reading of "Lapis Lazuli" to explicate this gaiety has produced some memorable formulations: Longley, for instance, characterizes it as "creative joy ... the formal 'energy' an artist summons when compelled to confront the worst" (66), while Paul Gordon links it to the vision of tragedy that Yeats shares with Nietzsche, "a form of rapturous overabundance that is synonymous with artistic creation in general" (39). Recasting the spirit of such descriptions within a utopian frame, one might regard this gaiety as epitomizing the artistic will to harmony, the Shelleyan legislative drive to transmute difference into correspondence, to draw the world—or, in Yeats's case, Ireland, and then all history itself—into a kind of artifactual unity. While Auden saw this drive as dangerous—"Every good poem" may be "very nearly a utopia," but to live inside a poem would be nightmarish—Yeats repeatedly displays a willingness to entertain serious analogies between poetic and societal forms (even at the expense of liberty: witness his eugenicist juxtaposition in "Under Ben Bulben" of the "well made" poem with those "Base-born products of base beds" whose very corporeal existences seem in defiance of formal propriety). In setting out the ideal of "Tragedy wrought to its uttermost," Yeats exalts the artist's capacity to set to work upon the bare facts of human suffering and mortality.[1] Out of the acceptance that "All men have aimed at, found and lost ... cannot grow by an inch or an ounce"—i.e., that given the cyclical vision of history, our bereavements can increase neither in quantity nor in existential heft—are born the most truthfully "wrought" of our imaginative expressions. Those who lack this acceptance are driven to make philistinic demands of art, as though it ought to simply reflect the reality of our condition rather than transfiguring it.

As itself a transfigurative work of art, "Lapis Lazuli" undertakes a dialectical exploration of the relationships between audience and artist, reality and tragedy, the individual work of art and the vast inexorable turns of history. The third stanza opens with an evocation of civilizational overturn: "On their own feet they came, or on shipboard, / Camel-back, horse-back, ass-back, mule-back, / Old civilizations put to the sword. / Then they and their wisdom went to rack" (25–8). The transformation of "they" across these four lines, from destroyers to destroyed, speaks to "their" status as all of us, rendered blurrily indistinguishable—conquerors from conquered—by the whirring of history's gyres. As the passive voice suggests, "Old civilizations put to the sword" is an action so inevitable as to be voided of its agential force. Even the greatest of artworks can be likewise turned under by this anonymous harrower:

No handiwork of Callimachus
Who handled marble as if it were bronze,
Made draperies that seemed to rise
When sea-wind swept the corner, stands;

> His long lamp chimney shaped like the stem
> Of a slender palm, stood but a day;
> All things fall and are built again
> And those that build them again are gay. (29–36)

Coming as it does immediately after the speaker's assertion of humanity's essential impermanence, the introduction of the valorizing proper noun "Callimachus" can strike us as jarring. Even once we are told that despite his preternatural transmutative talents, none of his "handiwork … stands"—and indeed that his lamp for the Erechtheum in Athens "stood but a day"—we seem to have digressed quite markedly from the poem's opening impetus as a refutation of an alarmed audience's propagandistic demands. Do the textural qualities of Callimachus's "draperies" and "stem[s]" represent an aestheticist assertion of creative autonomy in the face of a public that would subordinate art to political imperatives? Does Callimachus himself serve to emblematize the artist who, despite knowing that his work may succumb, even almost instantly, to the pinch of ephemerality, undertakes it nonetheless? Does Yeats thus deploy him in order to highlight the paradox that his very name survives to retain an artifactual significance even in the physical absence of his art, and thus to imply that tragic gaiety, the quintessential artistic virtue, lingers in the world to transfigure it even in the absence of the monuments to which it gives rise? "All things fall and are built again, / And those that build them again are gay": in other words (and this is the poem's most ambitious rejoinder to the doomsayers of the first stanza), gaiety is the regenerative force of civilizations.

Just as the dread of reality is transfigured by gaiety into authentically tragic art, so are the resultant artworks ground by the pressure of history into the dust of dread reality, requiring new transfigurative exertions of the gaiety that birthed what was lost and will no doubt be lost again, ad infinitum. The poem's first three stanzas chart this cyclical dialectic, unfolding a panoramic stage upon which the gay poet plays the parts of tragic hero and stoic legislator, embodying both the anonymous humanity upon whom history inexorably acts and the singular artist for whom such actions serve as the raw material for his history-making creative performances. The poem's final two stanzas shift into the ekphrastic mode, with the poet audiencing himself to an ancient, lasting work of art within his more precarious modern one:

> Two Chinamen, behind them a third,
> Are carved in Lapis Lazuli,
> Over them flies a long-legged bird
> A symbol of longevity;
> The third, doubtless a serving-man,
> Carries a musical instrument. (37–42)

The perfect iambic tetrameter of the second and fourth lines—especially in a poem in which such metrical regularity is so infrequent—inescapably yokes the statue's semi-precious medium to the idea of "longevity," a formal choice that both draws upon a perhaps too-obvious symbolic connotation of stone and (more esoterically) evokes the poem's rootedness in Yeats's reading of Nietzsche. Gordon notes that in his copy of the English translation of Nietzsche's *Morgenröte* (*The Dawn of Day*), Yeats specifically marked the following aphorism: "How we turn to stone. By slowly, very slowly growing hard like precious stones, and at last lie still; a joy to all eternity" (53). This dialogues with a set of ranging motifs of hardness and stillness both in Yeats's later work and in its critical reception, first given voice in Ezra Pound's 1914 characterization of his poetry after *The Green Helmet and Other Poems* as "becoming gaunter, seeking greater hardness of outline"—an image that finds ambivalent expression in the "stone" hearts of Rising leaders that "trouble the living stream" in "Easter, 1916," resurfaces in the "hammered gold" bird that the speaker will become in Byzantium's "artifice of eternity," and swells through to the profusion of marble and bronze statues, rocky faces and voices, and assortments of stone that populate these last poems ("Later Yeats"). Throughout Yeats's later work, hardness and stillness converge to evoke a kind of timelessness, and in "Lapis Lazuli," this timeless convergence manifests in human terms as the transfigurative trait of gaiety. Just as in Nietzsche's aphorism the one who slowly grows as hard as precious stone at last attains the numinous stillness that makes him "a joy to all eternity," in Yeats's poem gaiety combines a stone-like impassivity with the precious glint of joy to allow those who embody it both to remain unhysterical in the face of history's upheavals and to infuse their handiwork with its sustaining clear gaze in the hope that, should the gaily forged artifact persist at any fortunate length along the gyres' procession, it might pass on its sustenance. This vision of a renewing cycle—with the audience gleaning the artwork's gaiety, and some among them thus becoming the artists who carry that gaiety forward—asserts for art a clear utopian function as the repository of that which fuels the building and rebuilding of civilizations. The poem's final stanza depicts the absorptive phase of this cycle, as the speaker's act of ekphrastic unfolding serves to renew his own artistic impetus:

> Every discolouration of the stone,
> Every accidental crack or dent
> Seems a water-course or an avalanche,
> Or lofty slope where it still snows
> Though doubtless plum or cherry-branch
> Sweetens the little half-way house
> Those Chinamen climb towards, and I
> Delight to imagine them seated there;
> There, on the mountain and the sky,
> On all the tragic scene they stare.
> One asks for mournful melodies;
> Accomplished fingers begin to play.
> Their eyes mid many wrinkles, their eyes,
> Their ancient, glittering eyes, are gay. (43–56)

That the erosions wrought upon the carving by history—i.e., its "discolouration[s]" and "accidental crack[s] or dent[s]"—seem to the speaker integral to its aesthetic power, taking on the verisimilitude of "a water-course or an avalanche," serves to connote his awe in the face of the artifact's lastingness. Amidst the civilizational wrack the poem expounds, the sheer fact of the statue's being there lends it an edifying aura; indeed, the presence of "avalanche" hints at how narrowly this and any lasting artifact arrives to us through the gauntlet of historical circumstance. So evocative prove the marks of the carving's survival that the speaker's account of them shifts from the verisimilitudinous to the fanciful as, transfixed, he is transported beyond the empirical stasis of the lapis to construct for it a temporal scenario, imagining that "it still snows" on the "lofty slope," convincing himself that "doubtless plum or cherry-branch / Sweetens the little half-way house," and admittedly taking "Delight" in these fabrications. As with all ekphrastic speakers, Yeats here pays tribute to art's evocative powers within an artwork itself designed to evoke; unique to Yeats's endeavor here, however, is the attempt to evoke in us the very gaiety invoked in him by the eponymous work in stone. In fact, the poem's final lines add another layer to this chain of evocation, accenting the poem's almost memetic vision of how the transfigurative force of gaiety is passed along through generations and across civilizations. "On all the tragic scene they stare," and as they stare, they long for art not to *renovate* their visions (in the sense of "make new") but rather to *make ancient* the scene before them, to transfigure it into timelessness—in effect to pack it (to borrow the phrasing of a famous late-Yeatsian aphorism) in "ancient salt." And so "Accomplished fingers begin to play," transforming what at the touch of lesser hands might be simply "mournful melodies" into another edifying conduit for the driving force of civilizational renewal: "Their eyes mid many wrinkles, their eyes, / Their ancient, glittering eyes, are gay." The two discerning "Chinamen" thus prove "lofty" not just spatially but temperamentally, and the poem ends by reveling in the very gaiety for which the poets are scolded by their naysayers in its bitter opening lines—a trait that has been rhetorically recast over the course of five canny stanzas not just as not a flaw, but as humanity's chief creative virtue.

I have gestured to the utopian function that the poem assigns to art as the means of conveying this virtue through history. It would be fair to ask, however, whether the brand of gaiety that Yeats theorizes and valorizes throughout the poem could be said to be achievable by the common run of humanity—or whether, in keeping with the hierarchical cast of Yeats's thought in general, the poem implies that it is the sad lot of most of us to be enslaved to reality, while only an elect caste of artists possesses the capacity to ennoble that enslavement, through the transfigurative power of gaiety, into something authentically tragic. On the other hand, one might more generously detect a kernel of progressive optimism amidst the poem's bleak vision of endless civilizational overturn rendering anonymous the great mass of humanity: for as our store of artworks builds, should not also our opportunities to learn their sustaining lesson? At the very least, "Lapis Lazuli" is proleptically defiant of Auden's claim that poetry makes nothing happen—and yet the transfigurative potential with which it invests art seems troublingly anti-social, especially given the wider historical circumstances of its composition. As Michael Valdez Moses notes, the poem was written in the same month (July 1936) that Hitler pledged military support to Franco in the Spanish Civil War; for Valdez Moses, this makes it "a painful instance of Yeats's ethically irresponsible and politically misguided response to the growing threats of fascism and wider war in Europe" (273). Consequently, he claims, "Any defence of Yeats's poem rests on an implicit acceptance of the Nietzschean view that the highest duty of the artist is to transform the violence and cruelty of human existence into an object worthy of aesthetic and philosophic contemplation" (273–4). In setting forth so absolute a condemnation, however, Valdez Moses neglects both the extent to which Yeats believed such "violence and cruelty" to be historically inevitable and the extent to which "Lapis Lazuli" implies that the artistic transfiguration of these inevitabilities may contain a progressive dimension. Even by the end of his life, Yeats remained unresolved as to the depth of his historical fatalism; in *On the Boiler*, his last major prose work, he declares that "civilization rose to its high-tide mark in Greece, fell, rose again in the Renaissance but not to the same level," going on to assert that "we may, if we choose, not now or soon but at the next turn of the wheel, push ourselves up, being ourselves the tide, beyond that first mark" before correcting himself to conclude: "But no, these things are fated; we may be pushed up" (*Late* 240). "Lapis Lazuli" poetically embodies this ambivalence, on the one hand asserting that human calamity "cannot grow by an inch or an ounce" while on the other hand holding out hope that our store of misfortune might actually *shrink*, and that poetry itself—and all art, as a repository of edifying gaiety—might abet this ameliorative dwindling. That this possibility is resonant for Yeats with the concept of utopia is clear from his admission, elsewhere in *On the Boiler*, that "In my savage youth I was accustomed to say that no man should be permitted to open his mouth in Parliament until he had sung or written his *Utopia*, for lacking that we could not know where he was taking us, and I still think that artists of all kinds should once again praise or represent great or happy people" (249). The slippage here from utopia—usually thought of as a concept inextricable from collectivity (as in the example of More's *Utopia* that Yeats cites)—to the markedly more individualistic "great or happy people" can be seen to encapsulate the shift from Yeats's early-career cultural nationalism to the aristocratic outlook of his later work. Viewed in light of "Lapis Lazuli," however, we might see this "greatness" and "happiness" as amalgamated in *gaiety*, and infused with the hope that, in the face of history's inevitable catastrophes, those who best embody this trait in their art and in their bearing might convey its transfigurative force forward to effect an upward push, however fleeting or infinitesimal, in humanity's fortunes.[2]

In keeping with his aristocratic proclivities, Yeats saw this gaiety as heroic, and when he set about explaining his adherence to such an individualistic conception in a time of societal strife, he alluded by way of contrast to none other than W. H. Auden. In a letter to Dorothy Wellesley in July 1935, he evokes his fin-de-siècle compatriot Ernest Dowson's exaltation (in his poem "Villanelle of the Poet's Road") of "Us the bitter and gay," using Dowson's epithet as a springboard from which to theorize what would become the central theme of "Lapis Lazuli":

'Bitter and gay,' that is the heroic mood. When there is despair, public or private, when settled order seems lost, people look for strength within or without. Auden, Spender, all that seem the new movement, *look* for strength in Marxian Socialism, or in Major Douglas; they want marching feet. The lasting expression of our time is not this obvious choice but in a sense of something steel and cold within the will, something passionate and cold. (*Letters* 837)

In citing Auden as chief among those younger poets who look for strength externally, whether in Marxism or Douglas's Social Credit movement, Yeats implicitly folds him in with the materialists whose pursuit of utopia through the concrete redistribution of wealth so often drew the older poet's disdain (the details of which I discussed in Chapter 2). The desire for "marching feet" that Yeats attributes to Auden and company can be linked to the imperative for "drastic action" expressed by the "hysterical women" of "Lapis Lazuli"; these are the "obvious choice[s]" that lack the "steel and cold within the will" that Yeats comes to valorize in the form of gaiety. Yeats would return to this theme in his October 1936 broadcast for the BBC, "Modern Poetry," in which he chides Auden and his circle (who he acknowledges are seen by many critics to be "the poetry of the future") for their "overwhelming social bitterness"—i.e., the obverse of the gaiety he champions in this period (*Later* 95–6). As the most renowned representative of "the new movement" in poetry, Auden can thus be seen as a veiled antagonist of "Lapis Lazuli," which thus becomes not just an assertion of artistic autonomy in the face of histrionic demands for propaganda, but also a combative *ars poetica* formulated to defend Yeats's aristocratic inward mode against what he saw as the flagrantly outward approach of a younger generation that, in perhaps giving the modern audience the engaged art it asks for, threatens to supersede him.

Poetry's Gratuitousness

Despite his sustained engagement with socialist ideas during the 1930s, Auden was much less a poet of political action than his popular reputation at the time would imply, nor was he as bluntly desirous of "marching feet" as Yeats's comments suggest. In fact, a chief preoccupation of Auden's mid-1930s poetry is the way in which our individual desires and behaviors find societal expression, therefore alerting us to our potential complicity in collective-sphere upheavals that would appear to be beyond our sway. This places him in dialogue with Yeats's emphasis, in both the above-quoted letter and "Lapis Lazuli," on the internal world's potentially determinate influence upon the external. In one of Auden's signal poems of the period, "Easily, my dear, you move, easily your head" (written in November 1934, eight months before Yeats's letter to Wellesley), the speaker meditates on the mutually permeable boundaries of public and private life, citizenship and amorous intimacy:

Ten thousand of the desperate marching by
Five feet, six feet, seven feet high:

5. Ekphrasis and the End(s) of Utopia   167

Figure 6 Yeats at the microphone at the BBC, London, March 1937. The poet delivered six BBC broadcasts in 1936 and 1937 (and ten in total, dating back to 1931).

>   Hitler and Mussolini in their wooing poses
>   Churchill acknowledging the voters' greeting
>   Roosevelt at the microphone, van der Lubbe laughing
>   And our first meeting.
>
>   But love, except at our proposal,
>   Will do no trick at his disposal;
>   Without opinions of his own, performs
>   The programme that we think of merit,
>   And through our private stuff must work
>   His public spirit. (*English* 153, lines 31–42)

Betraying his indebtedness here to the vision of Eros elaborated by Freud in *Beyond the Pleasure Principle* as tending "to combine organic substances into ever larger unities," Auden depicts a mass of "Ten desperate million" driven to mindless combinatory "marching," ripe to be manipulated by the "wooing poses" of stagey dictators (315). In casting the driving force of mass desire targeted by demagogues as the same erotic force that fuels the speaker's romantic relationship ("And our first meeting"), the first of these stanzas posits a cautionary unity of the political and the personal, implying that what we do in twos might somehow manifest among the anonymous millions living ostensibly beyond the amorous pale. Most darkly, this suggests that our capacity to be wooed in private is inseparable from our susceptibility to political manipulation: the same cocktail of vanity, bodily hunger, the longing to worship, and the basic desire to be wanted foments at the root of them both. At the same time, the second stanza above puts a positive spin on this inseparability, depicting a personified love as having "trick[s] at his disposal" and yet being "Without opinions of his own"—that is, as powerful and yet impersonal, capable of effecting change and yet amoral in his directionlessness. Love thus "performs / the programme we think of merit," taking his cues from "our private stuff"—with the nonspecific noun "stuff" here deftly capturing the inextricable snarl of psychosexual material that characterizes our erotic entanglements—in order to actualize "His public spirit." Love, then, is a kind of mimic, looking to the sphere of couplehood for gestures to enact on a larger scale in the arena of history. Such a model contains a kernel of utopian optimism, for if the personal is microcosmic of the political, then our individual behaviors matter immensely, and positive changes in those behaviors will ripple outward to the betterment of the social collective. This is at least somewhat analogous to the model Yeats sets out in "Lapis Lazuli," with the stoic gaiety of the artist transmitted through the artifact to the select artistic few who will become the future rebuilders of their endlessly wracked civilizations. A crucial difference, of course—and one very much in keeping with the two poets' divergent political outlooks, especially in the 1930s—is that while Yeats's vision of the personal transfiguring the political is rooted in individual embodiments of gaiety, Auden's corresponding vision hinges on the inherently communal force of love. This can be seen to roughly correspond to Yeats's elaboration in the letter to Wellesley of the difference between himself and the Auden generation; while the older poet looks inward to draw upon a "heroic" core of gaiety in times of civilizational strife, the younger ones look outward to a public sphere that, for this late version of Yeats, is too mired in philistinic dogmatism to offer anything other than disappointment or betrayal. On the other hand, both poets cast poetry as a means of (as Auden puts it in discussing Yeats himself soon after the latter's death) "mak[ing] personal excitement socially available"—and to the potential melioration of the collective (*English* 6). While Yeats's vision of gaiety's transfiguring potential through its embodiment in works of art remains largely implicit in a way that accords with his aristocratic aloofness, Auden's communalistic ethos in this period leads him (as I discussed at length in Chapter 3) to advance much more overtly grandiose conceptions, as in his envisaging (in the year before Yeats wrote "Lapis Lazuli") of a "parable-art, that art which shall teach man to unlearn hatred and learn love" (*English* 341–2). Nonetheless, in the decade leading up to the Second World War, both poets' work embodies with varying degrees of subtlety the hope that poetry might play a pedagogical role in helping either to avert the civilizational catastrophe that the times seemed to promise or to rebuild a sturdier civilization in that catastrophe's wake.

Yeats's death on the eve of war leaves us to wonder how the fact of its happening might have altered his conception of art's role amid social upheaval—especially given that the conflicts he did live through (the First World War, the Easter Rising, the Irish War of Independence, the Irish Civil War, etc.) were crucial motive forces behind the apocalyptic, fatalistic, and ultimately aristocratic overtones of his later work. (Might he have been driven even further out into the remorseless cosmos, for instance, becoming even more inclined to see art's role as that of limning cyclical inevitabilities?) With Auden, however, we can see concretely how his post–Second-World-War work reflects a fundamentally changed sense of art's capacities, and how this change is specifically conditioned by an acute awareness of the atrocities of the Holocaust and the mood of anti-idealism and moral futility that attended that awareness. Auden's first comprehensive biographer Humphrey Carpenter tells us, for instance, that throughout the post–Second-World-War era, "He remained convinced of the utter uselessness of trying to change the world through poetry, and when questioned about this would usually reply: 'I know that all the verse I wrote, all the positions I took in the thirties, didn't save a single Jew. These attitudes, these writings, only help oneself. They merely make people who think like one, admire and like one—which is rather embarrassing'" (413). In keeping with this disdainful attitude toward the taking of "positions" in art, one of his favorite words for describing poetry throughout this period is "gratuitous." In his 1947 essay "Squares and Oblongs," for instance, he explicitly rejects the notion "that writing—and this idea is, I think, particularly prevalent in regard to the writing of poetry—is a kind of religious technique, a way of learning to be happy and good," advancing in lieu of this echo of his earlier self the claim that "the writing of art is gratuitous, i.e. play" (*Prose II* 341). He further develops this idea of gratuitousness in "The Poet and the City," his most substantial published statement in the postwar era on the relationship between poetry and politics. In that essay, Auden claims that "the so-called fine arts have lost the social utility they once had"—which according to him inhered in their mnemonic and documentary functions—and that "they have, consequently, become 'pure' arts, that is to say, gratuitous activities" (*Dyer's* 74). Having set out this opposition between the utile and the gratuitous, he goes on to deploy it as a framework for explaining the inglorious place of poetry "in a society governed by the values appropriate to Labor" (with the acknowledgment that "capitalist America may be more completely governed by these than communist Russia"), arguing that whereas prior societies regarded gratuitous activities as sacred, "to Man the Laborer, leisure is not sacred but a respite from laboring, a time for relaxation and the pleasures of consumption" (75). As a consequence, then, society is "suspicious" of artists, which it regards at worst as "parasitic idlers" and at best as "trivial" (75). From this state of affairs, he derives a warning: "A poet and painter has to accept the divorce in his art between the gratuitous and utile as a fact for, if he rebels, he is liable to fall into error" (75). The "error" in question is the "heresy" of *l'art engagé*: "when poets fall into it," Auden avers, "the cause, I fear, is less their social conscience than their vanity; they are nostalgic for a past when poets had a public status" (76). In thus culminating this line of argument, Auden not only puts paid to the grand claims for poetry's ameliorative capacities that he himself made throughout the 1930s but also implicitly accuses his past *engagé* self (in a way that echoes his statements to Carpenter about poetry's impotence in relation to the Holocaust) of writing less out of social conviction than personal ambition. And yet, in the penultimate paragraph of "The Poet and the City," Auden gestures to poetry's importance in a way that, while not quite contradicting his dichotomy of utility versus gratuitousness, certainly problematizes it:

> In our age, the mere making of a work of art is itself a political act. So long as artists exist, making what they please and think they ought to make, even if it is not terribly good, even if it appeals to only a handful of people, they remind the Management of something managers need to be reminded of, namely, that the managed are people with faces, not anonymous numbers, that *Homo Laborans* is also *Homo Ludens*. (88)

If the act of artistic creation serves as a crucial reminder that humans are not just working beings but playing ones, then this leaves open the possibility that poetry's utility inheres precisely in its gratuitousness. For if indeed "managers need to be reminded ... that the managed are people with faces," and if the very act of writing poetry serves to satisfy this need, then like all acts of artistic making it would seem to play a useful role in de-anonymizing us, forestalling our subsumption into the numerical matrix. Here, then, at the rhetorical crescendo of an essay in which he has been at pains to cast as delusory his own past hopes for poetry as a political force, Auden allows the utopian implications of his characterization of poetry as "gratuitous" to come to the fore: the word, after all, derives from the Latin *grātuītus*, meaning free, spontaneous, voluntary—and so its deployment connotes the realm of artistic production as one of escape from the coercive regime of the useful.

Auden, Adorno, and Poetry after Auschwitz

Auden's ambivalence in this period—his insistence upon poetry's practical uselessness in societal matters, his keen sense of its impotence in the face of atrocity, and yet his unwillingness to fully consign poetry to a void of apolitical frivolity—places him in dialogue with perhaps the key thinker of their shared generation on the linkages between aesthetics and politics, his near-contemporary Theodor Adorno. While even more urgently concerned than Auden with the place of art in an administered society, Adorno shares with the poet both the conviction that art stands opposed to the dominant regime of utility and a complexly ambivalent outlook on the implications of this in terms of the artist's aims and obligations. In his *Aesthetic Theory*, Adorno opposes art to utility not by casting art as gratuitous, but by highlighting its immanence to the world it critiques and therefore its capacity to internalize, dismantle, and reform that world—a capacity he characterizes in specifically utopian terms:

> In the midst of a world dominated by utility, art indeed has a utopic aspect as the other of this world, as exempt from the mechanism of the social process of production and reproduction ... By its bare difference from the uniform, art is a priori the critic of the uniform, even when it accommodates itself to what it criticizes and effectively moves within its presuppositions. Unconsciously every artwork must ask itself if and how it can exist as utopia: always only through the constellation of its elements. The artwork transcends not by the bare and abstract difference from the unvarying but rather by taking the unvarying into itself, taking it apart, and putting it back together again; such composition is what is usually called aesthetic creativity. Accordingly, the truth content of artworks is to be judged in terms of the extent to which they are able to reconfigure the other out of the unvarying. (311-12)

Eschewing the connotations of freedom inherent in a word like "gratuitous," Adorno instead characterizes art as "exempt" (with its milder connotations of existing at a certain remove) from what he terms "the uniform" and "the unvarying"—i.e., the dominant logic of conformity and self-identity that sustains the utility regime. In his insistence that even in its capitulations to or co-optings by this logic, "art is a priori a critic of the uniform," Adorno echoes, in a higher philosophic register, Auden's claim that in a world in which human beings are reified as workers, "the mere making of a work of art is itself a political act." In emphasizing art's "utopic aspect as the other of this world" and underlining the imperative for every work of art to "ask itself if and how it can exist as utopia," however, Adorno goes well beyond the vagueness of Auden's "political act" to assert that artistic form (i.e., the artwork's "constellation of elements," its "composition") constitutes a means of "reconfigur[ing] the other out of the unvarying": in other words, the forms of works of art are the spectral utopian others to the prevailing forms of sociopolitical relations, casting over What Is the ineffable shadow of the Not Yet.

This may seem to shade rather closely toward the delusional equation between poetic and social forms that Auden cautions against in asserting that while "Every good poem is very nearly a Utopia," this can only be "an analogy, not an imitation" because given poetry's aesthetic imperatives of "beauty, order, economy and subordination of detail to the whole," a poem-like society would be "a nightmare of horror" (*Dyer's* 71, 85). For Adorno, however, art's otherness in relation to uniformity—i.e., its utopian dimension—derives not from virtues like beauty, order, and economy, but from the precarious promise of autonomy it harbors. As he puts it elsewhere in *Aesthetic Theory*:

> Because for art, utopia—the yet-to-exist—is draped in black, it remains in all its mediations recollection; recollection of the possible in opposition to the actual that suppresses it; it is the imaginary reparation of the catastrophe of world history; it is freedom, which under the spell of necessity did not—and may not ever—come to pass. (135)

Utopia is "draped in black" in the sense that what has not yet been can only be envisioned by means bequeathed to us from what has been or is: the enshrouded future is only imaginable in light of past presents. In performing the work of "recollection [read: *re-collection*, gathering up, reassembling] of the possible in opposition to the actual that suppresses it," art thus highlights both the contingency of "the catastrophe of world history" (i.e., by continually alerting us, through its imaginative, speculative, reconfigurative dimensions, that events might readily have transpired otherwise) and the evitability of future catastrophe—the alternative potentialities that always reside within the actual. Crucially, however, Adorno admits that such potentialities may forever remain concealed, that the "freedom" art embodies "may never … come to pass." Rather than conceiving of art as gratuitous, then, Adorno might be said to conceive of it as *questing after* its gratuitousness—that is, as holding out a sliver of possibility that a world might be achieved in which it can sufficiently extricate itself from the regime of utility and uniformity so as to both warrant the label of "gratuitous" and wear with dignity its residual connotations of freedom. If, for Adorno, "Art is the ever broken promise of happiness," the scope of his thought urges us to question the extent of the gap between making and breaking, hoping that the promise is not broken in the selfsame instant of being made, for it is in the space that might be glimpsed between them that utopia finds its delicate purchase (136).

It is this vein of negativity in Adorno's aesthetic thought—this sense of art as "a possibility promised by its impossibility" (136)—that links him most pointedly to the later Auden, for whom (as I discussed at length in Chapter 4) "poetry makes nothing happen" can be seen to take on utopian dimensions as a claim about the artform's capacity to lend presence to the space between aspiration and actuality, between (as the specifically religious context of *The Sea and the Mirror* has it) "the ungarnished offended gap between what you so questionably are and what you are commanded without any question to become." In fact, Adorno—who himself gestures to "The humiliating difference between art and the life people lead" (16)—can be seen as elaborating within a secularized, late-Marxist framework an alternate version of the negative poetics set out within a Christianized, Kierkegaardian framework by Auden during and after the Second World War.

Given Auden's frequent recourse to the Holocaust as the index of poetry's powerlessness, he and Adorno can also be linked through the latter's most renowned claim (and the twentieth century's only other statement about poetry that competes in prominence with Auden's "poetry makes nothing happen"), mounted in its original form in Adorno's 1951 essay "Cultural Criticism and Society": "To write poetry after Auschwitz is barbaric" (*Prisms* 34). As with Auden's statement, Adorno's is often isolated as an aphorism voided of context, making it seem an unequivocal condemnation of the poetic act in the post-Holocaust world, an assertion of the primacy of urgent biopolitical concerns over frivolous artistic ones, and/or a lament for the ignominious status of art amid the all-encompassing rapacity of late capitalism. It is all these things to a certain extent, but more complexly and only with qualification, as its fuller context within the final sentences of "Cultural Criticism and Society" makes clear:

> The more total society becomes, the greater the reification of the mind and the more paradoxical its effort to escape reification on its own. Even the most extreme consciousness of doom threatens to degenerate into idle chatter. Cultural criticism finds itself faced with the final stage of the dialectic of culture and barbarism. To write poetry after Auschwitz is barbaric. And this corrodes even the knowledge of why it has become impossible to write poetry today. Absolute reification, which presupposed intellectual progress as one of its elements, is now preparing to absorb the mind entirely. Critical intelligence cannot be equal to this challenge as long as it confines itself to self-satisfied contemplation. (*Prisms* 34)

In this context, society is becoming "total" in the sense that the logic of exchange that dominates late capitalism renders everything fungible, subjecting even minds to reification. In such a situation, we are liable to transmit even our "extreme consciousness of doom" in the form of mere "idle chatter" because that very consciousness—which ought to harbor the seeds of critique—is utterly subsumed into the conditions that give rise to it. Criticism faces the paradoxical task, then, of pronouncing as if from without upon a culture in which it is utterly enmeshed—as though, in an undersea kingdom, certain mer-people were to assume the mantle of offering an above-water perspective, despite never having tasted air themselves. Recognizing that the dialectic of culture and barbarism is driven by "intellectual progress"—i.e., that under late capitalism, scientific and even artistic advancement are inextricable from the refinement of ever-more efficient means of extermination—Adorno labels poetry "barbaric" because, as an artform perched airily at the eminent heights of Western cultural achievement, it is also thereby complicit in that culture's most accomplished acts of depravity. It is therefore "impossible to write poetry today" in the sense that poetry is too enmeshed in what *is* to fulfill its utopian function of imaging what *might be*. Even the conditions of its own impossibility are becoming more and more invisible to it, as "[a]bsolute reification ... is now preparing to absorb the mind entirely." Looked at from this Adornian perspective, Auden's account of poetry's gratuitousness is emptied of any connotations of freedom, with poetry consigned to being a frivolous emanation of the status quo, impotent even to be meaningfully self-reflexive about its own status as a commodity. To Auden's claim that, as an expression of "*Homo Ludens*", poetry serves to "remind the Management of something managers need to be reminded of, namely, that the managed are people with faces, not anonymous numbers," this version of Adorno might well reply that late capitalism actually prefers faces to numbers: not only are they more readily susceptible to commodification through the regimens of marketing, but they also provide a humanizing façade that conveniently obscures the reality of reification, their individual expressiveness offering assurances that both the minds behind them and the products of those minds alike have not been fully subsumed into objecthood—when in fact, this Adornian perspective would assert, *Homo Ludens* is a kind of wind-up toy, its "play" no more self-authorized than the metronomic drumming of a tin monkey.

But this extreme pessimism is not the only perspective on post-Auschwitz poetry Adorno offers, and the addition of his later, more hopeful, formulations places his overall outlook more fully in line with the ambivalence about poetry's utopian capacities that we find in Auden from the 1940s onward, whereby poetry is incapable of altering the barbarous course of history—indeed is likely complicit in fueling barbarity through its illusory pose of self-authorization (what Auden in a Christian register terms "auto-idolatry")—and yet still harbors the potential to illuminate the gap, too often papered over by the mystifications of progress and inevitability, between the What Is and the Not Yet. In revisiting his "after Auschwitz" claim a decade after its first iteration, in his 1961 essay "Commitment," Adorno avers, "I have no wish to soften the saying that to write lyric poetry after Auschwitz is barbaric; it expresses in negative form the impulse which inspires committed literature" (84). Protestations aside, however, this *is* a softening—at least as compared to his earlier account of poetry's dismal obliviousness to its own impossibility. If, as Adorno implies here, the "after Auschwitz" claim embodies in inverse form the impetus behind politically engaged literature, then the claim itself stands as an implicit expression of the utopian desire that poetry might escape its enmeshment in late capitalist totality, and of the hope that its state of reification might not be as hermetic as originally claimed. The essay "Commitment" is not, it should be emphasized, a statement in favor of "committed literature" in its overt opposition to the status quo—or at least not straightforwardly. It is instead a nuanced working-through of the competing claims of committed and autonomous art, the opposition between which poses an "antithesis" whose "menacing thrust" serves as "a reminder of how precarious the position of art is today" (76). Adorno claims that whereas in prior ages, art has been animated by the dialectical tension between these two extremes, the situation of European art in the 1960s is one of undialectical polarization:

> Each of the two alternatives negates itself with the other. Committed art, necessarily detached as art from reality, cancels the distance between the two. "Art for art's sake" denies by its absolute claims that ineradicable connection with reality which is the polemical *a priori* of the very attempt to make art autonomous from the real. Between these two poles, the tension in which art has lived in every age until now, is dissolved. (76)

The zero-sum scenario Adorno lays out in this passage is the consequence of the post-Auschwitz condition of societal totality elaborated a decade earlier. Under this condition, art is reified either by its reactionary *detachment from* reality—which only serves to display its beholdenness to the status quo—or, inversely, by its no less reactionary *engagement with* reality, which displays a beholdenness of a different order, though not of a different magnitude. Much of "Commitment" is spent framing and reframing this impasse. Rather than build toward a quietist acceptance of art's impotence in the face of its own total reification, however, the essay's last paragraph evokes art's utopian function in terms that acknowledge both its tenuousness and its urgency: "The moment of true volition ... is mediated through nothing other than the form of the work itself, whose crystallization becomes an analogy of that other condition which should be. As eminently constructed objects, works of art, even literary ones, point to a practice from which they abstain: the creation of a just life" (89). In positing form as the crystallization of true volition, analogous to that utopian "other condition which should be," Adorno not only positions himself in the Schillerian lineage of linking form and utopia, but he also joins Auden in that lineage, echoing with his "eminently constructed objects" that "point to ... the creation of a just life" Auden's claim that "every good poem is very nearly a utopia." In claiming that works of art "point to a practice from which they abstain," Adorno also echoes Auden's caution that the linkage between poem and utopia is purely analogical and should therefore not be taken to fuel the delusion that "because all is well in the work of art, all is well in history" (*Dyer's* 71). For Adorno, works of art "abstain" from the practice of creating a just world not voluntarily but inevitably, as function of both their subsumption into the status quo and their material impotence in the face of what Adorno termed "the coarsest demand" (and the only demand in which "tenderness" is to be found): "that no-one shall go hungry anymore" (*Minima* 156). Nonetheless (and as with Auden, who as I discussed in Chapter 4 ultimately conceives of "making nothing happen" as illumination rather than capitulation), in *pointing* to the practice of creating a just world, works of art are thus conceived of as indispensable in proleptically evoking futures in which that practice will be undertaken in earnest.

Denying Consolation in "The Shield of Achilles"

While rooted in divergent ideological perspectives—with Adorno's Frankfurt School leftism far more radical than Auden's increasingly Americanized liberalism (which by the 1950s evidences only the barest residue of his earlier Freudo-Marxist inclinations)—both see poetry as at an impasse: on the one hand, it is impotently entangled in the system of total reification most horrifically exemplified by the Holocaust; on the other hand, it harbours glimmers of a potential to illuminate the rifts between what is and what could be—to (as Adorno puts it in his 1957 essay "On Lyric Poetry and Society") "give voice to what ideology hides" (*Notes* 39). In tracing Adorno's shift from utter pessimism as to poetry's mere possibility in "Cultural Criticism in Society" to the more utopian accounts of its capacities in "Lyric Poetry and Society" and "Commitment," Michael Rothberg points to a "dual theory of poetry" in his work, as the "revelatory notion of art as expression" contends with "the earlier idea that 'poetry after Auschwitz' mystifies knowledge of the social" (38). We can see just such a dual theory in Auden in this later period, most overtly in his landmark "The Shield of Achilles," a poem first published in the year after Adorno's first iteration of the "after Auschwitz" claim, and one in which the tensions between committed and autonomous literature, poetry's impossibility and its utopian potential are almost systematically allegorized.

The vehicles of this allegorization are characters drawn from the *Iliad*, Achilles's entreating mother Thetis and the obstinate blacksmith god Hephaestos, with the former embodying the audience's desire for a poetry of consolation and the latter the post-Auschwitz poet's repudiation of the consolatory. As with Yeats's "Lapis Lazuli," the poem begins by evoking a female–male dynamic of expectation and refusal:

> She looked over his shoulder
> > For vines and olive trees,
> Marble well-governed cities
> > And ships upon untamed seas,
> But there on the shining metal
> > His hands had put instead
> An artificial wilderness
> > And a sky like lead. (*Collected* 594, lines 1–8)

Thetis is looking for a utopia of sorts—a world that neatly balances nature cultivated for human benefit ("vines and olive trees") with nature left wild ("untamed seas") and a settled civic life ("Marble well-governed cities") with a peripatetic questing one ("ships on untamed seas"). Seeking this harmoniousness (the delusoriness of which is formally embodied in the almost farcical "trees"/"cities"/"seas" end-rhyming), she finds instead "An artificial wilderness": that is, rather than a work celebrating art's capacity to create more ideal worlds, Hephaestos confronts her with one that foregrounds not only its own artifice but the artificiality of concepts like "wilderness" itself—which, in setting human society off against nature, serves to obscure the fact that we *are* nature and thereby to disavow our animality, with all the embodied capacity for brutality and vulnerability that comes with it.[3] Thus in Hephaestos's hands the "shining metal" becomes "lead" in the sense that the artistic medium is voided of its capacity for ideality, rendered leaden in order to better represent the burdensome conditions attendant not only upon war (for in the *Iliad*, of course, the shield is being forged for Achilles to carry into battle) but also citizenship in the post–Second-World-War era—which is depicted in the next two stanzas as typified by ugliness, discomfort, isolation, oppression, cheerless obedience, and ultimately, ruination:

> A plain without a feature, bare and brown,
> > No blade of grass, no sign of neighborhood,
> Nothing to eat and nowhere to sit down,
> Yet, congregated on its blankness, stood
> > An unintelligible multitude,
> A million eyes, a million boots in line,
> Without expression, waiting for a sign.

> Out of the air a voice without a face
>   Proved by statistics that some cause was just
> In tones as dry and level as the place:
>   No one was cheered and nothing was discussed;
>   Column by column in a cloud of dust
> They marched away enduring a belief
> Whose logic brought them, somewhere else, to grief. (9–22)

In contrast to Thetis's utopia of fine food, monumental architecture, and good government against a backdrop of sublime nature, the world Hephaestos depicts is barren, inhospitable, and utterly lacking in the pleasures of verdancy and companionship—a place of "blankness." The "unintelligible multitude" that inhabits it is defined solely in terms of its capacity for spectatorship and militarism ("A million eyes, a million boots in line"), "Without expression" in both the literal sense of betraying no visible emotion and the figurative sense implied by their "waiting for a sign": as consumers rather than creators, they are so wholly subsumed into the reified totality as to be effectively incapable of "expression," reduced instead to reactionarily attending the signals that will spur their obedience. They are therefore "unintelligible" because—like poetry after Auschwitz as Adorno initially frames it—any expression they might venture to offer by way of distinguishing themselves would arise out of a state of reification so absolute as to amount to little more than an anonymous emanation of the status quo's overriding barbarism. While the multitude have been rendered fungible as faces without voices, that to which they listen is "a voice without a face"—as though by explicitly shedding its bodily humanity, an entity has installed itself above those who have been only implicitly and unwittingly so divested. Armed with "statistics" (which serve as both the results and the tools of fungibility and reification), this commanding voice has reformulated the question of what is "just" as one susceptible to quantification; "nothing was discussed" because the aim of such technocracy ("Whose logic brought them, somewhere else, to grief") is to mobilize the apparent indisputability of the numerical to foreclose the verbal nuance that discussion would entail. Just as the previous stanza's "congregated" and "waiting for a sign" highlight Auden's concern with Christianity's dilution (i.e., the implied congregation here is not a divine-oriented community of worship, but rather one evocative of fascist rallies or Orwell's dystopian "Two Minutes Hate"), the fact that the multitude marches off "*enduring* a belief" tacitly acknowledges that the statistics that serve to impel their marching are post-ethical in their manner of subsuming individual human beings into countable nonentities, and that a belief rooted in such an awareness can never be fully embraced but rather only endured. (This is similar to how, three stanzas later, the executed trio are said to have "died as men before their bodies died," as though figuratively killed by the keenness of their awareness of their status as killable (44).)

   In its concern with the human as a civic being as distinct from the human as a body—and indeed with the eclipse of the former by the latter—"The Shield of Achilles" can be readily characterized as a poem interested in *biopolitics*. A decade after he wrote it, in "The Poet and the City," Auden would systematize in prose the essence of the poem's more elusively expressed biopolitical critique:

> What is peculiar and novel to our age is that the principal goal of politics in every advanced society is not, strictly speaking, a political one, that is to say, it is not concerned with human beings as persons and citizens but with human bodies, with the precultural, prepolitical human creature. It is, perhaps, inevitable that respect for the liberty of the individual should have so greatly diminished and the authoritarian powers of the State have so greatly increased from what they were fifty years ago, for the main political issue today is concerned not with human liberties but with human necessities. (*Dyer's* 87)

This is precisely the shift—from a politics "concerned with human beings as persons and citizens" to one focused on "human bodies" and the "human creature"—charted by the poem. The classical world conjured by Thetis's expectations through the use of praeteritio—i.e., the rhetorical device by which material is emphasized by being allegedly omitted, in this case embodied in how the act of describing Thetis's unfulfilled expectations succeeds in fulfilling them for the reader—envisions its inhabitants not only in terms of citizenship, as we have seen (inhabiting "Marble well-governed cities") but also, further on in the poem, in terms of aesthetic and spiritual fulfillment of a specifically communal character. In the fourth stanza, for instance, she envisions a religious rite solemnized by "ritual pieties, / White flower-garlanded heifers, / Libation and sacrifice" (24-6), while in the seventh stanza (her next appearance in the poem), she evokes the more purely sensuous rituals of "athletes at their games, / Men and women in a dance / Moving their sweet limbs / Quick, quick to music" (46-9). In both cases, what Hephaestos has forged in place of Thetis's expectations—i.e., what, within the poem's dialogic structure, reads as his "response"—registers as an explicit rejection of her hopes, and even as a condemnation of their inexcusably blinkered naivety. In response to her decorative vision of ritualized animal sacrifice, for instance, he presents her with an "arbitrary spot" bounded by "Barbed wire" in which "three pale figures were led forth and bound / To three posts driven upright in the ground" (36-7), and in place of the binding communal act of devotion, he images a scene "Where bored officials lounged (one cracked a joke) / And sentries sweated for the day was hot" while "A crowd of ordinary decent folk / Watched from without and neither moved nor spoke" (32-5). While Thetis's portrait of religious communion so much assumes the spiritual equality of the participants that the people present are not themselves enumerated, Hephaestos's counter-portrait depicts a rigidly hierarchized order of surveillance and violence, with "officials" (who possess the privilege of telling "joke[s]" at an execution) presiding over "sentries," then "ordinary decent folk," and finally the abjected "three pale figures," who have "died as men before their bodies died"—in the sense, too, of having been animalized in the process of their condemnation. While Thetis envisions a halcyon humanity united by its spiritual superiority to its nonhuman animal brethren, Hephaestos asserts—in line with Auden's critique of the shift from politics proper to biopolitics—a post-Auschwitz condition typified by the authoritarian tendency to see humans as reducible to bare animal life.[4] Similarly, in response to Thetis's envisioning of the sportive revelries of athletes and dancers, Hephaestos describes the archetypal progeny of the age's barbarity:

> A ragged urchin, aimless and alone,
>   Loitered about that vacancy; a bird
> Flew up to safety from his well-aimed stone:
>   That girls are raped, that two boys knife a third,
>   Were axioms to him, who'd never heard
> Of any world where promises were kept,
> Or one could weep because another wept. (53–9)

The contrast here to Thetis's communally oriented visions is so stark as to be almost programmatic: instead of the dancers' "sweet limbs," we get a "ragged urchin"; instead of heifers "garlanded" in sacred dignity, we get "a bird" taking flight from a "well-aimed stone"; instead of "Men and women in a dance," we get a world where "girls are raped" and "two boys knife a third," all of which culminates in an absence of both futurity ("Of any world where promises were kept") and empathy (the possibility that "one could weep because another wept")—the two of which are connected, of course: for in a world in which nothing awaits its denizens but obedience, grief, degradation, and death, the Not Yet is a place of emptiness, insusceptible to the investment of utopian desire, and so other people are merely emanations of the hopeless void. Throughout the poem, Hephaestos's vision highlights this connection between futurelessness and friendlessness—to which one might add featurelessness, as he seems to depict the exploitative character of political and personal relationships as arising, like stunted trees, out of the shield world's distinctly anti-utopian topography.

On the other hand—and as with "Musée des Beaux Arts," another poem that (as I discussed in the Introduction) might be read as strictly anti-utopian on the surface—there are hints even in the Hephaestos sections, specifically in aspects of the stanzas' form, of utopian possibilities being held out. Note how in the above-quoted stanza, for instance (the poem's penultimate stanza and Hephaestos's last), the second line is enjambed to leave the word "bird" suspended at line's end ("Loitered at that vacancy; a bird"), as though not only giving the lie to the place's "vacancy" by its animal presence but also holding out the possibility of flight and freedom inherent in its avian nature. Note, too, how despite resonating with hopelessness within the full framework of the sentence, the last two lines can be seen to resonate hopefully by virtue of their positioning *as* individual lines ("Of any world where promises were kept, / Or one could weep because another wept")—as though, in being arrayed by formal circumstance into this state of horizontal suspension, the possibility of their positive achievement is kept waveringly alive. The way such formal details can be seen to connote the presence of latent utopian undercurrents in tension with the stanzas' manifest content should further urge us to examine the poem's overall structure—specifically the fact that while Thetis envisions a harmonious world in irregularly stressed eight-line stanzas in the mongrel rhyme scheme of ABCBDEFE, Hephaestos depicts a fractured world in virtuosically sewn rhyme royal, in which each stanza consists of seven lines of iambic pentameter rhyming ABABBCC. Stan Smith casts this "contradiction" inherent in Hephaestos's stanzas as attesting to the poem's exaltation (even despite itself) of poetry's transfigurative capacities: "For this work in heavy metal, exhaustingly produced by hard labour, and depicting an ugly and problematic world, manages to achieve the transformation of pain and disorder into art" (193). And indeed, one might see the tension between the formal harmony of rhyme royal and the discordancy of the scenes the stanzas depict as being perfectly in line with the later Auden's negative poetics, according to which poetry's utopian function inheres in its capacity to illuminate the Calibanian "gap" between the world as it is and the world as imaged by divine decree. Smith offers a secularized version of this analysis in claiming that "Poem and shield both force open a division between the beauty of the representation and the ugliness it represents, translating 'shining metal' into 'a sky like lead' in a way which both affirms and conceals its artifice under the success of its illusion" (193). In other words, the poem is both celebratory and wary of (to adopt Helen Vendler's terms as I discussed them in the Introduction) the contrast between the *serenity of form* and the *anguish of content*. On the one hand, form can serve to conceal and therefore to deceive, while on the other—and this is where Smith's analysis can dovetail with the poetics of utopia I have been elaborating—in "forc[ing] open a division between the beauty of representation and the ugliness it represents" (and especially in enforcing our *awareness* of this division), form can fulfill the functions Adorno posits for poetry, of "giving form to the crucial contradictions in real existence" and "giv[ing] voice to what ideology hides" (*Notes* 39). "The Shield of Achilles" can thus be read as a poem that deploys form counterfactually, registering utopia's presence as against unreconciled reality while leaving its contours "draped in black."

As with "Musée des Beaux Arts," though, "The Shield of Achilles" raises ethical questions as to whether a poetics of utopia can take shape in the teeth of depictions of extreme suffering. Once again—and in keeping with how closely the two thinkers' concerns seem to hew in this era despite their considerable ideological differences—Adorno's work harbors insights that can help us to understand Auden's. In a section of "Commitment" entitled "The Problem of Suffering," Adorno reflects on precisely the issue that the formal virtuosity of "The Shield of Achilles" raises—that is, whether art's responsibility to give suffering a voice supersedes the risk of rendering that suffering aesthetically pleasurable. Adorno avers that suffering "demands the continued existence of art while it prohibits it; it is now virtually in art alone that suffering can still find its own voice, consolation, without immediately being betrayed by it" (85). Thus, it would seem that while recognizing the danger of betraying suffering by commodifying it, Adorno unequivocally affirms the necessity that it be represented. And this is true—but as so often with Adorno, only with intricate qualification. Further down the same paragraph, in discussing Arnold Schoenberg's cantata *Survivor of Warsaw*, he elaborates:

The so-called artistic representation of the sheer physical pain of people beaten to the ground by rifle-butts contains, however remotely, the power to elicit enjoyment out of it. The moral of this art, not to forget for a single instant, slithers into the abyss of its opposite. The aesthetic principle of stylization, and even the solemn prayer of the chorus, make an unthinkable fate appear to have had some meaning; it is transfigured, something of its horror is removed. This alone does an injustice to the victims; yet no art which tried to evade them could stand upright before justice. (85)

Read in light of this passage, "The Shield of Achilles" is revealed as harboring a deep ethical ambivalence. Which is more defensible: to aspirationally envision a world of harmony and communal fulfillment in a form whose discordancy hints at the counterfactual naivety of the vision's conception—or to hard-headedly depict a world of disharmony and near-universal suffering in a form whose harmoniousness risks detaching that depiction from its underlying realities to the extent of rendering suffering pleasurable? Adorno would very likely say the latter, but only barely—for the musicality and structural seductiveness of a form like rhyme royal certainly risks occasioning the forgetting that leaves even the most resolutely ethical poem "slither[ing] into the abyss of its opposite." This is the function of the Thetis sections—to serve as a less formally seductive yet at the same time less ethical alternative to Hephaestos's aestheticized depictions of suffering, thus prodding the reader toward the conclusion that while the beauty of the blacksmith's stanzas might risk "an injustice to the victims," the evasive alternative cannot "stand upright before justice."

That said, critics have too often read "The Shield of Achilles" as straightforwardly condemnatory of Thetis's aspirational naivety, with the result that Hephaestos emerges from the analysis a more unproblematically praiseworthy figure than the poem warrants. Lucy McDiarmid, for example (always among the most insightful of Auden's critics), reads the poem as a study in "undepictability," asserting that "its subject is what art cannot do"—namely, depict the spiritual (131, 127). While acknowledging the poem's persistent use of praeteritio as a means of depicting what is ostensibly undepictable, McDiarmid focuses on the many instances in the poem at which what is purportedly shown on the shield could not possibly be—for example, the fact of the multitude "waiting for a sign" and their "enduring a belief," the assertion that the condemned men "could not hope for help" and that they "lost their pride," the urchin's acceptance of rape and murder as "axioms," and so on— and thereby interprets the poem as evidencing Auden's conviction in this period that poetry is "a means of disenchantment, through which our expectations for the absolute are answered with the contingent and the derivative" (130). In other words, in ludicrously flouting literal possibility through its claims of Hephaestos having depicted undepictable inner matters of emotion and belief, the poem highlights its own incapacity to encapsulate the spiritual—Caliban's gap again— while asserting that "if art's subject is always its own incapacities, then it will always disenchant those who come to it seeking the fulfillment of their wishes" (130). In this reading, of course, Thetis's desire to see her hopes for harmony manifested in art is unambiguously wrong, and Hephaestos is the unequivocal bringer of rightness, authoritatively marshaling unpleasant yet necessary truths: "The harshness of the denial reflects the excess of the wish" (131). Because her reading does not attend to the tensile interplay of form and subject matter in the poem, however, McDiarmid cannot account for the way it generates its meanings—and indeed its utopian energy—dialectically, out of the mutual entanglement of the two characters' stances of engagement and autonomy. The last stanza is ostensibly Thetis's but brings the cast together in a way that troubles firm accounts of where rightness and wrongness in the poem reside:

> The thin-lipped armorer,
>   Hephaestos, hobbled away,
> Thetis of the shining breasts
>   Cried out in dismay
> At what the god had wrought
>   To please her son, the strong
> Iron-hearted man-slaying Achilles
>   Who would not live long. (60–7)

While Hephaestos being "thin-lipped" is often taken to connote his puckishly inhabiting a victorious silence (in combination with his "hobbl[ing] away," a kind of mic drop), this physical trait can also be read as signaling—especially given his proverbial ugliness, deformity, and jealousy—a puritanical asceticism in contrast to the sensuous physicality connoted by Thetis's "shining breasts." Remembering that (as McDiarmid points out) in Homer's account, the shield Hephaestos forges depicts *two* cities, one in which a wedding is taking place amid a scene of civic order and the other besieged by war, we might suspect Auden's Hephaestos of being a fetishist of suffering, warped by his own bitterness into disavowing the harmonious and fulfilled aspects of life. Seen in this way, Thetis's stanzas serve not only to present the delusory alternative next to which Hephaestos's clear-eyed realism, however dismal, seems ethically preferable, but also to ensure that the utopian desire for better ways of living and being is lent concrete presence not just in the poem's form but (albeit imperfectly) in its subject matter. This highlights the poem's fundamentally dialectical structure: for just as the naivety of Thetis's visions casts Hephaestos's depictions into sharper ethical relief; and just as the irregularity of her stanzas illuminate, by contrast, the virtuosity of his; so do subject matter and form operate cross-dialectically, with, for instance, Thetis's images of conciliation priming us to notice their formal analogue in Hephaestos's beautifully wrought rhyme royal. Any reader so attuned to this dialectical interplay cannot possibly accept the poem's closing words ("Achilles / Who would not live long") at face value. No, art will not save our lives, but as the poem has so intricately demonstrated, poetry at least continues to harbor the capacities to aspire, transfigure, and ennoble, not only in ways that are ideologically compromised by being too fully rooted in an inexorably reified totality, but in ways that—in dialectically prizing open the gaps between form and content, representation and reality, aspiration and responsibility—afford us sustaining glimpses of utopia's obscure light.

History's Silence and the Ends of Utopia

It is a key aspect of this chapter's argument that Yeats's "Lapis Lazuli" and Auden's "The Shield of Achilles" employ the ekphrastic mode to offer irreconcilable visions of poetry's utopian capacities, and that this irreconcilability is at least partly a function of their different historical positioning vis-à-vis the Second World War. Writing on the eve of that war, Yeats depicts his audience as demanding his poetry's engagement with the encroaching violence—demanding, in other words, what Adorno would call "committed" literature—but in response, Yeats not only asserts art's autonomy but argues that the sublime manifestation of that autonomy, namely the virtue of *gaiety* possessed by exceptional artistic individuals, is an enduring force for civilizational amelioration—a *utopian* force, transmitted and expanded through its embodiment in the aesthetic artifact. Writing in the war's aftermath, on the other hand (and particularly in the shadow of the Holocaust), Auden casts his audience as demanding the opposite of what Yeats's audience demands—and in fact Thetis can be seen as craving precisely the kind of rarified autonomous artifact that Yeats exalts in "Lapis Lazuli"—but in response, Auden asserts the necessity of commitment, implying that to adopt a stoic pose in the face of suffering (or, worse, to simply wish it away and replace it with visions of harmony) is to betray those who suffer—to make the pejoratively "utopian" mistake of assuming that "because all is well in the work of art, all is well in history" (*Dyer's* 71).

As should by now be clear, however, it would be wrong to infer from this contrast that Yeats offers a utopian vision of poetry's capacities while Auden offers an anti-utopian one. For as I have discussed, Yeats's utopianism in "Lapis Lazuli" and elsewhere is seriously qualified by both his determined individualism and his deterministic view of history, both of which operate in tension with the communalistic thrust of the concept of utopia—which is itself of course also ever-present as an important current in Yeats's poems, particularly in their recurrent emphasis on the collectivities of class, nation, society, and civilization. Furthermore, on Auden's side, though by the postwar era he is hostile both to the Yeatsian aesthetic of the artifact as a repository of utopian virtues and to his younger self's grandiose visions of poetry's meliorative potential, his negative poetics—according to which poetry's utopian function resides in its capacity to illuminate gaps: between poem and world, form and content, the What Is and the Not Yet, and so on—places him firmly in line with the vanguard utopian thinkers of the age, Bloch and Adorno in particular, the essence of whose utopianism is encapsulated in the latter's claim that "Even in the most sublimated work of art there is a hidden 'it should be otherwise'" ("Commitment" 89).[5] In other words, even works that seem to remain sublimely aloof—the carving in lapis lazuli that serves as the poem's ekphrastic object, for instance—resonate with utopian desire. This book has striven to illuminate that while both Yeats and Auden consistently embody this desire in their work, they do so distinctly both from each other and at different points in their career.

We might say that while Yeats sees utopian desire as embodied in the artifact itself, Auden (at least the later Auden, once he has sloughed off his early Yeatsian idealism) sees such desire as inherent in the gaps the artifact illuminates. Put another way, Yeats advances a positive poetics of utopia while Auden advances a negative one—or yet another way: for Yeats the poem is a vehicle of enchantment, while for Auden it is one of disenchantment. Despite its many permutations, Yeats's vision of art's world-altering power is remarkably consistent. In 1900, at the peak of his early career, he writes: "I am certainly never certain, when I hear of some war, or of some religious excitement or of some new manufacture, or of anything else that fills the ear of the world, that it has not all happened because of something that a boy piped in Thessaly" (*Early* 116). Almost four decades later, in the last year of his life, he concludes "The Statues" (another exercise in ekphrasis) by asserting the communal resolve of his nation to seek its apotheosis in the rarefied realm of artifactual stasis:

> We Irish, born into that ancient sect
> But thrown upon this filthy modern tide
> And by its formless, spawning fury wrecked,
> Climb to our proper dark, that we may trace
> The lineaments of a plummet-measured face. (28–32)

The "formless, spawning fury" of the "filthy modern tide" can only be transcended—and the promise of that "ancient sect" fulfilled—by "trac[ing] / The lineaments of a plummet-measured face"—that is, by deriving the lessons of the Pythagorean ratios that throughout the poem are credited with inspiring, through the "lineaments" of the artworks to which they give rise, not only sexual desire but also, because that desire is objectively justified, genetic and therefore civilizational excellence. The "proper dark" to which the Irish will "[c]limb" is thus another Yeatsian space of artifactual purity, akin to the "artifice of eternity" in "Sailing to Byzantium" or to the "glittering eyes" as the embodiment of gaiety in "Lapis Lazuli"—a transfigurative state of exaltation that can only be reached through the utopian conduit of art. Auden, on the other hand, shifts radically from his early aspiration (one that might readily be termed Yeatsian) toward "parable-art, that art which shall teach man to unlearn hatred and learn love" to the negative poetics inaugurated by his claim (aptly framed, of course, in relation to Yeats) that "poetry makes nothing happen" (*English* 341-2). For Yeats, that "nothing" is the "proper dark" of "The Statues"—a space of withdrawal from the "spawning fury" of modernity, as if to say, "If this filthy modern tide is 'something,' then I invite you to ascend to this place of nothingness, where everything of import in fact happens." I have already explored at length what, by contrast, this "nothing" is for Auden—the many ways in which the gap at the nexus of his negative poetics is a place of happening. This aesthetics of the gap receives its most radical expression in the title poem of the 1965 collection so denigrated by Larkin for its lack of "poetic pressure," *Homage* to Clio (*Collected* 608). Addressing Clio, characterized as "Muse of the unique / Historical fact" and "Muse of time," Auden offers his most unequivocal account of art's incapacities (66, 81). While Aphrodite and Artemis—who function in the poem to metonymize the forces of desire and reproduction on the one hand and those of death and predation on the other—"[c]an be represented in granite" (56), Clio—"who look[s] like any / Girl one has not noticed and show[s] no special / Affinity with a beast" (60–2)—is unrepresentable, despite presiding over the very substance of reality: "Lives that obey you move like music, / Becoming now what they only can be once, / Making of silence decisive sound" (77–9). In tacit response to Walter Pater's claim that "All art constantly aspires towards the condition of music," Auden would assert that aspire though it may, that aspiration is bound to be thwarted, for art is not equipped to capture things as "they can only be once" and is too dependent on presence to register the flow of time and the procession of history as processes of "Making of silence decisive sound." That is, while art can very well represent sound (and object and event and other indices of presence), its capacities founder in the face of the silence (or emptiness or absence) that serves as history's backdrop. There is a tautology here, but a productive one: the poem asserts that whatever is represented in art is no longer a "unique / Historical fact"—i.e., it has been rendered repeatable, reiterable, and therefore no longer what it could only be once—and so what art cannot do is represent the silent passage of history because once something is represented, it is no longer silent. In other words, the poem's critique of art amounts to accusing it—absurdly yet powerfully—of being unable to represent what is not represented by it. The closing lines cast this failure as a reason for the muse of history to ignore poetry: "Approachable as you seem, / I dare not ask you if you bless the poets, / For you do not look as if you ever read them, / Nor can I see a reason why you should" (89–92). Clio is "Approachable" because, as she who presides over history itself, nothing eludes her approach—unlike poetry, which tears events out of their historical uniqueness and into an artifice of recurrence. Even here, however—amid a critique of poetry's limitations so extreme as to be both absurd and irrefutable—the poem's manner of illuminating this gap between art's mode of presencing and actual historical presence attests to poetry's propensity to futurity: its conjuration, even if only by admitting its own failure to conjure, of what has not come to pass, what is not yet upon us, but toward which we might orient our desire, knowing (as poems so often teach us) that what *is* lies perpetually in the shadow of what could be.

Notes

1   Along these lines, Ramazani sees the mysterious interjection "Black out" as signalling "a kind of momentary death"—"a staged confrontation with death" that is the initial step in the exaltation of the sublime ("Tragic Joy" 164). Ramazani links this to Yeats's rumination, in the 1937 essay published posthumously as "A General Introduction for My Work," on Shakespearean tragic ecstasy: "The heroes of Shakespeare convey to us through their looks, or through the metaphorical patterns of their speech, the sudden

enlargement of their vision, their ecstasy at the approach of death" (*Later* 213). In light of this analysis, one might see "Tragedy wrought to its uttermost" as conveying how tragedy, in being so "wrought"—i.e., in so meticulously staging confrontations with death—serves to cultivate the transcendent trait of gaiety.

2 Yeats's tendency to link happiness and greatness—and to cast an exceptional capacity for happiness in utopian terms—can be traced back to his early career. His first theorization of happiness as a utopian virtue occurs in his 1902 essay "The Happiest of Poets," which focuses on William Morris, praising him for "mak[ing] his poetry out of unending pictures of a happiness that is often what a child might imagine, and always a happiness that sets mind and body at ease" (*Early* 47) and going on to praise him as an embodiment of "a time when poets and artists have begun again to carry the burdens that priests and theologians took from them angrily some few hundred years ago" (49) and as "among the greatest of those who prepare the last reconciliation when the cross shall blossom with roses" (50). Though the exaltation of childhood and the Rosicrucian mysticism that permeate these claims are aspects of this early stage in Yeats's career that by the 1930s he had long left behind, one can still draw a firm conceptual line between the utopian implications of the "ease" born of happiness he eulogizes here and his account of the renovating force of gaiety in "Lapis Lazuli."

3 The classic account of the artificiality of the concept of wilderness comes from the environmental historian William Cronon, who claims of wilderness that "far from being the one place on earth that stands apart from humanity, it is quite profoundly a human creation—indeed, the creation of very particular human cultures at very particular moments in human history" (7). Most relevantly to my analysis here, Cronon later asserts (in terms that echo the poem's critique of Thetis's delusional naivety) that "The flight from history that is nearly the core of wilderness represents the false hope of an escape from responsibility, the illusion that we can somehow wipe clean the slate of our past and return to the tabula rasa that supposedly existed before we began to leave our marks on the world" (16). In light of this analysis, Hephaestos's "artificial wilderness" represents a forceful exposure of the violence inherent in Thetis's escapist expectations.

4 Giorgio Agamben, of course, provides the most robust theorization of the tyrannical uses to which the category of "animal" has been put, particularly in his concept of a "state of exception" according to which sovereign power uses the law to establish a zone as paradoxically outside of that law, thus rendering those consigned to that excepted zone as what he calls "bare life." Agamben defines bare life as "an unsacrificable life that has nevertheless become capable of being killed to an unprecedented degree" (114). Taking as his signal example the Holocaust, in which (he claims) "the Jews were exterminated not in a mad and giant holocaust but exactly as Hitler had announced, 'as lice', which is to say, as bare life" (114), Agamben draws our attention to how sovereign power evokes and mobilizes the category of the animal to desacralize murder into simple killing, often animalizing those of whom it wishes to dispose.

5 I group Bloch and Adorno together here despite their important differences as utopian thinkers because they crucially share the conviction that art's utopian function inheres in its difference from what is—i.e., they share a *negative utopianism*. That Bloch is the major philosophical spur to the emphasis on utopia throughout Adorno's work is acknowledged by the latter when, in an interview focused on utopia that he conducted alongside the former (which is published as the first chapter of *The Utopian Function of Art and Literature*), he credits Bloch as "the one mainly responsible for restoring honor to the word 'utopia'" (1).

CONCLUSION: SHADOWS OF FUTURITY

Poetry aspires. This broad claim resonates at the core of this book, evidenced in such myriad ways across Yeats's and Auden's bodies of work that, admittedly, it might risk dissipating into vagueness. In the hope of rendering this aspiring more tangible, I have repeatedly characterized the aspirational poses taken by the two poets' work under the rubric of "affirmative futurity"—a label that encompasses a broad continuum of future-oriented desires, from the haziest of undefined longings, through wishing and hoping, to the more pointed modes of prophesy and even advocacy. Still, however, one might ask whether all art does not aspire in this way, whether the very existence of a work of art does not serve to testify to an impelling conviction of the world's incompletion, or at least a tacit intuition that to bring a work of art into the world is an act of affirming the future as a space of potentiality. This book has certainly proceeded from the premise that yes, art in general—whether undertaken with the insular aim of attaining personal satisfaction or the communal one of effecting social change (or anything in between)—is a repository of aspiration. Though some art embodies values that may strike us as dubious or even reprehensible, one would be hard-pressed to find a work of art worthy of the name that explicitly embodies the desire that the world be worse than it was before the work entered into it.

That the previous statement of course runs up against the subjective imprecision of "worse" points to the usefulness of the analytical framework of *utopia* that structures this book, as it serves as a means by which the ostensibly personal stances of affirmative futurity embodied in works of art can be assessed in relation to their engagement with communal, social, and political aspirations—in other words, in relation to their capacity to embody concepts such as Levitas's "desire for a better way of living and being" and Bloch's "anticipatory illumination" in the collectivist senses inherent in such formulations.[1] And as I discussed in the Introduction, the origins of utopia in a work and a genre of literature make it an apt category within which to view specifically poetic manifestations of "social dreaming," serving to anchor their more elusive aspirational dimensions within a literary-historical framework. Despite its neglect within the body of utopian scholarship, poetry in particular can be seen as a quintessentially utopian artform in the way it bridges utopia as *desire* and utopia as *genre*. On the one hand, poetry conveys through its sonic and rhythmic aspects the immediacy and evanescence gestured to in Pater's signal maxim "all art constantly aspires to the condition of music" (106), embodying in its essential unparaphraseability the pregnant negativity of the Blochian strain of iconoclastic utopianism epitomized by Adorno's account of art as "recollection of the possible in opposition to the actual that suppresses it"—that is, as glimmering with a utopian potentiality that cannot be fully reified, even under the conditions of late-capitalist totality (*Aesthetic Theory* 134).[2] On the other hand, as a verbal artifact, poetry has the capacity to depict, to figure, to chronicle, to imply, to declaim, and so on—all of which capacities it shares with the mainstream narrative utopian tradition in a line inaugurated by More. Poetry is thus singular, I would argue, in its capacity to at once explicitly advance utopian ideas in the generic, blueprintist sense and inherently possess the negative utopian potential—that sense of evental ephemerality, of ineffable otherness in relation to the world that is—that the iconoclastic tradition holds so sacrosanct.

As the preceding chapters have explored, both Yeats and Auden embody *in* their poetry and envision *for* poetry just such utopian capacities. Depending on which stage of each's career one examines, one can encounter them—in both their poetry and their prose about poetry—expressing the desire for a more ideal future, meditating on the perpetuity and futility of that desire, figuring the contours of that desire's object, or limning a role for poetry in making that object manifest to the benefit of the collective. Both poets can be said to move from the physical to the metaphysical, to begin by envisioning a material role for poetry in forging a better society and then abandoning that vision in favor of a more immaterial, transcendent conception of poetry's capacity for social melioration. Thus Yeats begins by claiming for poetry a concrete role in forging Ireland into national unity, then shifts to seeing poetry as expressing in essence the ceaseless idealistic striving at the root of all that he finds best in history and culture, before arriving at a vision of great artworks, poems paramount among them, as repositories of the clear-eyed transfigurative gaiety that fuels all civilizational renewal. Despite crucial differences in ideology, nationality, and historical positioning, Auden begins similarly, envisioning for poetry a role in diagnosing and potentially healing the modern affliction of disunity, shifting to see poetry as teaching us about good and evil—and thereby potentially serving as a vehicle of moral conditioning—before abandoning such tangible aspirations in favor of a Christianized negative poetics, first casting poetry as serving to illuminate the aspirational gap between humanity and divinity and then recasting that gap as a figuration of history's silence in the face of art's aspiring. Across this protean range of conceptions of how poetry's impact is actualized in the world (rather than, say, in the minds of its solitary readers), neither Yeats nor Auden ever ceases to frame this actualization in relation to a wider collective, whether nation, society, humanity, history, or some other communal category. In other words, both poets' poses of affirmative futurity retain, in permutations more or less immanently recognizable as such, a utopian dimension. This book's titular *poetics of utopia*, then—rooted in the sense of *poiesis* as the act of making or bringing into being—resonates on multiple levels, encompassing poetry's capacity to envision more ideal worlds, poetry's possible role in making the actual world a better place, and poems themselves as aesthetic exemplars of the utopian impulse, embodying in their formal pursuit of novel coherencies an analogue to the desire for social harmony. The poetics of utopia thus comprehends the complex of ways in which the bringing into being of poems, particularly modern poems, is undertaken in the shadow not just of the future but also of futurity, not just the time to come but also the desirous drive toward that coming time as a place of conciliatory potential.

I am not claiming that Yeats and Auden are somehow representative of modern poetry as a whole; as I indicated in the Introduction, to do so would be to neglect, on the one hand, the extent to which they share certain formalist commitments that place them at odds with the more experimentalist dimensions of the modernist avant-garde and its inheritors and, on the other hand, the extent to which they are too extraordinary to be representative, particularly in the longevity and depth of their common determination to probe poetry's social role. What I do want to claim, however, is that some of the shaping conditions under which Yeats and Auden enact their respective poetics of utopia also inform the work of many of their contemporaries across the early decades of the twentieth century (certainly in the Anglo-American sphere), and therefore it can be illuminating to approach the work of those contemporaries within the framework of utopia that I have set out in this book, extending the species of attention I have paid to Yeats's and Auden's poses of affirmative futurity to those of other poets of the era as a way of further nuancing our sense of modern poetry as a utopian artform.

In looking back at the preceding chapters, we can identify three crucial conditions that shaped Yeats's and Auden's work and would also generally be shared by modern poets in the Anglo-American sphere in a manner potentially productive of alternative poetics of utopia. First, we see in Yeats and Auden alike a keen sense of societal disunity as both exerting a determinate influence on their poetry and presenting an obstacle that must be overcome if that poetry is to prove effective in the world. This sense is encapsulated, for instance, in Yeats's rhetorical question in his essay "The Galway Plains" (1903)—a question echoed in many permutations throughout his Celtic Revival period: "Does not the greatest poetry always require a people to listen to it?" (*Early* 158). Though Auden lacks the cultural nationalist impetus that shapes Yeats's purview within the Irish context, we find this core concern with social division reiterated from his distinctly British point of view throughout his early career, as in his assertion in "Writing" (1932) that "whenever society breaks up into classes, sects, townspeople and peasants, rich and poor, literature suffers" (*English* 312). In fact, much of the gravitational pull that Yeats exerts on Auden can be attributed to the latter's recognition that, however much he may find his own worldview to be fundamentally irreconcilable with that of the elder poet, they share at certain points in their careers an urgent sense that poetry cannot flourish amid societal disunity. Auden tacitly acknowledges his sympathy with Yeats on this score in "The Public v. the Late Mr. William Butler Yeats" (1939), when he has the Counsel for the Defence opine of Yeats's poems that "from first to last they express a sustained protest against the social atomization caused by industrialism, and both in their ideas and their language a constant struggle to overcome it" (*English* 393). As the above-cited quotations make clear, the second key condition that shapes Yeats's and Auden's work (and potentially that of their contemporaries) is conceived of by both poets as a result of the first: the diminished audience for poetry. As I have explored at many points throughout this book, whether in terms of Yeats's work in the service of Irish independence or Auden's less concrete aspirations to repair our dividedness, unity is pursued by the poet not purely as a social good but also as a means by which to hopefully secure the widest possible audience for poems. This brings us to the third condition informing Yeats's and Auden's poetics of utopia, which is that the politically charged atmosphere in which both worked—most marked in the 1930s but prevailing through much of their careers—imposed the virtual imperative upon poets, if not to directly politicize their work, at least to confront the question of poetry's relation to politics (even if only to dismiss the possibility of any such relation). We can see this condition as virtually inextricable from the other two, with social atomization dialectically both giving rise to and resulting from the competing ideologies that make the early decades of the twentieth century such a politically charged era, and this in turn—in combination with rampant socioeconomic inequality and the increased availability of more instantly gratifying forms of entertainment, among other factors—results in a shrinking of poetry's audience. (I should say here that as this is a work of literary criticism and not of social history, the set of interrelated conditions I have mapped out—of a politically charged era, a diminished audience for poetry, and an atomized society—is necessarily oversimplified; the important thing for my purposes is that Yeats, Auden, and other modern poets *perceive* this convergence of conditions as exerting a potentially determinate pressure on their work, and their various iterations of a poetics of utopia take shape out of the encounter with that pressure.) Thus we can see the more overtly sociopolitical, meliorating, and indeed utopian conceptions of poetry's role that both Yeats and Auden advance in their early careers as taking shape in relation to the amalgam of ideology, audience, and atomization that prevails within their respective historical circumstances—1880s and 1890s Ireland on the one hand, 1920s and 1930s England on the other—while seeing their later repudiation of those hopes for poetry as a concrete force for betterment not as the rejection of utopian aspirations but as their enactment on a higher, transhistorical plane. We can see, for example, how a combination of a refusal to cede one's art to the demands of propaganda and a sense of having failed to cultivate a unified audience produces in both poets an outlook of futility vis-à-vis poetry's usefulness as an agent of palpable social change, which in turn leads both to conceive of poetry's effects according to more expansive categories, shifting, for instance, from nation to history or from society to humanity—a trajectory that, again, signals not the abandonment of a poetics of utopia but its intensification, a raising of the stakes of poetry to civilizational or celestial levels.

Eliot, Stevens, and the Poetics of Utopia

While, as I have said, Yeats and Auden are too extraordinary to be representative, we can certainly see other poets as working in response to these same prevailing conditions—social disunity, a diminished audience for poetry, the imperative to be socially and politically useful—in ways that lead them to frame their work in terms of its relation to a collective. In his 1933 book *The Use of Poetry and the Use of Criticism*, for instance—a title that itself attests to the pressure to be useful—T. S. Eliot dismisses questions as to the "nature" or "essence of poetry" as being the province of "the study of aesthetics" and therefore beyond the poet's purview, before highlighting what *does* properly occupy the latter: "The poet is much more vitally concerned with the social 'uses' of poetry, and with his own place in society; and this problem is now perhaps more importunately pressed upon his conscious attention than at any previous time. The uses of poetry certainly vary as society alters, as the public to be addressed changes" (149–50). Eliot thus acknowledges the perhaps unprecedented extent to which poets in the 1930s find themselves freighted with the expectation of social engagement, and rather than assert poetry's independence or timelessness in the face of this, he acknowledges the decisiveness of societies and their publics as historically specific factors in shaping poetry's role. And like Yeats and Auden, Eliot sees social disunity at his moment in history as both exerting a limitation upon and presenting a challenge to poetry: "The most useful poetry, socially, would be one which could cut across all the present stratifications of public taste—stratifications which are perhaps a sign of social disintegration. The ideal medium for poetry, to my mind, and the most direct means of social 'usefulness' for poetry, is the theatre" (152–3). Eliot's exaltation of the theater here (which of course betokens his own imminent shift in emphasis from poetry- to play-writing) can be seen as a tacit acknowledgment of poetry's inability to reach a satisfactorily wide audience in a disintegrated society. Indeed, in acknowledging further on that "Every poet would like, I fancy, to be able to think that he had some direct social utility," Eliot once again highlights the theater as the venue in which the poet is most likely to fulfill this hope: "He [the poet] would like to convey the pleasures of poetry, not only to a larger audience, but to larger groups of people collectively; and the theatre is the best place in which to do it" (154). While explicitly not broaching the question of *what* poetry should convey or *how* it might be useful and instead taking recourse to the vaguely phrased "pleasures of poetry" as that which the poet longs to share with the collective, Eliot nonetheless makes it clear that a larger audience for poetry is desirable, that social disintegration makes such an audience difficult to come by, and that the pressure of this scarcity is felt all the more keenly by poets in an age that seems to demand their extra-poetic engagement.

    In the Introduction, I discussed Douglas Mao's essay on utopian dimensions in the 1930s and 1940s work of Eliot and Wallace Stevens (virtually the only scholarly treatment before this book of modern poetry within a utopian framework), an analysis that hinges on what he sees as the two poets' shared aversion to how the competing political ideologies of the era served "to channel mass belief towards the present and visible," their shared conviction that "the best human future would minister to the claims of the unseen as well as the seen," and their shared determination "to outline the terms of their reconciliation" (210). In Mao's account, Eliot's attempts toward this reconciliation of the seen and the unseen are most powerfully glimpsed in his dramatic works; in plays like *The Rock* and *The Family Reunion*, for example, the poet uses the material accoutrements of stagecraft to suggest the presence of an unseen world shimmering divinely behind the seen one of human action. Extending Mao's analysis by placing it in dialogue with both Eliot's acknowledgment (in *The Use of Poetry and the Use of Criticism*) of the pressure exerted upon poets to be socially useful and his concomitant exaltation of the theater's communal possibilities, we can see how Eliot's use of the genre of poetic drama as a means of contrasting the impoverishment of the seen, material, temporal world to the plenitude of an unseen, immaterial, divine one allows him at once to assert poetry's aesthetic independence from the regimen of the utile and to stake out for poetry a function that transcends mere utility: for if poetry in dramatic form can serve as a means through which we are urged to orient our fallen existences in the seen world toward the redemption of the unseen, then it becomes not just socially useful but also spiritually necessary. This places Eliot in dialogue with both Auden's negative poetics—according to which poetry serves as a bulwark against auto-idolatry by alerting us to the unfordable gap between the life we live and a redeemed one—and Adorno's vision of art as the un-reifiable other of late-capitalist totality, alerting us to the potential contours of a poetics of utopia that might be discerned in his work more widely.

We can similarly extend Mao's analysis of Stevens—for whom "there is no seeing of reality undeformed by the play of imagination" and therefore "in a rigorous sense the world remains unseen, something we believe in rather than know" (Mao 199)—by placing it in dialogue with the poet's prose theorizations of poetry's role in society, in order to more pointedly highlight the utopian cast of his thinking. In his 1941 lecture "The Noble Rider and the Sound of Words," Stevens (like Eliot in *The Use of Poetry* eight years earlier) both attests to the extraordinary pressure exerted upon poets to be socially useful and asserts poetry's fundamental independence from such pressure:

> I do not think that a poet owes any more as a social obligation than he owes as a moral obligation, and if there is anything concerning poetry about which people agree it is that the role of the poet is not to be found in morals. I cannot say what that wide agreement amounts to because the agreement (in which I do not join) that the poet is under a social obligation is equally wide. Reality is life and life is society and the imagination and reality; that is to say, the imagination and society are inseparable. (27–8)

Here Stevens may seem to dismiss any notion—such as that held at one stage by the early Auden, for instance, for whom poems could teach us about good and evil—of poetry as a force for moral education and therefore social conciliation. But the word "obligation" is crucial here; for what Stevens is denying is not that poetry *can* exert positive moral or social influence but rather that it is pledged, bound, or constrained to exert such influence. If "life is society and the imagination and reality," and if this means (i.e., "that is to say") that "the imagination and society are inseparable," then poetry, as a product of the imagination's shaping encounter with reality, is not only fundamentally social in the sense of being formed through the mind's dialogue with that which lies outside itself, but is also a concrete verbal manifestation of our sociality, our gregariousness, as a fundamentally creative disposition. Stevens builds on this later in the essay, casting poets not only as exemplars of the inextricability of reality, society, and the imagination but as fashioning, through their acts of gregarious creation, the world to come:

> There is, in fact, a world of poetry indistinguishable from the world in which we live, or, I ought to say, no doubt, from the world in which we shall come to live, since what makes the poet the potent figure that he is, or was, or ought to be, is that he creates the world to which we turn incessantly and without knowing it and that he gives life to the supreme fictions without which we are unable to conceive of it. (31)

One can discern the contours of a poetics of utopia here by parsing out Stevens's elusive use of the word "world," which appears four times in this single circuitous sentence, carrying four different valencies: "a world of poetry," "the world in which we live," "the world in which we shall come to live," and "the world to which we turn incessantly and without knowing it." Though verbally and conceptually discrete—corresponding roughly to the world of art, the present world, the future world, and the world for which we yearn—these four worlds are effectively, according to Stevens, synonymous: that is, poetry makes explicit the performance of world-building that is always already being undertaken by anyone who lives in the present, thereby affording us insight into how the worlds of the future might be built to more satisfactorily align with our as-yet unarticulated yearnings. When Stevens claims of the poet elsewhere in "The Noble Rider and the Sound of Words" that "His role, in short, is to help people to live their lives" (29), it is this complex capacity to model the cocreative encounter between poetry and reality—and the way in which this act of cocreation analogizes on the aesthetic plane the decidedly un-quotidian work of living as imaginative, desirous beings—that lies beneath this deceptively simple claim.

Both Stevens and Eliot frame their aspirations for poetry in communal terms—i.e., in terms of "people" or "larger groups of people collectively" in the examples discussed earlier—while at the same time asserting poetry's independence in the face of the pervasive pressure exerted upon poets of their era to turn their work to social advantage. In fact, for both, it is precisely by remaining refinedly aloof from questions of direct utility that poetry proves its social value: while Eliot holds out the possibility that the undefined and perhaps undefinable "pleasures of poetry" might "cut across all the present stratifications of public taste," Stevens goes further by asserting poetry's capacity "to help people to live their lives" by "creat[ing] the world to which we turn incessantly and without knowing it." Though space does not permit an exploration of how Eliot's and Stevens's wider poetic oeuvres reflect the poetics of utopia whose contours we glimpse in the prose discussed earlier, it is evident that crucial insights could be shed upon their work by viewing their poems within the utopian framework I have set out here and elsewhere in this book—which as far as Eliot and Stevens are concerned (and at certain points, indeed, Yeats and Auden) can be summarized as follows: in a socially fragmented world in which poets at once find their audience withheld, their stature perhaps unprecedentedly precarious, and their art under coercion to pronounce on the sources of and remedies for the world's fragmentation as a potential means of regaining that lost audience and stature, they are inclined both to turn haughtily away from the world's demands, avowing the autonomy of poetry, and, paradoxically, to frame this autonomy as the very source of poetry's efficacy as a meliorating force in the world. Eliot's own discussion of Yeats praises him in terms that evoke precisely this dynamic:

> Born into a world in which the doctrine of "Art for Art's sake" was generally accepted, and living on into one in which art has been asked to be instrumental to social purposes, he held firmly to the right view which is between these, though not in any way a compromise between them, and showed that an artist, by serving his art with entire integrity, is at the same time rendering the greatest service he can to his own nation and to the whole world. (*Selected Prose* 257)

Particularly interesting here is Eliot's claim that the path "between" *l'art pour l'art* and socially instrumental art is "not in any way a compromise between them." What Eliot seems to be claiming, in other words, is that Yeats did not come to see art as partly for its own sake and partly for society's but rather that—as with Stevens's vision of "a world of poetry indistinguishable from the world in which we live" (or for that matter Auden's "every good poem is very nearly a utopia")— poetry's aesthetic autonomy as and for itself makes it socially useful to the extent that it serves to analogize states of freedom, coherence, harmony, and so on, which are as yet unachievable in the world as it is. The "service" rendered by poetry like Yeats's, both "to his own nation and the whole world," then, it that of modeling a cocreated world in miniature that, through its achieved integrity, spurs our aspirations for the greater world that contains it.

Modernism and Presentism

There is an unmistakable dimension of futurity to the theorizations of poetry we find in Eliot and Stevens (and, of course, Yeats and Auden), and it is part of my goal in this conclusion to urge consideration of just how pervasive this futurity— and the variations on a poetics of utopia that take shape through it—may be in modern poetry, particularly in the early decades of the twentieth century, when the converging factors of the pressure to be socially useful, increasingly fragmented societies, and a seemingly ever-dwindling audience for poetry produce poetic responses that cast the utile autonomy of poetry as urgently relevant to our strivings after better future worlds. There are, however, other dominant strains of thought among modern poets, most pertinently a kind of what I will call *presentism* that seems to reject the post-Romantic impulse to futurity that prevails in the poets I have discussed so far in favor of an allegiance to and an exaltation of poetry's capacity to rivet us in the present moment, to celebrate the intensity of being in the Now. This presentism is particularly prevalent among the modernist avant-garde, which tends to envision poetry in terms of its capacity to epitomize, through experimentalism, an achieved modernity—and thus to position the poet as an emblematic specimen of an actually advanced humanity rather than as a forward-looking figure whose art emerges foremost out of an awareness of the imperfections of the present and is therefore fundamentally aspirational. In theorizing Imagism, for example, Ezra Pound repeatedly employs presentist rhetoric, as in his famous "A Few Don'ts by an Imagiste," first published in *Poetry* magazine in March 1913, which begins: "An 'Image' is that which presents an intellectual and emotional complex in an instant of time" (*Imagist Poetry* 130). The exaltation of instantaneity in this basic definition is expanded upon as Pound goes on to elaborate the effects of a well-wrought image: "It is the presentation of such a 'complex' instantaneously which gives that sense of sudden liberation; that sense of freedom from time limits and space limits; that sense of sudden growth, which we experience in the presence of the greatest works of art" (130). The diction itself here is telling: "presentation," "instantaneously," "sudden" (twice), "presence." For Pound, the poetic image—and, by extension, the Imagist poem—achieves its impact through an immediacy conceived of in almost transcendent terms, eliciting in its readers a "sense of freedom from time limits and space limits"—a "liberation" from material bounds, a "sense of sudden growth" that aggrandizes the Now in a way that would seem to foreclose any aspiration toward the Not Yet. In "Vorticism," first published in the *Fortnightly Review* in September 1914, Pound makes it clear that poets themselves are the possessors of and conduits for this transcendent presencing capacity. After citing early on in the essay a version of Pater's tenet that "all art constantly aspires towards the condition of music" (which he misquotes as "all arts approach the conditions of music"), Pound is at pains to theorize Imagist poetry as analogous to music and painting in its formal rigor and immediacy of aesthetic impact:

> The Image is the poet's pigment. The painter should use his colour because he sees it or feels it. I don't much care whether he is representative or non-representative. He should depend, of course, on the creative, not upon the mimetic or representational part in his work. It is the same in writing poems, the author must use his image because he sees it or feels it, not because he thinks he can use it to back up some creed or some system of ethics or economics.

To the first of these sentences, Pound appends a footnote citing his own earlier definition of the poetic image in "A Few Don'ts" (discussed earlier), a citation that indicates his conviction that the instantaneity of the Imagist image allows it to operate in a way analogous to pigment in painting, meeting the eye and mind of the poem's reader much as color meets a painting's viewer or (in keeping with Pound's own emphasis elsewhere in the essay on music) as timbre meets a listener. It is notable that in setting out this analogy, Pound does not advocate for one aesthetic approach over another; though he lauds by name the painters Picasso and Wyndham Lewis and the sculptors Jacob Epstein and Henri Gaudier-Brzeska (as well as, in music, Bach and Mozart), he explicitly declines to favor strategies of abstraction, saying of the artist "I don't much care whether he is representative or non-representative" and prioritizing instead an authenticity of vision and the autonomy of that vision from extra-artistic concerns: "the author must use his image because he sees it or feels it, not because he thinks he can use it to back up some creed or some system of ethics or economics." While on the one hand, this is a commonplace fulmination against warping art toward the ends of propaganda; on the other, in the context of Pound's wider theorization of Imagism, it also embodies the pervasive presentism that crucially informs his poetics, for if the image emerges because the poet "sees it or feels it," then what occasions the Imagist poem, above all else, is the immanence and immediacy of the author's phenomenological experience—not wishing, or desiring, or aspiring, or any of the other manifestations of affirmative futurity that I have shown to so decisively shape Yeats's and Auden's and others' work, but rather the poet's achieved specialness as a purveyor of instantaneous visionary insight designed to rivet the reader in the here and now, eclipsing any thought "of ethics or economics" or other such unaesthetic concerns.

As the foregoing discussion of Pound's Imagist poetics of presentism makes clear, the exaltation among the modernist avant-garde of phenomenological immediacy as poetry's overriding objective often entails a concomitant fetishization of poets themselves as preternaturally equipped both to live intensely in the present and to communicate that intensity of vitality through up-to-date poetic means. Pound himself, for instance, formulates his "don'ts"—as with so much of his poetic theory—explicitly against what he saw as the "viewy" excesses of the nineteenth century; though he mandates that any prospective poet engage in staggeringly wide reading across history and language communities, he envisions Imagism as a resolutely modern movement, akin to Cubism or Expressionism in painting. Mentioning the latter two movements by name, for instance, he announces his intention in "Vorticism" to "explain 'Imagisme,' and then proceed to show its inner relation to certain modern paintings and sculpture"—thus positioning his own and the work of his compatriots in poetry as advancing a comparably vanguard mode of artistic expression. We see this convergence of a presentist poetics, a celebration of poets as incomparably tuned-in to the immediacy of experience, and a self-conscious sense of vanguardism in other representatives of the modernist avant-garde, to the extent that they can be seen to form a kind of anti-utopian counter-tradition in contrast to the various manifestations of a future-oriented poetics of utopia that I have mapped out through Yeats and Auden. In her 1925 essay "Modern Poetry," for example, Mina Loy delineates this convergence more or less programmatically:

> More than to read poetry we must listen to poetry. All reading is the evocation of speech; the difference in our approach, then, in reading a poem or a newspaper is that our attitude in reading a poem must be that of listening to and looking at a pictured song. Modern poetry, like music, has received a fresh impetus from

contemporary life; they have both gained in precipitance of movement. The structure of all poetry is the movement that an active individuality makes in expressing itself. Poetic rhythm, of which we have all spoken so much, is the chart of a temperament. (*Lost Lunar* 157)

Like Pound, Loy takes recourse to an analogy between poetry and music that also extends to encompass the visual arts, claiming that "our attitude in reading a poem must be that of listening to and looking at a pictured song" —a characterization that, again as with Pound, emphasizes poetry as above all an artform of the immediate present, both in the sense of its capacity to communicate in an unmediated way directly to the senses (thus achieving the Paterian "condition of music") and in the sense of having "received a fresh impetus from contemporary life" (thus earning through its up-to-dateness the approbatory label of "modern"). Evidencing her prior Futurist allegiances (another of her key prose works is her 1914 "Aphorisms on Futurism," written during her association in Florence with Futurist pioneers F. T. Marinetti and Giovanni Papini), Loy emphasizes modern poetry's gains in "precipitance of movement"—the implication being that the increased velocity and technological multifariousness of early-twentieth-century urban life has bequeathed to poetry new rhythms, cadences, dynamics, and other heretofore unavailable musical resources. Poets are thus defined by their capacity to marshal these fresh resources in negotiation with the speed of modern living: "The structure of all poetry is the movement that an active individuality makes in expressing itself. Poetic rhythm … is the chart of a temperament." The essay as a whole is saturated in this relentlessly individualistic conception of poetry as an artform: elsewhere we are told of poets that "the formation of their verses is determined by the spontaneous tempo of their response to life" (157–8), and in singling out exceptional individuals, including Pound ("To speak of the modern movement is to speak of him; the masterly impresario of modern poets" (158)), Loy tends to imply an achieved or even inherent superiority (what she terms elsewhere the poet's "organic personality" (160)), as when she claims of E. E. Cummings, for instance, that "fundamentally he is a great poet because his verse wells up abundantly from the foundations of his soul; a sonorous dynamo" (160). Overall, then, Loy's "Modern Poetry" stands as an exemplar of how a presentist poetics—that is, a poetics that envisions poetry's aesthetic ends in terms of its capacity to rivet us in the Now—entails not only a triumphalist vision of the present moment in history (in a way that Futurism, for example, is very explicit about) but an exaltation of poets as exceptional individuals capable of navigating and plumbing that present moment not just because of artistic savvy but because of special qualities of "individuality," "temperament," and "soul."

I am not claiming that the variations on a presentist poetics to be found among the modernist avant-garde lend themselves uniquely to exalted conceptions of the poet's exceptionality; what I am claiming, however, is that because such presentist poetics tend to rely upon triumphalist notions of the new, the now, the up-to-date, and so on—i.e., notions that emphasize the present as a place of achievement rather than of aspiration—they tend to conceive of poets (and their poems) in a similar way, as achieving in themselves rather than outwardly aspiring. Compare, for instance, Loy's characterization of Cummings as a "great poet because his verse wells up abundantly from the foundations of his soul" to Auden's claim (in "The Public v. the Late Mr. William Butler Yeats") that "poetic talent ... is the power to make personal excitement socially available" (*Prose II* 6). For Loy, greatness resides in the poet and his soul, of which poems are the upwelling expression, leaving one to wonder whether her conception of poetry even requires an audience. Auden, on the other hand, while emphasizing the potentially inherent traits of "talent" and "power"—though certainly these are less fundamentally innate than "soul"—singles out the movement from the personal to the social, asserting that while poems originate in talented individuals, their aims are ultimately communal. Even Yeats's most grandiose statements of the artist's power—as with his 1898 declaration that "the arts are, I believe, about to take upon their shoulders the burdens that have fallen from the shoulders of priests" (*Early* 141)—are usually offered in this communal tenor, harboring the conviction that poetry must embody the collective impulse to future melioration in order to prove its worth. This is starkly at odds with the insular focus on "good" and "bad" poetry, "dos" and "don'ts," and pithy aphorisms, no matter how potentially correct (e.g., "Music rots when it gets *too far* from the dance. Poetry atrophies when it gets too far from music" (*ABC of Reading* 61)), that we find in Pound's theorizing, not just in his early Imagist period but throughout his career. It is part of my contention here, first, that a poetics of presentism—which is also often a poetics of individualism, insularity, vanguardism, and so on—too often conceives of poetry as the poet's achieved engagement with the Now to the neglect of an alternative conception of poetry as potentially embodying communal aspirations toward the Not Yet, and second, that this latter conception affords a richer account of what poetry, as a form-forward verbal medium, is capable of doing more effectively and compellingly than other artforms, which is to simultaneously advance articulated ideas through its semantic and figurative dimensions and analogize new forms of harmony and coherence through its formal and musical ones.[3]

Lawrence and "The Poetry of the Present"

This is not to say that a presentist poetics must necessarily lack a utopian dimension. One might argue, for instance, that a fidelity to the Now and the individual's singular attempt to forge something autonomous and lasting out of that welter of ephemerality is in fact utopian at its core, born of an insistence on the value of our lives as they are lived from moment to moment—a sanctity too often lost sight of in a Western capitalist regimen built on dreams and promises. Indeed, the most overt statement of a poetics of presentism to emerge from the modernist era, D. H. Lawrence's "The Poetry of the Present" (1919), is at least partly amenable to such a utopian reading. Lawrence opens the essay by evoking the Romantic emblems of the skylark and nightingale, claiming of the former's song that it flows "straight on into futurity" and of the latter's that it hymns "the perfected past" (*The Bad*

Side of Books 77). He continues: "So it is with poetry. Poetry is, as a rule, either the voice of the far future, exquisite and ethereal, or it is the voice of the past, rich, magnificent" (77). Singling out Shelley and Keats by name, Lawrence links their allegiance to future and past, respectively (or what he calls elsewhere "the poetry of the end" and "the poetry of the beginning" (78)), to the formal choices that shape their poems:

> This completeness, this consummateness, the finality and the perfection are conveyed in exquisite form: the perfect symmetry, the rhythm which returns upon itself like a dance where the hands link and loosen and link for the supreme moment of the end. Perfected bygone moments, perfected moments in the glimmering futurity, these are the treasured gem-like lyrics of Shelley and Keats. (78)

While it makes some intuitive sense to frame the past as a place of "completeness," "finality," and "perfected moments," Lawrence's framing of not only the past but the *future* in this way is puzzlingly idiosyncratic. Even while tacitly acknowledging the time to come as a space of aspiration and potentiality through the phrasing "glimmering futurity," he persists here in conflating past and future as equally "gem-like" in their finishedness, in seeing the impulse to futurity not in kinetic terms—as fueled by the restless desire for a better way of being, for instance— but in terms of seeking out a stasis ("the supreme moment of the end"). This conceptual move allows him to ally both past- and future-oriented registers to a formalist poetics that seeks out "perfect symmetry" and "the rhythm that returns upon itself like a dance." It becomes clear as the essay continues that one of central purposes of "The Poetry of the Present" is to advance a theory of poetic form according to which the poetries of pastness and futurity—typified by formal strategies such as stanzaic patterning, rhyme schemes, and metrical regularity— are subordinated to the titular poetry of the present, which employs free verse as a means of announcing its fidelity to an instantaneity variously characterized in memorable Lawrencian formulations such as "the living plasm," "the quick of the ever-swirling flood," "the incarnate disclosure of the flux," "the still, white seething, the incandescence and coldness of the incarnate moment," and so on (78–9). Naming Whitman (whom he would lionize more thoroughly several years later in his *Studies in Classic American Literature* (1923)) as the signal poet whose "heart beats with the urgent, insurgent Now" (80), Lawrence mounts an argument for free verse not just as a means of "break[ing] the stiff neck of habit"—of pruning away both verbal and rhythmic clichés and infusing spontaneity into poetry— but as a mode with "its own *nature*," one that is "instantaneous like plasm," that "just takes place" (81–2; italics in original). It is in this culminating account of free verse's distinctive "nature" that the potentially utopian dimension of Lawrence's poetics of the present can be discerned:

> For such utterance any externally applied law would be mere shackles and death. The law must come new each time from within. The bird is on the wing in the winds, flexible to every breath, a living spark in the storm, its very flickering

> depending upon its supreme mutability and power of change. Whence such a bird came: whither it goes: from what solid earth it rose up, and upon what solid earth it will close its wings and settle, this is not the question. This is a question of before and after. Now, *now*, the bird is on the wing in the winds.
>
> Such is the rare new poetry. One realm we have never conquered: the pure present. One great mystery of time is terra incognita to us: the instant. The most superb mystery we have hardly recognized: the immediate, instant self. The quick of all time is the instant. The quick of all the universe, of all creation, is the incarnate, carnal self. Poetry gave us the clue: free verse: Whitman. Now we know. (82)

In line with his emphasis on free verse's unique "nature," Lawrence takes recourse to natural imagery here in the form of the "bird," ostensibly revising Shelley's skylark and Keats's nightingale into a figure illustrative of the pulsing vitality of the natural, animal, elemental world, whose "living spark" of "supreme mutability" cannot be apprehended by "any externally applied law." If we read Lawrence's exaltation of the bird's moment-to-moment existence as signaling a reverence for the individual animal, a refusal to consign that individual to the realm of the emblematic or symbolic, and a concomitant acknowledgment of the intrinsic value of living things, then his thinking here can be seen to harbor a productively ecological and indeed utopian dimension, evoking as it does a more equitable and less exploitative relation between the human and nonhuman worlds by highlighting their essential unity and interdependence as coexisting in a shared life-space. On the other hand, two aspects of Lawrence's rhetoric here, if not negate, at least seriously mitigate, its progressive ecological utopianism. First, the second paragraph of the above passage makes clear that while the reverence for the nonhuman world's intrinsic vitality that Lawrence displays here and elsewhere may contain authentically ecological dimensions, its primary purpose in "The Poetry of the Present" is to stake out a vanguardist claim on poetic (and therefore necessarily anthropocentric) mastery: "the pure present" is "terra incognita," the "[o]ne realm we have never conquered." Not only do the frequent first-person plural pronouns in this passage clearly refer to human beings—thus diluting its ecological thrust by tacitly affirming our linguistic facility as an index of our hierarchical superiority—but both the repeated recourse to the individualistic conception of "self" and the reiterated tribute to the greatness of the singular "Whitman" place Lawrence firmly in line with the presentist avant-garde as exemplified by Pound and Loy, with its emphasis on poets as exceptional specimens uniquely equipped to capture and uphold the present in all its vital instantaneity (in this case by mastering the aptly protean medium of free verse). This brings me to the second way in which this passage undermines the potential ecological utopianism of Lawrence's vision in "The Poetry of the Present": if "[t]he quick of all the universe, of all creation, is the incarnate, carnal self," and free verse is the means of seizing that "quick" for the purposes of poetic depiction, then the question remains, to what end? Even if we generously grant that the "carnal self" conjured here encompasses human and nonhuman selves alike in a way that might imply their inextricability and thereby suggest a kind of proto-ecological ethic, how can that ethic be actualized within a framework that explicitly forecloses futurity? In other words, if the poetry of the present categorically excludes both past- and future-looking registers, how can it be anything more than the present for the present's sake, a kind of vitalist aestheticism?

Poetry in the Future's Shadow

Ultimately, the poetics proffered by Lawrence in "The Poetry of the Present" is too individualistic, too lacking in communal awareness, and indeed too determinedly presentist to contain anything more than the barest contours of a utopian dimension. While seeming to advance a vision of the underlying unity of all living things and of free verse as the means of broadcasting that vision, it finally offers only a paradoxically solipsistic ecology, an interconnectedness conceived of as only visible through the conduit of the poet's vital genius, achievable only in art and not in the world at large.[4] This solipsistic ecology—this strange combination of rampant individualism, a wondrous sense of the universe's intertwined expansiveness, and a belief in the poet's power to unlock the mysteries of that myriad expanse through language—dovetails with the poetics of Symbolism, that late-nineteenth-century resurgence of Romanticism in a new key that forms another of modern poetry's crucial backdrops. In the introduction to his widely influential 1899 book *The Symbolist Movement in Literature* (a book actually dedicated to Yeats), Arthur Symons sets out Symbolism's anti-materialist creed in a way that bears crucially on the poetics of presentism I have been discussing:

> We are coming closer to nature, as we seem to shrink from it with something of horror, disdaining to catalogue the trees of the forest. And as we brush aside the accidents of daily life, in which men and women imagine that they are alone touching reality, we come closer to humanity, to everything in humanity that may have begun before the world and may outlast it.
>
> Here, then, in this revolt against exteriority, against rhetoric, against a materialistic tradition; in this endeavour to disengage the ultimate essence, the soul, of whatever exists and can be realized by the consciousness; in this dutiful waiting upon every symbol by which the soul of things can be made visible, literature, bowed down by so many burdens, may at last attain liberty, and its authentic speech. (5)

The central idea here—that artists are "coming closer to nature" even as they "seem to shrink from it," that in "brush[ing] aside the accidents of daily life" they are actually "com[ing] closer to humanity"—operates according to an analogous logic as the presentism of Pound, Loy, Lawrence, and others. Just as the Symbolists, in Symons's account, believe that by stripping away "nature" and "exteriority" they can reach "the ultimate essence" and "attain liberty," the presentists among the modernist avant-garde strip away past and future in the name of capturing an instantaneity that is fetishized as the apogee of artistic achievement. In both cases, indispensable aspects of actual reality as we experience it need to be done away with in order for the heretofore unopened poetic gateway—the "essence" on the one hand or the "present" on the other—to shed forth its numinous insights. There are crucial differences, to be sure: while the Symbolists forsake the material world in pursuit of an immaterial revelation, the presentists fetishize the material world as a fount of images—whether drawn from nature, the trappings of urban modernity, or other phenomenological sources—which they cast as portals to that revelation, the illumination of the present in all its pulsing vitality. In other words, the modernist avant-garde can often be seen as re-injecting the material world into the shell of a Symbolist poetics that imagines the poet as a being of superior perceptiveness and the making of poems as a starkly individual act, the privileged disclosure of glimpses of a hidden law. To a certain extent, this pose is understandable for historical reasons I have already discussed; in an age in which poetry's audience was diminishing, it seems reasonable that some poets would react by casting their marginality as a sign of their rarefied superiority in a vulgarly material world. In his pioneering study of Symbolism and its decisive influence on modern literature, *Axel's Castle* (1931), Edmund Wilson notes of the Symbolists' haughty anti-materialism that "One of the principal causes ... for this withdrawal of the *fin de siècle* poets from the general life of their time, was the fact that in the utilitarian society which had been produced by the industrial revolution and the rise of the middle class, the poet seemed to have no place" (213). For the Symbolists' inheritors, then, the question becomes how and where to mark out a place for the poet in such a society, and thus it can be a productive way of approaching modern poets to consider how they answer this question. While the presentists choose to place the poet above and away from society, Yeats, for example—while indeed conceiving of his vocation as a priestly one and so maintaining the Symbolists' vision of the poet as a revealer of mysteries—never ceases to frame his role in relation to a collective, whether the Irish nation in his early career or less concretely political formations such as aristocracy or the "gay" builders and rebuilders of civilizations in his later. Auden, too, continually positions his work in relation to a collective; even after relinquishing his early hopes for poetry as capable of teaching us the nature of good and evil, he advances a negative poetics that casts poetry as potentially a key bulwark against auto-idolatry—i.e., against forgetting both our essential fallenness as human beings and our consequent obligation to seek out the transfigurative power of grace. Put simply, unlike many of their more avant-garde contemporaries, Yeats and Auden both answer the question of the poet's place in an atomized capitalist, industrial, utilitarian society by asserting that that place is a singular one only to the extent that poetry can be thought of as registering a palpable, meliorating influence in communal terms.[5]

In closing, I want to step back to assert in relation to poetry generally and modern poetry in particular that it ought to make a difference to us as critics and readers whether the poems we encounter, either individually or as bodies of work, assert a role for poetry in improving our lives, not just in terms of providing us with pleasure or entertainment but in embodying the aspirational impetus at the core of all positive change—if not affording us glimpses of paths to better collective futures then at least spurring our desire to forge those paths. What is at stake in this assertion is poetry's place among the arts, its singularity as a mode of harboring and transmitting aesthetic, ethical, and perceptual values. As an artistic medium that inherently foregrounds questions of form to an unusual degree, that utterly depends upon the capacity of the figurative to bring together that which may appear to be irretrievably apart, and that fully retains the power to communicate ideas and images literally and lucidly, poetry is uniquely capable of being utopian in the blueprintist and iconoclastic senses at once, offering us, through its combination of matter and music, manifestations of the desire for better ways of living and being that are both concrete and un-reifiable, incapable of being wholly subsumed into the trivializing matrix of the culture industries. As the preceding chapters have made clear, Yeats's and Auden's work exemplifies poetry's aptness and flexibility as a utopian artform in myriad ways; and though these two poets are exceptional in the breadth and depth of their expressions of affirmative futurity, the questions I have asked of their work—and also, of course, derived from it—can be productively posed of all poetry, especially in the twentieth century and beyond. What does this poetry aspire to? Does it acknowledge the latter-day marginality of poetry among the arts, and if so, what does it assert in response to this neglect? Can we discern in it a meaningful relationship between poetic form and affirmative futurity? Do its desires, its dreams, its wishes, and so on register as simply individual ambitions, or do they resonate in relation to a wider collective? How does it hope that poetry can help us? What prospects if any does it afford us of better futures together? This is of course only one set of questions that we might ask of poetry, representing only one of countless frameworks that might valuably inform future critical inquiry. But I would offer that such questions are asked far too infrequently, and that in overlooking them—in forgoing our opportunities to constellate the many possible poetics of utopia that await discernment and illumination in the annals of modern poetry and beyond—we risk ceding the capacity to perceive poetry in all its singular urgency, losing sight of what it can do that other arts cannot, of how its unique capacities relate to our deepest shared aspirations, and of why its marginality poses a threat not just to higher-order literacies but to our essential sociality. As we face the imperative to expand our spheres of community to include virtually the entire planet and all its inhabitants, poetry's attunement to invisible correspondences and unforeseen harmonies can be of vital use to us. More than ever, perhaps, we are living in the future's shadow, but that still may not need to be as ominous as it seems.

Notes

1 In light of my citing "communal, social, political aspirations"—i.e., the deliberate separating out of "social" and "political"—it is worth noting here the useful distinction that Hannah Arendt offers between the social and the political in *The Human Condition* (1958). Allying the social with our household, familial, and ultimately

animal existences and the political with our public, civic, and authentically human selves, Arendt argues that—as compared with the ancient Greeks, for instance—twentieth-century life in the West conflates the political and the social, and, as a consequence, most of us simply do not partake in the authentically human sphere of action. This set of distinctions between the social and the political, the animal and the human, the realm of the household and the realm of action, also accords with a distinction between labor (i.e., activities undertaken to secure basic necessities and sustain one's life processes) and work (i.e., activities that produce lasting artifacts, such as works of art). Just as, in Arendt's account, most of us do not partake of *action*, then, most of us also do not perform *work*. As Auden puts it in his review of the book (a review that initiated a lifelong friendship between himself and Arendt): "Public Life, in the Greek sense, has been replaced by social life, that is to say, the private activity of earning one's bread is now carried on in public" (*Prose IV* 189). I do not cite Arendt's distinctions because I agree with them wholesale, but rather because (1) they provide compelling justification for considering the social as separate from the political, and (2) they directly influenced Auden's later thought. In any case, it is clear that works of art engage aspirationally with both the social (familial, household, animal, labouring, etc.) and the political (civic, public, humanistic, working, etc.) aspects of our existence.

2 The fuller context of Pater's aphorism in his book *The Renaissance: Studies in Art and Poetry* is too infrequently cited. The book first appeared in 1874, but the following is drawn from the 1893 text, published the year before Pater's death:

> *All art constantly aspires towards the condition of music.* For while in all other works of art it is possible to distinguish the matter from the form, and the understanding can always make this distinction, yet it is the constant effort of art to obliterate it. That the mere matter of a poem, for instance—its subject, its given incidents or situation; that the mere matter of a picture—the actual circumstances of an event, the actual topography of a landscape—should be nothing without the form, the spirit, of the handling; that this form, this mode of handling, should become an end in itself, should penetrate every part of the matter:—this is what all art constantly strives after, and achieves in different degrees. (106)

Imagism—and indeed all the forms of presentism I describe here—can be seen as attempting to "obliterate," in the matter described by Pater, the "distinction" between "matter" and "form." This partly explains the avant-garde fetishization (in Pound, for example), of free verse, which because it abandons the trappings of artifice in the form of stanzaic patterning, rhyme schemes, metrical regularity, and so on, can be taken as a means of collapsing form into matter, rendering them so interpenetrating as to be indistinguishable. As I elaborated in the Introduction, however, poetry's aptness as a utopian artform often depends upon the dialectical interplay between subject matter and form, with the tension between them generating aspirational resonances.

3 Laura Riding and Robert Graves's fascinating critical study *A Survey of Modernist Poetry* (1927) approaches poetry in a similarly individualistic manner to Pound and Loy (and, as we shall see, Lawrence). Championing the avant-garde—and, like Loy, setting out E. E. Cummings as an exemplar of modern poetic achievement—Riding and Graves caution against mistaking for the truly new that which is merely newfangled in its engagement with societal trends: "It is … always important to distinguish between what is historically new in poetry because the poet is contemporary with a civilization of a certain kind, and what is intrinsically new in poetry because the poet is a new and original individual, something more than a

mere servant and interpreter of civilization" (163). While their exaltation of the true modernist poet as "a new and original individual" dovetails with the presentists' emphasis, they would, however, take issue with Loy's celebration of poetry that takes "a fresh impetus from contemporary life," seeing this precisely as breeding "what is historically new in poetry because the poet is contemporary with a civilization of a certain kind." Indeed, elsewhere in their study they castigate Pound as a producer of "up-to-date conduct-poetry" (187).

4 Because my analysis of Lawrence's anti-utopian individualism here is so firmly rooted in "The Poetry of the Present," it might be said to neglect the extent to which, elsewhere in his work, the proto-ecological utopianism we detect in the essay is rendered to a more thoroughgoing and less compromised extent. The poems of *Birds, Beasts and Flowers* (1923), for instance, often challenge anthropocentrism and assert an essential kinship among human and nonhuman animals in ways that could be fittingly characterized as utopian. For an account of the utopian dimensions of Lawrence's poem "Fish," for example, see my chapter on poetry in the *Edinburgh Companion to Vegan Literary Studies*.

5 It would be too much to claim that a formalist poetics that retains musical regularities of stanza, meter, rhyme, and so on—and thus can be more readily analogized not only to the communal activities of song, ritual, ceremony, and so forth, but also to visions of heretofore unachieved social harmony—is inherently more fitting to a poetics of utopia than a poetics rooted in free verse, with its insistence on individual dynamism, but the relatively stark differences in formal strategy between poets in whom a poetics of utopia can be discerned and those who adhere to a more presentist orientation at least raises this question of the relationship between form and affirmative futurity.

WORKS CITED

Adams, Hazard. *The Book of Yeats's Poems*. Florida State UP, 1990.
Adorno, Theodor. *Aesthetic Theory*. 1970. Translated by Robert Hullot-Kentor, U of Minnesota P, 1997.
Adorno, Theodor. "Commitment." Translated by Francis McDonagh. *New Left Review*, vol. 1, nos. 87–88, 1974, pp. 75–89.
Adorno, Theodor. "Lyric Poetry and Society." 1957. Translated by Bruce Mayo in *The Adorno Reader*, edited by Brian O'Connor, Blackwell, 2000, pp. 211–29.
Adorno, Theodor. *Minima Moralia: Reflections from Damaged Life*. Translated by E. F. N. Jephcott, Verso, 1978.
Adorno, Theodor. *Notes to Literature Volume 1*. Translated by Shierry Weber Nicholson, Columbia UP, 1991.
Adorno, Theodor. *Prisms*. Translated by Samuel and Shierry Weber, MIT, 1983.
Agamben, Giorgio. *Homo Sacer: Sovereign Power and Bare Life*. Translated by Daniel Heller-Roazen, Stanford UP, 1998.
Alpers, Paul. *What Is Pastoral?* U of Chicago P, 1996.
Anderson, Benedict. *Imagined Communities: Reflections on the Origin and Spread of Nationalism*. Revised Edition. Verso, 1983.
Arendt, Hannah. *The Human Condition*. 1958. Second Edition. U of Chicago P, 1998.
Auden, W. H. *Collected Poems*. Edited by Edward Mendelson, Modern Library, 2007.
Auden, W. H. *The Complete Works of W. H. Auden. Prose Volume 1, 1926–1938*. Edited by Edward Mendelson, Princeton UP, 1996.
Auden, W. H. *The Dyer's Hand and Other Essays*. Random House, 1962.
Auden, W. H. *The English Auden: Poems, Essays, and Dramatic Writings 1927–1939*. Edited by Edward Mendelson, Faber, 1977.
Auden, W. H. *Forewords and Afterwords*. Selected by Edward Mendelson, Vintage, 1974.
Auden, W. H. *Prose Volume II 1939–1948*. Edited by Edward Mendelson, Princeton UP, 2002.
Auden, W. H. *Prose Volume III 1949–1955*. Edited by Edward Mendelson, Princeton UP, 2008.
Auden, W. H. *The Sea and the Mirror: A Commentary on Shakespeare's* The Tempest. Edited by Arthur Kirsch, Princeton UP, 2005.
Auden, W. H. *Selected Poems*. Edited by Edward Mendelson, Vintage, 1990.
Auden, W. H., and Christopher Isherwood. *Journey to a War*. 1939. Paragon House, 1990.
Augustine, Saint, Bishop of Hippo. *Confessions*. Translated by Henry Chadwick, Oxford UP, 1992.
Ayers, David, et al. *Utopia: the Avant Garde, Modernism, and (Im)possible Life*, De Gruyter, 2015.
Bloch, Ernst. *The Principle of Hope*. Volume 2. Translated by Neville Plaice, Stephen Plaice, and Paul Knight, MIT, 1995.

Bloch, Ernst. *The Utopian Function of Art and Literature*. Translated by Jack Zipes and Frank Mecklenburg, MIT Press, 1988.

Bloom, Harold. *Yeats*. Oxford UP, 1970.

Bornstein, George. *Yeats and Shelley*. U of Chicago P, 1970.

Bradford, Curtis. "Yeats's Byzantium Poems: A Study of Their Development." *PMLA*, vol. 75, no. 1, 1960, pp. 110–25.

Caesar, Adrian. *Dividing Lines: Poetry, Class and Ideology in the 1930s*. Manchester UP, 1991.

Callan, Edward. *W. H. Auden: A Carnival of Intellect*. Oxford UP, 1983.

Carey, John, editor. *The Faber Book of Utopias*. Faber, 1999.

Casanova, Pascale. *The World Republic of Letters*. Translated by M. B. Debevoise, Harvard UP, 2004.

Castiglione, Baldesar. *The Book of the Courtier*. Penguin, 1976.

Caudwell, Christopher. *Illusion and Reality: A Study of the Sources of Poetry*. 1937. Lawrence & Wishart, 1973.

Cole, Stewart. "Love and Other Gods: Personification and Volition in Auden." *Twentieth-Century Literature*, vol. 60, no. 3, 2014, pp. 367–96.

Cole, Stewart. "Poetry." *The Edinburgh Companion to Vegan Literary Studies*, edited by Laura Wright and Emelia Quinn, Edinburgh UP, 2022, pp. 193–202.

Crick, Bernard. *In Defence of Politics*. Continuum, 2000.

Cronon, William. "The Trouble with Wilderness or, Getting Back to the Wrong Nature." *Environmental History*, vol. 1, no. 1, 1996, pp. 7–28.

Cullingford, Elizabeth. *Yeats, Ireland, and Fascism*. Macmillan, 1981.

Davenport-Hines, Richard. *Auden*. Random House, 1995.

Davis, J. C. *Utopia and the Ideal Society: A Study of English Utopian Writing 1516–1700*. Cambridge UP, 1981.

Deane, Seamus. *Celtic Revivals: Essays in Modern Irish Literature 1880–1980*. Faber, 1985.

DeGrave, Analisa. "Ecoliterature and Dystopia: Gardens and Topos in Modern Latin American Poetry." *Confluencia*, vol. 22, no. 2, 2007, pp. 89–104.

Donoghue, Emma. "'How Could I Fear and Hold Thee by the Hand?' The Poetry of Eva Gore-Booth." *Sex, Nation, and Dissent in Irish Writing*. Edited by Éibhear Walshe, Cork UP, 1997, pp. 16–42.

Eagleton, Terry. "First-Class Fellow-Travelling: The Poetry of W. H. Auden." *New Blackfriars*, no. 57, 1976, pp. 562–6.

Eagleton, Terry. *Heathcliff and the Great Hunger: Studies in Irish Culture*. Verso, 1995.

Eagleton, Terry. *The Ideology of the Aesthetic*. Blackwell, 1990.

Eagleton, Terry. *Marxism and Literary Criticism*. Methuen, 1976.

Eliot, T. S. *Selected Essays*. Edited by Frank Kermode, Farrar, Straus and Giroux, 1975.

Eliot, T. S. *The Use of Poetry and the Use of Criticism*. 1933. Faber and Faber, 1964.

Ellmann, Richard. *Yeats: The Man and the Masks*. Norton, 1979.

Empson, William. *Some Versions of Pastoral*. Chatto & Windus, 1950.

Firchow, Peter Edgerly. *W. H. Auden: Contexts for Poetry*. U of Delaware P, 2002.

Foster, R. F. *Paddy and Mr. Punch: Connections in Irish and English History*. Allen Lane, 1993.

Freud, Sigmund. "Beyond the Pleasure Principle." Translated by James Strachey in *Penguin Freud Library Volume 11 On Metapsychology: The Theory of Psychoanalysis*, edited by James Strachey, Penguin, 1991, pp. 269–338.

Frye, Northrop. "Varieties of Literary Utopias." *Utopias and Utopian Thought*, edited by Frank E. Manuel, Houghton Mifflin, 1966, pp. 25–49.

Fuller, John. *W. H. Auden: A Commentary*. Princeton UP, 1998.
Gifford Terry. *Pastoral*. Routledge, 1999.
Gordon, Paul. *Tragedy after Nietzsche: Rapturous Superabundance*. U of Illinois P, 2000.
Gore-Booth, Eva. *Poems of Eva Gore-Booth: Complete Edition*. 1929. Chadwyck-Healey Electronic Edition, 2000.
Gray, John. *Black Mass: Apocalyptic Religion and the Death of Utopia*. FSG, 2007.
Gregory, Rosalyn, and Benjamin Kohlmann, editors. *Utopian Spaces of Modernism: British Literature and Culture, 1885-1945*. Palgrave Macmillan, 2012.
Grigson, Geoffrey, editor. *New Verse*, nos. 26-27, November 1937.
Grigson, Geoffrey, editor. *New Verse*, no. 29, March 1938.
Heard, Gerald. *Social Substance of Religion: An Essay on the Evolution of Religion*. Harcourt, Brace, 1931.
Hecht, Anthony. *The Hidden Law: The Poetry of W. H. Auden*. Harvard UP, 1993.
Hodgson, Gregory. *America in Our Time: From World War II to Nixon—What Happened and Why*. 1976. Princeton UP, 2005.
Hynes, Samuel. *The Auden Generation: Literature and Politics in England in the 1930s*. Viking, 1977.
Imaz, Maria Lourdes Otaegi. "Looking for Paradise. Utopia as a Social Issue in Basque Poetry." *Bulletin of Hispanic Studies*, vol. 93, no. 10, 2016, pp. 1173-95.
Jacoby, Russell. *Picture Imperfect: Utopian Thought for an Anti-Utopian Age*. Columbia UP, 2005.
Jacobs, Alan. *What Became of Wystan: Change and Continuity in Auden's Poetry*. U of Arkansas P, 1998.
Jameson, Fredric. *Archaeologies of the Future: The Desire Called Utopia and Other Science Fictions*. Verso, 2005.
Jameson, Fredric. "The Politics of Utopia." *New Left Review*, no. 25, 2004, pp. 35-54.
Jarrell, Randall. "Freud to Paul: The Stages of Auden's Ideology." *Partisan Review*, vol. 12, no. 4, 1945, pp. 437-57.
Jeffares, A. Norman. *A Commentary on the Collected Poems of W. B. Yeats*. Stanford UP, 1968.
Jones, Peter, editor. *Imagist Poetry*. Penguin, 1972.
Kermode, Frank. *Romantic Image*. Routledge, 1957.
Kiberd, Declan. *Inventing Ireland*. Jonathan Cape, 1995.
Kirsch, Arthur. *Auden and Christianity*. Yale UP, 2005.
Larkin, Philip. *Required Writing: Miscellaneous Pieces, 1955-1982*. U of Michigan P, 1999.
Lawrence, D. H. *The Bad Side of Books: Selected Essays*. Edited by Geoff Dyer. NYRB, 2019.
Lawrence, D. H. *Fantasia of the Unconscious* and *Psychoanalysis and the Unconscious*. Penguin, 1971.
Leighton, Angela. *On Form: Poetry, Aestheticism, and the Legacy of a Word*. Oxford UP, 2007.
Levitas, Ruth. *The Concept of Utopia*. Philip Allan, 1990.
Lewis, Gifford. *Eva Gore-Booth and Esther Roper: A Biography*. Pandora, 1988.
Longley, Edna. *Yeats and Modern Poetry*. Cambridge UP, 2013.
Loy, Mina. *The Lost Lunar Baedeker*. Edited by Roger L. Conover, FSG, 1996.
Mannheim, Karl. *Ideology and Utopia, An Introduction to the Sociology of Knowledge*. 1929. Harvest, 1967.
Mao, Douglas. "The Unseen Side of Things: Eliot and Stevens." *Utopian Spaces of Modernism: British Literature and Culture, 1885-1945*, edited by Rosalyn Gregory and Benjamin Kohlmann, Palgrave Macmillan, 2012, pp. 194-213.

Marcus, Phillip L. *Yeats and Artistic Power*. Macmillan, 1992.
Marinelli, Peter V. *Pastoral. The Critical Idiom*. Methuen, 1971.
McDiarmid, Lucy. *Auden's Apologies for Poetry*. Princeton UP, 1990.
Mendelson, Edward. *Early Auden*. FSG, 1981.
Mendelson, Edward. *Later Auden*. FSG, 1999.
More, Thomas. *Utopia*. 1516. Translated by Robert M. Adams. Norton, 1991.
Morton, A. L. *The English Utopia*. Lawrence & Wishart, 1952.
Moses, Michael Valdez. "Nietzsche." *W. B. Yeats in Context*, edited by David Holdeman and Ben Levitas. Cambridge UP, 2010, pp. 266–75.
Moylan, Tom, and Raffaella Baccolini, editors. *Utopia Method Vision: The Use Value of Social Dreaming*. Peter Lang, 2007.
Mumford, Lewis. *The Story of Utopias*. 1922. Bibliobazaar, 2008.
Nersessian, Anahid. *Utopia, Limited: Romanticism and Adjustment*. Harvard UP, 2015.
Newlands, George. *The Transformative Imagination: Rethinking Intercultural Theory*. Ashgate, 2004.
Nic Dhiarmada, Bríona. "Aspects of Utopia, Anti-utopia, and Nostalgia in Irish-Language Texts." *Utopian Studies*, vol. 18, no. 3, 2007, pp. 365–78.
"The Nobel Prize in Literature 1923." *The Nobel Prize*, https://www.nobelprize.org/prizes/literature/1923/summary/.
O'Dwyer, Manus. *Memory and Utopia: The Poetry of José Ángel Valente*. Legenda, 2020.
Pater, Walter. *The Renaissance: Studies in Art and Poetry*. Edited by Donald L. Hill, U of California P, 1980.
Patterson, Annabel. *Pastoral and Ideology: Virgil to Valéry*. U of California P, 1988.
Pound, Ezra. *ABC of Reading*. New Directions, 1960.
Pound, Ezra. "The Later Yeats." *Poetry*, May 1914, https://www.poetryfoundation.org/poetrymagazine/articles/65892/the-later-yeats-5f3ab833c5262
Pound, Ezra. "Vorticism." *Fortnightly Review*, September 1, 1914, https://fortnightlyreview.co.uk/vorticism/.
Pryor, Sean. *W. B. Yeats, Ezra Pound, and the Poetry of Paradise*. Ashgate, 2011.
Ramazani, Jahan. *The Hybrid Muse: Postcolonial Poetry in English*. U of Chicago P, 2001, pp. 21–48.
Ramazani, Jahan. "'A Little Space': The Psychic Economy of Yeats's Love Poems." *Criticism*, vol. 35, no. 1, 1993, pp. 67–89.
Ramazani, Jahan. *Poetry of Mourning: The Modern Elegy from Hardy to Heaney*. U of Chicago P, 1994.
Ramazani, R. Jahan. "Yeats: Tragic Joy and the Sublime." *PMLA*, vol. 104, no. 2, 1989, pp. 163–77.
Reeve-Tucker, Alice, and Nathan Waddell, editors. *Utopianism, Modernism, and Literature in the Twentieth Century*. Palgrave Macmillan, 2013.
Replogle, Justin. "Auden's Marxism." *PMLA*, vol. 80, no. 5, 1965, pp. 584–95.
Riding, Laura, and Robert Graves. *A Survey of Modernist Poetry*. Heinemann, 1927.
Said, Edward W. "Yeats and Decolonization." *Nationalism, Colonialism, and Literature*, edited by Terry Eagleton, U of Minnesota P, 1990, pp. 69–95.
Salvadori, Corinna. *Yeats and Castiglione: Poet and Courtier*. Alan Figgis, 1965.
Schiller, Friedrich. *On the Aesthetic Education of Man*. 1795. Translated by Reginald Snell, Dover, 2004.
Schiller, Friedrich. *On the Naïve and Sentimental in Literature*. 1795. Translated by Helen Watanabe-O'Kelly, Carcanet, 1981.

Selby, Nick, editor. *T. S. Eliot: The Waste Land: Essays, Articles, Reviews*. Columbia UP, 2001.
Shakespeare, William. *The Tempest*. Edited by Stephen Orgel. Oxford UP, 2008.
Shelley, Percy Bysshe. *Shelley's Poetry and Prose*. Edited by Donald H. Reiman and Sharon B. Powers, Norton, 1977.
Smith, Stan. *W. H. Auden*. Blackwell, 1985.
Stevens, Wallace. *The Necessary Angel: Essays on Reality and the Imagination*. Vintage, 1951.
Symons, Arthur. *The Symbolist Movement in Literature*. 1899. Introduced by Richard Ellmann, E. P. Dutton, 1958.
Trilling, Lionel. *The Liberal Imagination*. 1950. NYRB Classics, 2008.
Vendler, Helen. *Our Secret Discipline: Yeats and Lyric Form*. Harvard UP, 2007.
Vendler, Helen. *Yeats's Vision and the Later Plays*. Harvard UP, 1963.
Whitaker, Thomas R. *Swan and Shadow: Yeats's Dialogue with History*. 1964. Catholic U of America P, 1989.
Wilson, Edmund. *Axel's Castle: A Study of the Imaginative Literature of 1970-1930*. 1931. Introduction by Mary Gordon. FSG, 2004.
Winter, Jay. *Dreams of Peace and Freedom: Utopian Moments in the Twentieth Century*. Yale UP, 2006.
Yeats, W. B. *Autobiographies*. Edited by William H. O'Donnell and Douglas N. Archibald. Scribner, 1999.
Yeats, W. B. *The Collected Letters of W. B. Yeats*. Electronic Edition. InteLex Corporation, 2002.
Yeats, W. B. *The Collected Poems of W. B. Yeats*. Revised Second Edition. Edited by Richard J. Finneran, Scribner, 1996.
Yeats, W. B. *Early Essays*. Edited by George Bornstein and Richard J. Finneran, Scribner, 2007.
Yeats, W. B. *Explorations*. Macmillan, 1962.
Yeats, W. B. *Later Essays*. Edited by William H. O'Donnell, Scribner, 1994.
Yeats, W. B. *Letters*. Edited by Allan Wade, Macmillan, 1955.
Yeats, W. B. *Memoirs*. Edited by Dennis Donoghue, Macmillan, 1972.
Yeats, W. B. *Uncollected Prose, Volume 1*. Edited by John P. Frayne, Macmillan, 1970.
Yeats, W. B. *Uncollected Prose Volume 2*. Edited by John P. Frayne and Colton Johnson, Macmillan, 1975.
Yeats, W. B. *A Vision*. 1925. Edited by Catharine E. Paul and Margaret Mills Harper, Scribner, 2008.
Yeats, W. B. *A Vision*. 1937. Macmillan, 1961.

INDEX

Adams, Hazard 50
Adorno, Theodor 5, 26, 50, 61 n.2, 170–6, 177, 180–1, 183, 186 n.5, 188, 192
   Aesthetic Theory 5, 171, 172
   "Commitment" 174–5, 180–1
   "Cultural Criticism and Society" 172–3, 175
   "Lyric Poetry and Society" 61 n.2, 175
   on poetry after Auschwitz 31, 172–6, 177
Aestheticism (movement) 42, 44, 53
Agamben, Giorgio 186 n.4
Agape 106, 109, 115, 123–4 n.6. *See also* Eros, love
aisling 55–7
Alighieri, Dante 82, 83, 93 n.9, 118
   Paradiso 118
Alpers, Paul 38
Anderson, Benedict 62 n.8, 78
   Imagined Communities 62 n.8
Arendt, Hannah 149, 155, 203–4 n.1
   The Human Condition 155, 203–4 n.1
aristocracy 53, 58, 59, 60, 68, 70, 71, 73–6, 78, 79, 80, 82, 83, 89, 93 n.7, 165, 166, 168, 169, 202
Auden, W. H.
   "Art and Morals" 152 n.1, 152 n.2
   "Atlantis" 3, 29, 134–9, 140, 147, 148, 153 n.8
   against auto-idolatry 18, 29, 140, 147, 148, 149, 152, 155, 157, 174, 192, 202
   Berlin Journal 28, 96–102, 104–5, 120, 123 n.3
   "A Bride in the 30's" *see* "Easily, my dear, you move, easily your head"
   and Christianity 12, 19, 21, 29, 95, 120–2, 124 n.9, 125, 135, 137, 139, 140, 145, 148, 172, 174, 177, 188
   "Dingley Dell and the Fleet" 39, 148–9
   The Dyer's Hand 152 n.1
   "Easily, my dear, you move, easily your head" 166–7

"The Fall of Rome" 158
Homage to Clio 17, 155, 184
"Homage to Clio" 31, 185
"Horae Canonicae" 133, 149–50
I Believe (essay contribution) 118, 127, 133
"In Memory of W. B. Yeats" 1, 3, 17, 22, 29, 32 n.1, 127–30, 131, 146, 152 n.3, 152 n.5
In Time of War 29, 95, 112, 119–22
islands in 109–10
Journey to a War 119
"Lecture Notes" (as "Didymus") 137–40
letters of 118, 123 n.2, 124 n.12, 139, 140, 153 n.9
Letter to Lord Byron 118
Look, Stranger! see *On This Island*
"Memorial for the City" 158
"Mimesis and Allegory" 137
"Musée des Beaux Arts" 11–15, 179
"Nature, History, and Poetry" 152 n.1, 152 n.2
"On This Island" 3, 15, 108–10
The Orators 105, 123 n.5
"Paysage Moralisé" 29, 110
Poems (1928) 19
Poems (1930) 98, 108
on poems as "very nearly" utopias 3, 16, 29, 126, 128, 132, 148, 150, 161, 171, 175, 194
Poems of Freedom (Introduction) 126–7, 130
"The Poet and the City" 133, 156, 169–70, 173, 178
"poetry makes nothing happen" 1, 17, 22, 29, 31–2 n.1, 127, 128, 130, 132, 134, 139, 145, 148, 164, 172, 184
The Poet's Tongue (Introduction) 28, 115, 126
"The Protestant Mystics" 153 n.9

"Psychology and Art To-day" 22, 28, 113–14, 116, 146, 169, 184
"The Public v. the Late Mr. William Butler Yeats" 1–2, 24, 29, 130–2, 151, 168, 189, 198
"Purely Subjective" 140
The Sea and the Mirror 29–30, 139–48, 157, 172
"The Shield of Achilles" 30, 31, 158, 175–83
"Spain" 112
"Squares and Oblongs" 25, 169
"Thinking What We Are Doing" 204 n.1
"Vespers" (from "Horae Canonicae") 149–50
"The Virgin and the Dynamo" 3, 16, 13, 29, 126, 128, 132, 133, 148, 150, 152 n.1, 161, 171, 183
"The Watershed" 28, 97–102
"Writing" (1932) 28, 102–7, 116, 189
"Writing" (from *The Dyer's Hand*) 126, 133
Yale Daily News banquet address 153 n.7
"Yeats as an Example" 151–2
"Yeats: Master of Diction" 152–3 n.6
"Yeats's Letters" 154 n.16
Ayers, David, et al., *Utopia: the Avant Garde, Modernism and (Im)possible Life* 6

Baccolini, Raffaella 61 n.1
Bacon, Francis 16
Barker, George 18
Bellamy, Edward 7, 16, 17, 69, 84
  Looking Backward 17
Berlin, Isaiah 155
Big House, Anglo-Irish 60, 70, 73–5, 78
Bishop, Elizabeth 141
Blake, William 36, 46, 52, 53, 137
Bloch, Ernst 4, 5, 7, 17, 69, 77, 107, 138–9, 156, 183, 186 n.5, 187, 188
  anticipatory illumination (and anticipatory consciousness) 4, 7, 70, 107, 187
  the Not Yet 4, 5, 10, 14, 77, 156, 171, 174, 179, 183, 195, 198
  The Principle of Hope 17, 138
  The Spirit of Utopia 17

Bloom, Harold 61–2 n.3, 93–4 n.13
Bornstein, George 50
Bradford, Curtis 93 n.13
Browning, Robert 42
Burdekin, Katharine, *Swastika Night* 17

Caesar, Adrian 124 n.12
Callan, Edward 99–100
capitalism 124 n.11, 157, 173
Carey, John, *The Faber Book of Utopias* 93 n.11
Carpenter, Humphrey 169
Casanova, Pascale 11, 32 n.3
  The World Republic of Letters 32 n.3
Castiglione, Baldassare 59–60, 63 n.10, 74
  Book of the Courtier 59, 63 n.10
Caudwell, Christopher 116–18, 119, 124 n.11
  Illusion and Reality 116–18
Celtic Revival (incl. Celtic Twilight) 5, 19, 27, 38, 44, 49, 54, 62 n.8, 67, 80, 93 n.7, 112, 159, 189
Celtic Twilight *see* Celtic Revival
communism 17, 18, 19, 21, 69, 83, 91, 107, 117, 155, 157, 169. *See also* socialism
Crick, Bernard 112
Cronon, William 186 n.3
Cullingford, Elizabeth 78
Cummings, E. E. 197, 198, 204 n.3

Davenport-Hines, Richard 104, 123 n.2, 124 n.12
Davis, J. C., *Utopia and the Ideal Society* 40
Day-Lewis, Cecil 18
Deane, Seamus 93 n.7
democracy 17, 27, 69, 70, 77, 78, 79, 80, 82, 83, 84, 86, 89, 90, 132, 150, 151
Donoghue, Emma 92 n.4, 92 n.5
Douglas, (Major) C. H. 166
Dowson, Ernest 43, 62 n.4

Eagleton, Terry 33 n.7, 53–4, 62 n.8, 124 n.11, 124 n.12
Easter Rising (1916) 22, 54, 72, 154 n.16, 163, 169
ekphrasis 12, 14, 15, 30, 31, 158, 162, 163–4, 183, 184
Eliot, T. S. 6–8, 191–2, 193–4

The Use of Poetry and the Use of Criticism 191
The Waste Land 8
Ellmann, Richard 94 n.14
Empson, William 37
Epstein, Jacob 196
Eros 102, 103, 108, 115, 123 n.8, 168. *See also* Agape, love

fascism 17, 21, 22, 78, 79, 93 n.8, 105, 118, 122, 155, 165, 177
Ferguson, Sir Samuel 44, 46
Firchow, Peter 157–8
First World War 17, 159, 169
Foster, R. F. 53
France, Anatole 69
Franco, Francisco 165
Frankfurt School, the 5, 175
Freud, Sigmund 21, 30, 96, 99–100, 102, 103, 108, 113, 115, 116, 123 n.3, 123 n.8, 146, 168, 175
   Beyond the Pleasure Principle 96, 100, 102, 123 n.3, 168
   The Ego and the Id 100, 123 n.3
Frye, Northrop 39, 40
Fuller, John 108–9, 123 n.2, 123 n.4, 123 n.6, 137
Futurism 197

Gaudier-Brzeska, Henri 196
Gifford, Terry 38–9
God 7, 12, 21, 29, 83, 86, 108, 135–8, 140, 141, 147, 148, 152, 153 n.10
Gonne, Maud 59, 60, 61, 77, 87
Gordon, Paul 161, 163
Gore-Booth, Eva 70–3, 83–4, 92 n.4, 92 n.5, 92 n.6
Graves, Robert 204–5 n.2
Gray, John 92 n.1, 149, 154 n.15
Greene, Graham 18
Gregory, Lady Augusta 63 n.10, 74, 75, 80
Gregory, Rosalyn, and Benjamin Kohlmann, *Utopian Spaces of Modernism* 6
Grigson, Geoffrey 18–19, 21, 123 n.2

Heard, Gerald 28, 104–6, 109, 115, 123 n.6
   Social Substance of Religion 105–6
Hecht, Anthony 109

Hitler, Adolf 165, 167, 186 n.4
Hodgson, Gregory 157
Holocaust, the 155, 156, 169, 170, 172–3, 175, 183, 186 n.4
Hopkins, Gerard Manley 42
Huxley, Aldous 17, 69, 118
   Brave New World 17, 118
   Island 69
Hynes, Samuel 18, 124 n.9

Imagism 195–6, 204 n.2
Irish Civil War 68, 79, 80, 154 n.16, 169
Irish War of Independence 169
Isherwood, Christopher 119, 120

Jacobs, Alan 153 n.13
Jacoby, Russell 5–6, 69–70, 107, 135–6, 138, 153 n.10, 155
James II 160
Jameson, Fredric 4, 5, 89
Jarrell, Randall 19, 123–4 n.8
Johnson, Lionel 43, 62 n.4
Jonson, Ben, "To Penshurst" 76
Jung, Carl 114

Kant, Immanuel 138
Keats, John 86, 199, 200
Kermode, Frank 92 n.6
Kiberd, Declan 54, 62 n.7
Kierkegaard, Søren 21, 121, 137, 139, 172
Kirsch, Arthur 139, 142, 153 n.12

Larkin, Philip 19, 155, 158, 184
Lawrence, D. H. 28, 31, 104–5, 198–201, 204 n.3, 205 n.4
   Birds, Beasts and Flowers 205 n.4
   and the ecological 200
   Fantasia of the Unconscious 104–5
   "The Poetry of the Present" 198–201
Leighton, Angela 12–13
Levitas, Ruth 6, 11, 27, 28, 39–40, 41, 48, 52, 70, 78, 107–8, 121, 123 n.7, 187
   The Concept of Utopia 6, 39, 123 n.7
Lewis, Gifford 71
Lewis, Wyndham 196
Liberal Consensus, the 30, 157
Longley, Edna 159, 161
love 8, 22, 45, 46, 48, 57–8, 59–61, 72, 78, 85, 87, 89, 92 n.3, 105, 106, 108–10,

111, 115, 123–4 n.8, 167–9, 184. *See also* Agape, Eros
Loy, Mina 31, 196–7, 200, 201, 204–5 n.3
"Modern Poetry" 196–7

Mannheim, Karl, *Ideology and Utopia* 5, 17
Mao, Douglas 6–8, 33 n.6, 191–2
Marcus, Phillip 45, 62 n.5
Markiewicz, Countess (Constance Gore-Booth) 72–3, 83, 92 n.6
Marinelli, Paul 38–9
Marinetti, F. T. 197
Marx, Karl, and Marxism 10, 15, 19, 21, 33 n.7, 48, 69, 80, 103, 107, 113, 115, 116, 118, 124 n.11, 156, 166, 172, 175
McDiarmid, Lucy 123 n.8, 133, 152 n.5, 153–4 n.14, 181–2
Mendelson, Edward 62 n.6, 102, 103, 104, 107, 115, 123 n.3, 123 n.4, 124 n.12, 128, 139, 140
Milosz, Czeslaw 12–13
modernism 6, 8, 52, 66, 104, 116, 189, 194–8, 201–2, 204–5 n.3
More, Thomas 4, 5, 16, 28, 69, 84, 138, 165, 188
Morris, William 7, 16, 17, 66, 68, 69, 84, 118, 186 n.2
News from Nowhere 17
Morton, A. F. 109
Moylan, Tom 61 n.1
Mumford, Lewis 4–5, 17, 66–70
The Story of Utopias 4–5, 17, 66–9
Mussolini, Benito 79, 167

negative poetics 29, 125, 134, 139, 142, 144, 148, 150, 172, 180, 183, 184, 188, 192, 202
Nersessian, Anahid, *Utopia, Limited* 16
New Verse (magazine) 18–22, 117
Nic Dhiarmada, Bríona 56
Niebuhr, Ursula 140, 153 n.9
Nietzsche, Friedrich 18, 68, 78, 160, 161, 163, 165
Morgenröte (*The Dawn of Day*) 163

Orwell, George, *Nineteen Eighty-Four* 17, 84, 177

Papini, Giovanni 197
pastoral 26, 27, 35–9, 40, 41, 42, 44, 48, 49, 52–3, 54–5, 56, 58, 60, 61, 88, 92 n.5, 103, 111, 116, 117
Pater, Walter 185, 187–8, 195, 197, 204 n.2
The Renaissance 204 n.2
Patterson, Annabel 38
Picasso, Pablo 196
Plato 66, 69, 108, 126–7
Republic 127
Popper, Karl 149, 155
Pound, Ezra 31, 32 n.4, 52, 97, 163, 195–6, 197–8, 200, 201, 204 n.2, 204–5 n.3
presentism 194–202
Protestant Ascendancy, the 71, 76, 80, 93 n.7, 160
Pryor, Sean, *W. B. Yeats, Ezra Pound, and the Poetry of Paradise* 32 n.4

Ramazani, Jahan 51, 53, 54, 92 n.3, 152 n.3, 185 n.1
Reeve-Tucker, Alice 6, 17
Replogle, Justin 113
Richards, I. A. 118
Rickword, Edgell 19
Riding, Laura, and Robert Graves, *A Survey of Modernist Poetry* 204–5 n.3
Romanticism 1, 16, 17, 22, 36, 37, 42, 43, 45, 49, 51, 52, 54, 61 n.2, 61 n.3, 72, 84, 93 n.12, 98, 126, 145, 153 n.13, 194, 198, 201
Roper, Esther 70, 72
Rothberg, Michael 175

Said, Edward 22, 33 n.8, 54
Salvadori, Corinna 63 n.10
Schiller, Friedrich 9–10, 12, 22, 33 n.7, 35, 47, 175
On the Aesthetic Education of Man 9
Schoenberg, Arnold 180
Second World War 1, 8, 30, 139, 151, 155, 156, 157, 158, 169, 172, 176, 183
Shakespear, Olivia 71
Shakespeare, William 75, 139, 141, 142, 185 n.1
The Tempest 139, 141, 142, 146, 153 n.11

Shelley, Percy Bysshe 22–5, 27, 36, 42,
    46–8, 49–50, 51, 52, 53, 54, 58, 62
    n.3, 68, 83, 121, 126–7, 153 n.13, 161,
    199, 200
  Defence of Poetry 23–5, 47–8, 126
  Prometheus Unbound 46, 48
Skinner, B. F. 5
Smith, Stan 119, 123 n.5, 128, 180
socialism 118, 131, 157. *See also*
    communism
  Auden on 113–4, 116
  Yeats on 78, 83, 166
Spanish Civil War 165
Spencer, Theodore 139
Spender, Stephen 166
Spenser, Edmund 36
sprezzatura 59, 60, 63 n.10, 74, 76
Stevens, Wallace 6–8, 31, 191, 192–4
  "The Noble Rider and the Sound of
    Words" 192–3
Symbolism (movement) 36, 47, 53, 57, 87,
    93 n.6, 97, 201–2
Symons, Arthur 43, 201
  *The Symbolist Movement in
    Literature* 201

Talmon, J. L. 155
Tennyson, (Lord) Alfred 42
Thomas, Dylan 18
Trilling, Lionel 30, 157
  The Liberal Imagination 157
Tynan, Katharine 45

utopia
  as affirmative futurity 2, 4, 7, 10, 14, 16,
    21, 27, 35, 48, 65, 92, 156, 187, 188,
    189, 196, 203, 205 n.5
  blueprint utopias 5, 6, 7, 10, 15, 31, 32
    n.6, 66, 69, 70, 92, 92 n.2, 107, 135,
    138, 156, 188, 203
  as desire for a better way of being 6,
    11, 12, 15, 21, 22, 26, 27, 28, 39, 40,
    41, 50, 52, 70, 95, 107, 121, 182, 187,
    199, 203
  as the education of desire 26, 49, 52–3,
    55, 62 n.5, 67, 112
  as *eutopia* (good place) 3, 28, 35, 66–9,
    70, 85, 90, 91, 94 n.13, 98, 121, 123
    n.2, 127, 139, 149, 150

  as genre 3, 4, 16, 17, 26, 32 n.4, 39, 70,
    109, 187
  as good place *see* eutopia
  iconoclastic utopianism 6, 31, 70, 107,
    135–6, 138, 188, 203
  as impulse 2, 4, 5, 6, 7, 9, 10, 11, 15, 27,
    28, 32 n.6, 33 n.7, 66, 69, 89, 91, 92,
    107, 110, 112, 118, 137, 138, 140, 156,
    189, 194, 199
  limited utopias 16
  minor utopias 15–16
  as no-place *see* outopia
  as *outopia* (no-place) 3, 28, 35, 66,
    70, 85, 90, 92, 94 n.13, 128, 134–5,
    142, 148
  and poetic form 4, 5, 8–11, 12–15, 16,
    22, 29, 47, 53, 112, 125, 126, 132–4,
    171, 175, 179–80, 182, 183, 189, 198,
    203, 204 n.2, 205 n.5

Valdez Moses, Michael 165
Vendler, Helen 12–13, 63 n.9, 75–6, 93
    n.10, 180
via negativa 135, 153 n.9
Villiers de l'Isle-Adam, comte de 36
Vorticism 195

Waddell, Nathan 6, 17
Weil, Simone, *La pensateur et la grace*
    153 n.9
Wellesley, Dorothy 165, 168
Wells, H. G. 7, 17
  A Modern Utopia 17
Whitaker, Thomas 93 n.12
Whitman, Walt 37, 199, 200
Wilde, Oscar 46
William of Orange 160
Wilson, Edmund, *Axel's Castle* 118, 202
Winter, Jay 15–17
Wordsworth, William 98, 153 n.13
  "Lines Composed a Few Miles above
    Tintern Abbey" 98

Yeats, George (née Bertha Georgie Hyde-
    Lees) 79, 82
Yeats, John Butler 43, 94 n.14
Yeats, William Butler
  "Adam's Curse" 27, 58–61, 63 n.10, 83
  as anti-utopian utopian 27, 65, 70, 156

on Auden 18, 165–6
Autobiographies 49, 51, 62 n.4, 68, 73, 82
"The Autumn of the Body" 25, 35, 46–7, 198
"Byzantium" 3, 28, 89–90, 93–4 n.13
Cathleen ni Houlihan 40
"The Celtic Element in Literature" 57, 67
"The Circus Animals' Desertion" 41
Crossways 41, 48, 49
and cultural nationalism 2, 21, 22, 25, 26, 27, 33 n.8, 39, 40–1, 44–6, 48, 51, 53–5, 58, 61 n.2, 62 n.8, 67, 68, 71, 78, 82, 97, 103, 159, 165, 189
on the Daemon (or Daimon) 80–1, 83, 89
"Down by the Salley Gardens" 45
"Easter, 1916" 45, 72, 73, 163
"Ego Dominus Tuus" 93 n.9
fascism, flirtation with 78–9
Four Years 67
"The Galway Plains" 25, 35, 82, 124 n.10, 189
"A General Introduction for My Work" 18, 185 n.1
The Green Helmet and Other Poems 59
"The Gyres" 152 n.3
"The Happiest of Poets" 186 n.2
on history's cyclicity 2, 22, 27, 58, 65, 68–9, 78, 79, 85, 88, 158, 161, 162, 169
"Hopes and Fears for Irish Literature" 35, 57
"If I Were Four and Twenty" 78, 82
"In Memory of Eva Gore-Booth and Con Markievicz" 70, 83
In the Seven Woods 59
"Ireland and the Arts" 47, 124 n.10
The Island of Statues 38
"J. M. Synge and the Ireland of His Time" 159
"The Lake Isle of Innisfree" 3, 15, 26, 49–51
"Lapis Lazuli" 30, 31, 158, 159–66, 168, 176, 183, 184, 186 n.2
"Leda and the Swan" 77
letters of 45, 53, 69, 71, 72, 73, 79, 165–6, 168
"The Madness of King Goll" 26, 41–5
"Man and Echo" 22

"The Meditation of the Old Fisherman" 45
Memoirs 62 n.8, 71, 73, 78
"Modern Poetry: A Broadcast" 18, 39, 166
"The Moods" 35
"Nineteen Hundred and Nineteen" 28, 68, 80–1, 83
and the Nobel Prize for Literature 19
"No Second Troy" 77
"On a Political Prisoner" 72
On the Boiler 67–8, 74, 92 n.2, 165
"Paudeen" 160
"A People's Theatre" 82
Per Amica Silentia Lunae 79–81, 159
"The Philosophy of Shelley's Poetry" 46
"Poetry and Tradition" 73
"The Poetry of Sir Samuel Ferguson" (1 and 2) 44–5
Introduction to *The Resurrection* 91
Reveries over Childhood and Youth 46
The Rose 48, 49
"Sailing to Byzantium" 2, 28, 85–90, 93 n.13, 144, 156, 163, 184
"The Second Coming" 45
The Seeker 38
"September 1913" 28, 76, 160
"The Song of the Happy Shepherd" 26, 35–8, 42, 61
"The Song of the Wandering Aengus" 26, 55–8
"The Statues" 31, 184
"The Stolen Child" 45
"The Symbolism of Poetry" 1, 97, 184
"To an Isle in the Water" 45
The Tower 81
"Under Ben Bulben" 45, 129, 161
and Unity of Being 81–5, 87–9, 93 n.9
"Upon a House Shaken by the Land Agitation" 28, 74, 160
"The Valley of the Black Pig" 46
A Vision 33 n.8, 68, 78–9, 80, 82–5, 87–90, 93 n.13, 160
and the Vision of Evil 68, 80
The Wanderings of Oisin 45
"The Wild Swans at Coole" 59–60
The Wind among the Reeds 48, 55, 59

Zamyatin, Yevgeny, *We* 17
Zipes, Jack 4

www.ingramcontent.com/pod-product-compliance
Lightning Source LLC
Chambersburg PA
CBHW052109300426
44116CB00010B/1595